Introducing Systems Design

Steve Skidmore
Brenda Wroe

NCC Blackwell

MANCHESTER • OXFORD

British Library Cataloguing in Publication Data

Skidmore, Steve
    Introducing systems design
    1. Computer systems. Design
    I. Title II. Wroe, Brenda
    004.2'1

ISBN 0-85012-638-X

First published in 1990 by:

NCC Blackwell Limited, 108 Cowley Road, Oxford OX4 1JF, England.

Reprinted 1991 (twice)

Editorial Office: The National Computing Centre Limited, Oxford Road, Manchester M1 7ED, England.

Typeset in 10pt Times Roman by Bookworm Typesetting, Manchester; and printed by Hobbs the Printers of Southampton.

ISBN 1-85012-638-X

Foreword

This book is the second of two texts about the development of computer systems. It presents a series of models and skills that should help the definition and delivery of appropriate, effective, maintainable and flexible information systems. This second book is primarily concerned with logical and physical design. The previous text *Introducing Systems Analysis* is primarily concerned with physical and logical analysis.

The book is aimed at:

- undergraduate and Higher National Diploma and Certificate students undertaking a module in Systems Analysis and Design;

- trainee Analysts studying for Professional qualifications or following professional development schemes.

The questions given at the end of each chapter serve to reinforce the point that this is essentially a *study textbook*. A short supplementary teaching guide for lecturers is available from the NCC.

The text concentrates upon the activities of Systems Analysis and Design and the skills and attitudes required to undertake them. It is not concerned with the organisation of the tasks. The terms 'analysis', 'design' and 'development' are used fairly interchangeably to describe the whole system activity. The different words are employed for textual variation rather than to suggest the title of the person undertaking the task. The different management arrangements of Data Processing (DP) or Information Systems (IS) have been explored elsewhere (Keen, 1981).

Similarly, the term 'user' is employed in the sense of embracing the clients, operators and victims of the computer system. The term is too standard for its replacement in a textbook.

A case study is used in most chapters to illustrate the models introduced in the earlier parts of each chapter. It must be stressed that the case study is not complete and does not stand on its own. It is used to present a common theme and environment, not as a complete analysis of an organisation. The case study concerns a developing company called InfoSys which offers computer and management training, publishing and consultancy. It has recently been taken over by a large multinational organisation, COMMUNIQUE, which specialises in this area. The Managing Director of the company is Paul Cronin and Jim McQuith is the Seminar Manager. InfoSys and COMMUNIQUE are completely fictitious companies but their operations illustrate the business systems orientation of the text.

In common with the companion text, this book does not adopt any of the proprietary development methodologies currently available in the commercial market-place. The reasoning behind this is discussed in more detail in the review in Chapter 8. However, it is worth stating that many proprietary methodologies now appear to be offering or indeed operating a 'toolkit' approach (Benyon, 1987). For example, in a survey of the use of SSADM in commercial and government sectors (Edwards, et al, 1988) it was found that 'less than half of the respondents use, or intend to use, SSADM in its entirety' and that 'some users of SSADM still have to realise that the methodology does not replace good analysts/designers by a set of rules to be followed religiously'. The survey concluded that SSADM provided guidelines, not rules, for the development of systems.

Finally, although we have attempted to provide a detailed teaching text, we strongly feel that this should be supported by case study practice. Systems Analysis and Design remains a practical subject with a significant tangible end product. Teaching Analysis without context can be both unrealistic and unfocused.

Benyon D, Skidmore S, *Towards a Tool Kit for the Systems Analyst*, The Computer Journal, vol 30 no 1, 1987

Edwards H, Thompson J, Smith P, *A survey of the use of SSADM in the commercial and government sectors*, Software Engineering Group, Sunderland Polytechnic, 1988

Keen J, *Managing Systems Development*, John Wiley, 1981

Acknowledgements

The following permissions to reproduce copyright material should be noted:

Quoin Computing Ltd has kindly granted permission for the reproduction of Figures 2.7, 2.11 to 2.13 inclusive and 2.15.

Marks & Spencer Financial Services for the copy statement in Figure 2.14.

Figure 2.21 (Form V10) is crown copyright and is reproduced with the permission of the Controller of Her Majesty's Stationery Office.

Digital Research (UK) Ltd, for permission to reproduce Figure 3.3.

Figure 4.3 (Form DPR.1 Application for Registration) is reproduced with permission from the Data Protection Registrar. The forms are available from Crown Post Offices and the Registrar's Office.

Contents

1 System Design Objectives

This chapter begins by examining the models and knowledge brought forward from analysis before introducing the objectives and constraints of system design. It concludes with an example system which will form the basis of design exercises in the rest of the book.

1.1 PICKING UP FROM ANALYSIS

The delivery of successful information systems requires three main activities:

- A thorough analysis of business information requirements based on clear strategic planning. A problem understood is half solved.

- From this foundation an effective manual or computer-based system is developed to meet those requirements in an efficient and effective way. This is the primary task of system design.

- The final activity is the successful implementation of the system in the user's environment. This demands training, management, planning and monitoring.

The nature of the systems analysis work, and techniques which may be used to undertake these tasks, were discussed in detail in the companion book *Introducing Systems Analysis*. This current text picks up at the point where the design of a new system starts. It is concerned with the work of the Analyst in translating information needs into the detailed design and implementation of an effective computer-based information system. It builds on the sound foundation of a thorough analysis of problems and requirements.

Before discussing the tasks of design it is useful to recap the nature and level of understanding of the system generated during analysis. The Analyst needs to assemble and convey knowledge of the system requirements to those undertaking the design. This knowledge is generally acquired by a study of the operations and activities of the enterprise and the current systems (if any) that seek to support these. Documentation techniques such as organisation charts, system flowcharts, and document specifications collectively model the Current Physical System. These will prove useful to the designer because they define current operations, expectations and responsibilities.

However, there is clearly a large step from modelling the current operations to designing a computer-based replacement. The gap between these two activities has been recognised by the development of logical models. These establish the requirements of the system *irrespective* of organisational arrangements, staff responsibilites and clerical procedures. These logical models support both the current system and its intended successor. They are described using data analysis (producing a static snapshot of the data structures needed) and data flow diagrams which focus on the transformation of data as it passes through the system. These are supported by ancillary techniques such as entity life histories and the data dictionary.

The design elements of the new information system are also conveyed by means of a series of models. The first set of models introduced in this book are those which support the specification of a New Logical System. This will include logical dialogue outlines, structure charts and action diagrams. However, the likely performance constraints of computer systems based directly on these models means that they may not provide a sound basis for physical implementation. Consequently, the design is 'flexed' to take hardware, software and operational constraints into account. The detailed design of the New Physical System is thus refined from this logical view by a process of iterative definition, evaluation and refinement. Hence, a second set of models is required to support and control this iteration. Entity attribute grids and logical access maps are representative of this second set of models. Figure 1.1 shows the role of the logical models in connecting analysis and design.

There are many candidate design models. This text selects and presents a range of tools and techniques from an extensive Analyst toolkit in preference to a prescriptive methodology. Several proprietary methodologies are available which aim at providing a packaged, structured set of techniques and guidelines for their application with an organisation. The approach taken in this book is essentially non-methodological in the sense that it does to adopt a prescriptive proprietary methodology. Techniques are included on the merit of being appropriate for a specific design task. The authors consider that it would be wrong to present a 'safe method' by implying that only one set of techniques will lead to successful information system development in all circumstances.

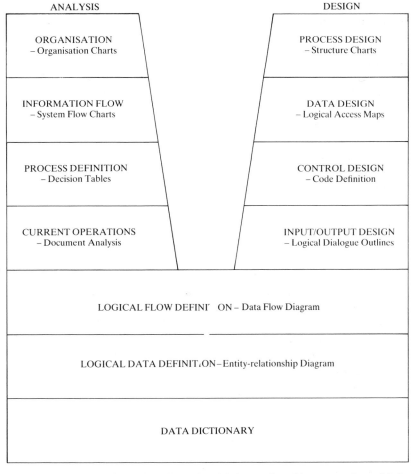

The diagram shows fundamental areas of analysis and design together with representative models for each area. The 'bedrock' of the system – the logical models – can be used to provide the bridge from analysis to design.

Figure 1.1   A Ravine Model of Analysis and Design

The techniques and models available to the practitioner from this toolkit vary in their level of detail and perspective. However, the distinction between physical and logical models (see *Introducing Systems Analysis*) remains important. Physical models reflect the technical and operational structure, ie how the current or future system works. Logical models show *what* the system needs to do to transform and manipulate input data into the required output. Thus they concentrate on *why* something must be done not who does it, when, and how. The emphasis in logical models on the underlying requirements of the information system makes them more stable over time and independent of the physical environment.

In general, good models of any viewpoint are simple, consistent, complete, accurate, hierarchical, and often graphical – a picture is worth a thousand words.

1.2   INFOSYS: A REVIEW OF THE SYSTEM REQUIREMENTS

InfoSys was introduced in *Introducing Systems Analysis*, and will be recalled as a small company with a wide range of interests in publishing and seminars. Analysis began with strategic planning to establish the appropriate information systems required by InfoSys to successfully achieve its business objectives. The Strategic Plan highlighted the following issues:

- The need for accurate information on seminar bookings. The associated tasks of material production, accommodation booking and catering were hampered by the absence of accurate, timely information.

- Greater quality control in seminar delivery. The seminars were not evaluated properly. There was no specific information on seminar popularity, lecturer performance, booking trends, customer characteristics, etc.

- The marketing of the seminar programme was hampered by the absence of any systematic record-keeping. Information about delegates was held in separate course folders and sometimes manually extracted for special mailshots. Enquiries were seldom recorded in any usable fashion. The impact of advertising the seminar programme in a variety of publications and magazines was not evaluated in any way.

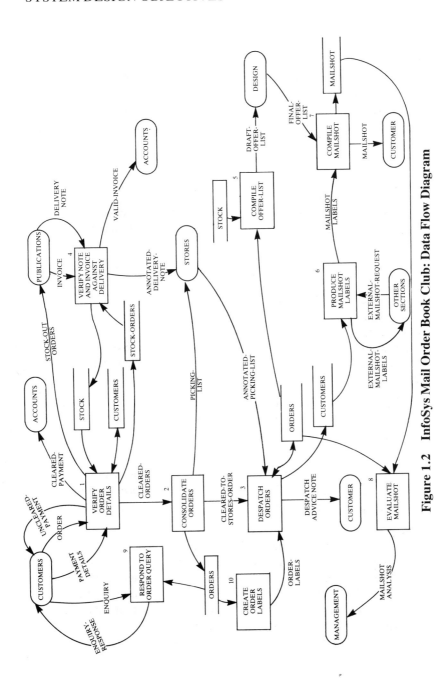

Figure 1.2 InfoSys Mail Order Book Club: Data Flow Diagram

It was subsequently agreed that a better information system was required to support a new, expanded seminars section, and a more efficient mailing system for the direct selling of computer-related titles. The mailing system will be necessary for, amongst other things, providing goods to customers, verifying that customers are fulfilling their terms of membership, and analysing mailshot responses and product sales.

A high level data flow diagram (Figure 1.2), an entity-relationship model (Figure 1.3) and a sample entity life history (Figure 1.4) have been extracted from the analysis documentation of the Current Logical System. These logical models will be referred to throughout the following chapters in the discussion of the design of an information system to meet the needs of InfoSys.

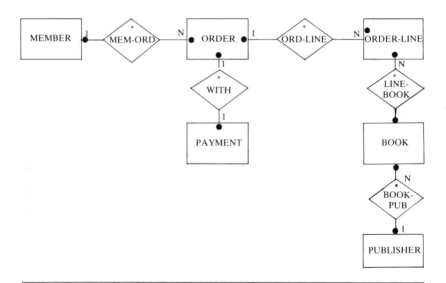

* Verification and clearance of order details
* Order consolidation and production of picking instructions
* Generation of member order despatch details
* Compilation of the offer list
* Compilation of a member mailshot and labels.

Figure 1.3   InfoSys Mail Order Book Club: Entity-relationship Diagram and Table

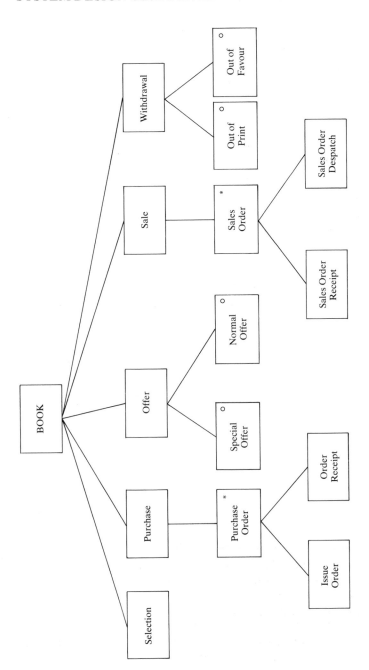

Figure 1.4 InfoSys Mail Order Book Club: 'Book' Entity Life History

1.3   WHAT IS SYSTEM DESIGN?

An information system design is a solution to a business problem. Design demands the translation of the requirements uncovered in analysis into possible ways of meeting them. There are many potential solutions to a specific problem and the Analyst will identify some of these and consider the relative merits of each in turn.

As with analysis, there are two levels of system design. *Logical design* produces a specification of the major features of the new system which meet the system objectives. The delivered product of logical design is a blueprint of the new system. It includes content requirements of the following system components:

- *Outputs* (reports, displays)

- *Input* (forms, screens, dialogues)

- *Procedures* (structure of procedures to collect, transform and output data)

- *Storage* (requirements for data to be stored in the database)

- *Control* (requirements for data integrity, security and procedures for recovery)

Physical design takes this logical design blueprint and produces the program specifications, physical file or database definition and user interface for a selected (or given) target hardware and software. These programs and files will fulfil the logical design requirements but may be subject to some constraints and compromises.

Sound logical design is important for the long term effectiveness of the system. It can be argued that the maintenance overheads of many companies is due to poor design, often resulting from a preoccupation with physical parameters and program fixes. Extensions and alterations to the system become progressively more difficult to incorporate and predict, leading to a large overhead that effectively stifles new systems growth. Martin (1984) reports that the US Department of Defence estimate that $16 million pa will be spent on maintenance by the end of the 1980s. On average, 60% of the lifetime software cost of a system is devoted to maintenance. Consequently, it is vital that the designer translates the requirements of the users into a physical design solution which fulfils system requirements, but in a way that imposes the least possible maintenance burden.

1.4 DESIGN OBJECTIVES

Design builds on the objectives set for the new information system in the Strategic Plan. Organisational objectives such as: increasing the business's profit, securing a larger market share, and improving customer service, are translated into specific business objectives. The Analyst seeks opportunities to support these by establishing a computer system contribution – such as information which is more rapidly accessed, up-to-date, accurate, and extensive or more logical processes and procedures. These are tightened up by adding criteria for success and delivery targets to form specific objectives which have to be met by the new system when it has been implemented.

The business goals for InfoSys are summarised in the following aims:

– to increase pre-tax profits by 25% within three years' time;

– to promote the European COMMUNIQUE image;

– to widen its service base.

These objectives are to be met by the establishment of a Mail Order Book Club supported by an information system which will:

– accurately identify targets for mailshots;

– produce mailing labels in a number of formats;

– analyse the success of each mailshot;

– process mail orders and maintain inventory records for the ordered goods.

There is of course, more than one way to achieve the requirements of the information system. A designer selects between many hardware, software and interface options in an effort to meet the objectives set. Similarly, these system objectives can be met by a simple, fairly crude solution or by a sophisticated implementation. The development of the *scope* of a design is addressed throughout the book. However, the achievement of the system objectives is only part of the story. There must also be a place for the overall elements of good design which are relevant to most applications.

The following list gives an indication of some of the desirable features of a 'good quality' design.

– *Functional*. Firstly, a system design should be functional in that it must successfully support the user's requirements. InfoSys requires a system which will accept members' orders for publications, and generate instructions for the assembly and despatch of individual orders. Specified hardware, software and business routines must enable the staff of InfoSys to effectively undertake their order-processing tasks. Programs which are less than fully functional in that they deal with only some of the tasks required will leave the staff to patch the system with their own efforts.

– *Efficient*. A system must also be able to meet the functional requirements within a specified time. A user of a system will quickly become disillusioned if delays are unacceptably long or agreed timescales are not achieved. This aspect of system quality may be measured in terms of:

- throughput (the ability to handle a specified number of documents per hour or day);

- response time (the ability to respond to a request for information within a given time limit);

- run time (the ability to undertake a whole processing task within a given time limit).

– *Flexible*. Many organisational systems are dynamic. They are affected by internal growth and politics, staff resignations and appointments, administrative reviews and re-arrangements, external takeovers, policies and pressures, and variations in customer preference and behaviour. Consequently, information systems designed to support the operational requirements should also exhibit flexibility, allowing users to adapt requirements to meet new needs as they become apparent. Systems that support static requirements may become progressively irrelevant.

– *Portable*. Portability is closely linked to independence. The rate of technological change means that investment in existing systems will only be preserved if the designer takes effective measures to ensure that only a minimum of conversion work is required to transfer a system from one computing environment to another. Systems built in this way can harness technical advances rather than reject them on the grounds of 'the cost of the re-write'.

– *Secure*. Data is a costly and hence valuable organisational asset and so any system which collects and processes it must be resistant to breaches of privacy and confidentiality. Systems must also be designed to meet legislative requirements for privacy. Ways in which an Analyst can ensure a system is designed to be secure are described in Chapter 4.

– *Reliable*. Integrity is a further feature of a good design. Parkin (1988) describes a system as having 'good integrity' when 'all the desired data is accurately recorded, without omission, and stored on the computer safely, so that it is not accidentally or deliberately corrupted or lost.' Thus a system must be trustworthy and accurate and it must exhibit these qualities to internal and external auditors who have the responsibility for checking the validity of the system.

– *Economical*. The need for a design which demands minimum storage for data and programs is probably a feature which has become less important as hardware costs rapidly decline. Nevertheless, minimising the amount of redundant data stored by a system reduces problems associated with amendment, insertion and deletion of data. These difficulties associated with data redundancy have been discussed more fully in Chapter 7 of *Introducing Systems Analysis*.

– *Usable*. Emphasis has recently been placed on the assessment of a design by the ease with which it may be learned and operated within acceptable levels of human discomfort, tiredness, effort, etc. Shackel (1986) suggests that the design process must be:

- User-centred
- Participative
- Experimental
- Iterative
- User-supportive

It is the people – systems developers and end users – who are the keys to successful applications of technology for business results. Schott and Olson (1988) state that a usable system may be defined as one that is not only user friendly but also feels 'normal' to use. This feature will be discussed more fully in Chapter 3.

Lists of criteria for good design (such as the one presented above), are very difficult to meet completely in a particular system project.

Furthermore, individual objectives may conflict. For example, a system which is very efficient in throughput may not be sufficiently secure for the user's requirements. Also, it may not be supported by on-line help features or even be flexible in the mode of operation it requires. The designer will have to make a compromise between these factors. Thus flexibility may be sacrificed for performance, and excessive functionality trimmed in the light of cost estimates.

1.5   DESIGN CONSTRAINTS

Constraints which will affect the designer are principally those of:

– *Budget*. The total system cost of meeting the objectives must be considered in the light of the available budget. 'Better' design – functionality, flexibility, portability, etc often incurs greater expense. Sophisticated secure hardware may be obtained and tight security procedures implemented to protect access to sensitive financial data. However, the overall cost of these measures may be prohibitive and indeed make the whole project infeasible.

– *Time*. The purchasers of computer systems usually have two primary questions: how much will it cost?, and when will it be delivered? Time taken to produce very usable systems will increase development costs and delay system delivery. It will also take a considerable time to design, build and thoroughly test adaptable interfaces which will enable the skill level of a user to evolve. This may produce a better design with enhanced long term productivity but its development cost and time may rule it out completely.

– *Integration with other systems*. Existing and planned systems may limit the options and features available. System development rarely takes place in a virgin site where there is no previous system to exert its influence and impose constraints. In nearly all cases the designer must interface with existing hardware, use available software tools and collect data from some previous manual or computer-based system.

– *Skills*. Limitations may arise from the range of skills and level of competence in both the design team and the planned users and operators of the system. Thus the design may reflect current strengths and practises of the data processing department (using COBOL rather than a 4GL for example) as well as incorporating procedures which recognise particular skill shortages in the workforce.

– *Standards*. Developments in workstation design involving a standard system architecture across personal computers and mainframes (Adie, 1988) will make it easier for the user to move from machine to machine. A common user interface will make machines more familiar.

Other internal standards may also drive the design task in a specified direction. For example:

- the hardware must be IBM;

- COBOL must be used for system development;

- all microcomputers must be IBM PS/2 compatible;

- the software must produce files accessible by dBase IV.

1.6 MEASURES OF DESIGN EFFECTIVENESS

Such objectives and constraints are normally defined in the requirements specification produced at the end of the analysis phase, and the design must be undertaken in this framework. Parkin (1988) states that these objectives must be measurable to ensure that they can be assessed. Objectives relating to performance may be specified in terms of throughput, response time, run time, etc. Usability is more difficult to consider objectively. However, Schott and Olson (1988) suggest that a system's usability may be measured in terms of:

– the time it takes to learn a system's basic concepts and master its operation;

– the rate of occurrence and ability to recover from errors of a specific type;

– the warm up time required to relearn after absence of the user;

– attitudes (ie user satisfaction). Usable systems have greater acceptance.

1.7 A ROAD MAP OF INTRODUCING SYSTEMS DESIGN

Figure 1.5 shows the structure and content of the following chapters in the form of a road map. However, it must be made clear that successful

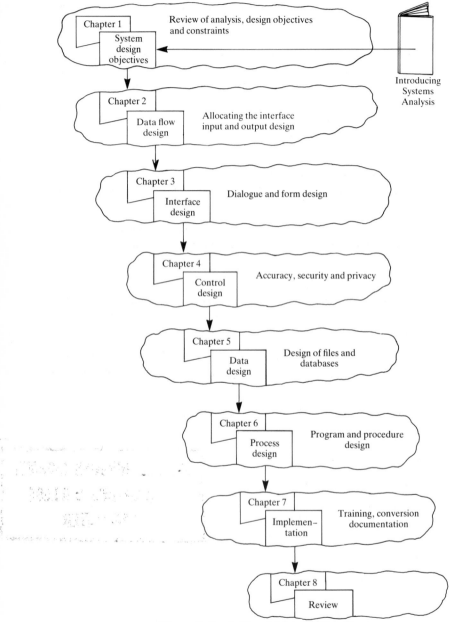

Figure 1.5   A 'Road Map' of this Text

information system design and development is not a linear process, achieved by simply progressing through the suggested stages without reflection or reassessment of what has been previously considered and decided. Design is an iterative activity and so readers are strongly urged to continually review their understanding of previous tasks so that they can strengthen their understanding of the whole design process.

1.8 SUMMARY

This chapter has:

- Suggested that system design is concerned with effectively and efficiently meeting the system requirements identified in the preceding analysis.

- Distinguished logical from physical design. Logical design is concerned with *what* and *why* rather than *how*. It provides a sound foundation for the subsequent physical design.

- Defined logical design as encompassing input, output, procedure, storage and control content. Physical design is primarily concerned with file and database definition together with specific interface tasks such as form and screen design.

- Established that certain models will support logical design definition whereas others will aid the transition to a physical implementation.

- Identified a number of general design objectives:

  - functional
  - efficient
  - flexible
  - portable
  - secure
  - reliable
  - economical
  - usable

which must be acknowledged in the design phase. However, it was also recognised that these will conflict with each other as well as with constraints of time, budget, skills, system integration and standards.

– Introduced the InfoSys case study and supporting analysis models as a basis for subsequent design discussion.

The point that physical design must be based upon sound logical foundations must be reinforced. The designer is planning for the future as well as fulfilling the immediate needs of the present. He or she is seeking to build substantial structures that will undergo modernisation and changes in use and ownership. This will be achieved by adaption not destruction. Shanty systems that support short term functions quickly become expensive long term problems.

1.9 PRACTICAL EXERCISES AND DISCUSSION POINTS

This text is concerned with the design of information systems. The interaction of these design issues, for example: file design affects program design, control design impacts upon input design, etc, led us to conclude that the main focus of the practical exercises should be a common case study using a library system.

The introduction of this common theme also gives us the opportunity to present three of the models introduced in the complementary text – *Introducing Systems Analysis*. Specifically:

– the rich picture;

– data flow diagrams;

– entity-relationship model.

These are used in the case study to further expand on the information given in the text.

Library Case Study

1.0 Initial Scenario

This case study concerns an imaginary library. It must be stressed that the case does not initially consider a complete system and all the probable requirements of a library system are not considered. For example, fines or the maintenance of a reference section are omitted.

The case study library is based in a small Professional Institute in Central London. It has the twin purpose of serving both qualified and student members of the Institute. It also provides a facility for schoolchildren to study the activity of the Institute with the aim of encouraging them to pursue the profession. This latter objective has led to the formation of the Elephant Club for children aged under 16 years of age, offering library facilities, newsletters and competitions.

The library receives applications on a standardised application form which requests name, address and status of the applicant. This last piece of information is used to ascertain how many tickets should be allocated to the applicant because there is a differential loan limit. For example, 'Academics' may borrow up to 10 books at a time, 'Juniors', only three. The date of joining the library is also recorded.

Vetting of applicants is restricted to requesting documentary proof of identity and status. The Librarian would like to see some method of identifying multiple applications and, more importantly, the identification of applicants who have previously been expelled from the library for disciplinary reasons. This is in the light of a recent offence when a 'Student' banned from the library for desecrating books re-enrolled five months later and destroyed copies of important manuscripts.

After the applicant has been vetted, he or she is allocated a certain number of tickets, with each ticket permitting the loan of one book. Thus an Academic is given ten tickets and a Junior three. The new library member is then free to borrow the appropriate number of books.

Once the books have been selected the member presents them to the library staff who take the cardboard identification slips out of each book and place them inside the borrower's tickets. One slip is placed inside one ticket. The tickets are then stored in a long wooden ticket box alphabetically within date order. Thus tickets for books due back today are nearer the front of the box than tickets for books due back tomorrow. It is not possible to borrow more than the loan limit because the borrower runs out of tickets! The book is then stamped with the return date and the borrower takes the book away.

When the borrower returns the book the date of return is checked and the appropriate ticket located in the wooden ticket box. This is done by first identifying the section containing tickets due back on the stamped return date and then searching alphabetically through this section. The identification slip is taken out of the ticket and tucked back into the book which is placed on a wheeled trolley ready for return to the shelves. The borrower's ticket is given back to the borrower who may then begin to peruse the book stock for his or her next selection.

Thus any system that replaces the current manual operations should permit the recording of a loan and its subsequent return. The Librarian feels that the present system works fairly well but that the information it gives is fairly limited. "You must understand", he says "that the present system is geared to date information because we need to quickly identify books which are overdue so that we can send these borrowers a reminder." However, this prevents the Librarian from seeing the complete borrowing record of a single borrower, ie which books are on loan to a given person at any one time. "To do this we would have to search through all the date due sections in the ticket box and extract a borrower's tickets individually".

Hence the replacement system should permit the identification of loans that have exceeded their return date and despatch overdue loan reminders. It should also give the opportunity of viewing a particular borrower's record.

A monthly book purchase brings new acquisitions into the library. These are recorded in a large foolscap 'acquisitions book' showing details of the book's title, author(s), publisher, publication date, price and ISB number. This latter entry refers to the International Standard Book Number (ISBN), a unique number allocated to a book and printed on its frontispiece. The code has four sections or facets; language, publisher, serial number and a check digit. The library also gives all acquisitions a unique code of its own called an accession number. This number is recorded in the accession book and also, along with the first author name and book title, on the cardboard identification slip that is placed inside the the book.

"There are a number of problems with this system" confides the Librarian. "But three really stand out. Firstly, the accession book is a very clumsy method of recording our stock and it begins to look even more amateurish when we start to do amendments and deletions – red crossings out all over the place. Secondly, the use of a removable cardboard slip is open to great abuse. A fair proportion of them seem to get lost or are switched between books, especially after the Saturday morning 'Elephant Club' for younger readers. We are constantly rewriting slips which requires time-consuming references to the acquisitions book."

The final problem identified by the Librarian concerns the valuation of the book stock. The Library Policy Sub-committee requires the Librarian to submit both the purchase and replacement costs of the book stock. This is needed for both accounting and insurance reasons. This request cannot be complied with at present. "It's headache enough just entering and totalling all the purchase prices, let alone maintaining the current price. I've told them it's impossible but they insist that their directive is followed. That's the problem when you get accountants interfering with matters that they don't understand."

Thus, it is clear that a replacement system must deal with the acquisition, deletion and maintenance of the book stock. Both purchase and current prices are necessary. The problem of lost slips seems to suggest a method of processing that does not require physical removal and storage.

"Reservations are a nightmare", claimed the Librarian, "in fact I have suggested to my staff that they tell enquirers that the service has been suspended due to staff cutbacks."

To process a reservation the library staff must:

- identify the present location of the book: this is done by searching the shelves and, if not found, looking at the borrowers' cards in the wooden ticket box;

- write to the present borrower requesting the immediate return of the book;

- chase the borrower if he fails to respond to the written request;

- match a returned book with the borrower who requested it;

- write to the person who made the reservation informing them that the book is now ready for their collection;

- chase the potential borrower to ask why he has failed to collect the book he reserved so urgently.

So the system should permit the speedy processing of requests, amendments and cancellation of reservations.

2.0 Modelling the Scenario

It is helpful to model problem areas so that we can begin to see the logical structure of the system that we are tackling. A first step might be to draw a Rich Picture of the library system. This is an attempt to illustrate important flows, boundaries and worries identified in the problem area. A possible Rich Picture for the library system is given as Figure 1.6. Rich Pictures can be used to show both the movements of physical objects (such as books) and the data flow that records such movements. In computerisation we are mainly concerned with this data flow and the opportunities it presents for automation. Figure 1.7 extends the Rich Picture to concentrate upon flows of information. The clouded areas are aspects of the system that we still know little about and these will all require clarification. This will usually be achieved by seeking further information from the users and operators of the library. Our aim is to build a logical model, using an appropriate modelling technique, which is free of these clouded areas of ignorance. The one we have chosen, and which is partly used in Figure 1.7, is the data flow diagram. A completed data flow model is given as Figure 1.8. A static view of the data structures of the case study is given in Figure 1.9.

3.0 Detailed Transaction List

From our models of the system we can identify ten major transactions that have to be supported.

1 *Store Details of a New Borrower.* This will require some checking of the record of previous offenders, probably based upon Name and Address.

An input screen will request Applicant Name, Applicant Address and Borrower Status. It will use this Borrower Status to determine the number of books that this member may borrow at any one time.

An option will also be required for amending borrower details (eg change of address) and status (moving from Junior to Academic).

2 *Store Details of a New Acquisition.* This will be done via an input screen that requests the Title of the book, Author(s), Publisher, Publication Date, ISBN and Purchase Price. It will also be necessary to permit the allocation of an Accession Number and

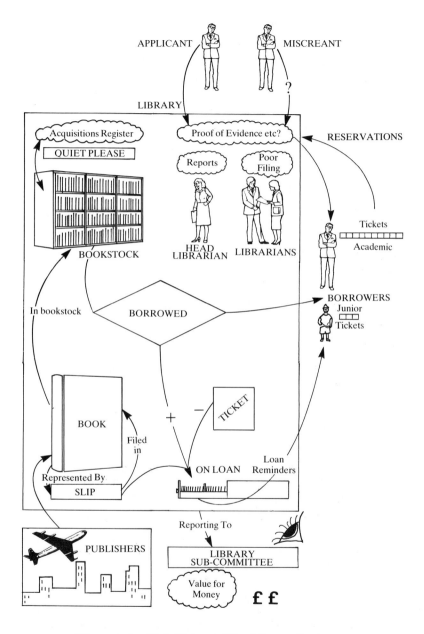

Figure 1.6   Rich Picture of the Library System

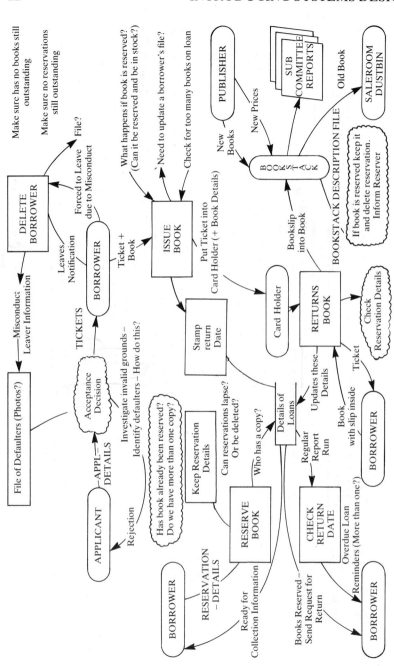

Figure 1.7   Information Flow Expanding the Rich Picture

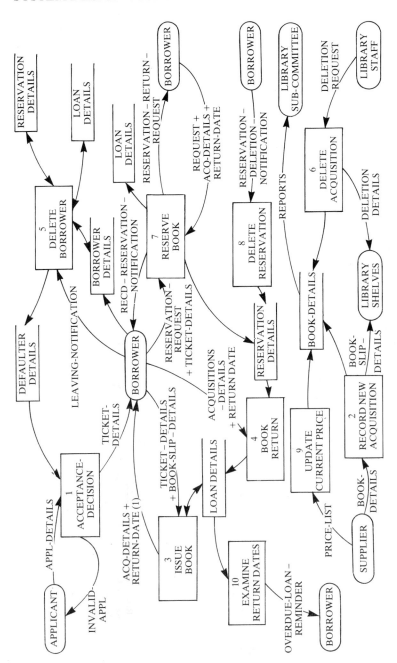

Figure 1.8 Top-level Data Flow Diagram – Library System

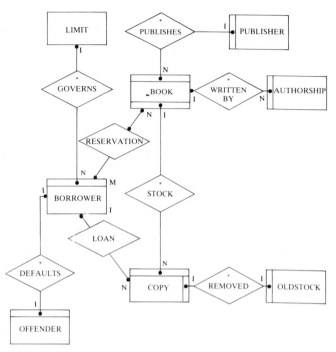

Tables

BORROWER: (<u>Borrower-Number</u>, Borrower-Name,
   Borrower-Address, Join-Date, Borrower-Status)

COPY: (<u>Accession-Number</u>, ISBN, Purchase-Price)

BOOK: (<u>ISBN</u>, Title, Publication-Date, Current-Price)

LIMIT: (<u>Borrower-Status</u>, Loan-Limit)

PUBLISHER: (<u>Publisher-Code</u>, Publisher-Name)

AUTHORSHIP: (<u>ISBN, Author-Name</u>)

OLDSTOCK: (<u>Accession-Number</u>, Acq-Delete-Code,
   Acq-Delete-Date)

OFFENDERS: (<u>Borrower-Name, Borrower-Address,</u>
   Borrower-Number, Leaving-Code, Leaving-Date)

LOAN: (<u>Accession-Number</u>, Borrower-Number, Loan-Date)

RESERVATION: (<u>Borrower-Number, ISBN</u>, Reservation-Date,
   Request-Date, Notification-Date)

Figure 1.9   Library Case Study – First Level Design

the Current Price as defined in the Library Sub-committee's requirements. It should additionally be noted that it is the library's policy to only stock one edition of a book. If a new edition is released then all copies of the previous edition are disposed of.

The facility to amend details will also be required. This can be done by showing all the details of the text and editing just the required field because the data should not change very often.

3 *Make a Loan*. The system should permit the retrieval of Borrower Name and Address and provide a template for the entry of books which the member intends to borrow. It is important that the system does not permit the Loan Limit to be exceeded. Books already on loan will *not* be displayed.

An additional facility will permit the retrieval of current information about a specific borrower. This screen will display Borrower Name, Address, Status and books currently on loan together with their Return Date. Current reservations will also be displayed. A printout of this report will be required.

4 *Record Return of Loan*. A facility is required to delete books from the borrower's record. Such a screen will look very similar to the loan screen but it does not require a process to check for overstepping of the Loan Limit. In this instance there will be an associated process which will determine whether the returned book is on reservation.

5 *Delete Borrower*. A screen giving the facility to delete borrowers from the system. This might include some visual checks to ensure that the wrong borrower is not deleted. It should not be possible to delete borrowers who still have outstanding loans. Such members are transferred to the defaulters' file for checking against future applications.

6 *Delete Acquisition*. Removal of a book from the book stock.

7 *Reserve Book*. Permits the reservation of a book by a borrower. It allows for the automatic location of the present position of this book and notification of this on the screen, together with the production of a letter requesting the urgent return of the book if it is out on loan.

It also lists recalled books not returned within a certain time so that action can be taken by the library staff to suspend borrowing rights.

Additionally it matches a requested book with the member who has requested it and automatically generates a letter informing the member that the text is ready for collection, listing reserved books that remain uncollected after a specified period of time for further action by the library staff.

8 *Deletion of Reservation*. Allows the deletion of a reservation. Editing details of a request are probably not required in the system because the change of any detail is likely to prove so comprehensive that it can best be dealt with by deleting the original request and creating a completely new one.

9 *Update Current Price*. The facility to update Current Price. To permit speedy input of price changes the amendment screen should only show the Title, Author, ISBN and Current Price.

10 *Send Overdue Loan Reminder*. Automatic production of loan reminders mailed to those borrowers whose loans have passed the stamped return date. Details should include Accession Number, Book Title and Author.

Inputs and Outputs

The transactions listed above will have certain input and output screens associated with them.

Transaction 1

    Required: Input details of new applicants
    Comment: To create a record for a Borrower
    Data items: Applicant Name
                 Applicant Address
                 Applicant Status
                 Date of Joining

    Required: Modify details of an applicant
    Comment: To modify Borrower details such as Address
    Data items: As above

Transaction 2

Required:	Input details of a new acquisition
Comment:	Create a record for a new acquisition
Data items:	Accession Number
	Title
	Author(s)
	Publisher
	Date of Publication
	Purchase Price
	ISBN

Required:	Amend details of an acquisition
Comment:	Change Acquisition details except for Current Price
Data items:	As above

Transaction 3

Required:	Insert details of a loan transaction
Comment:	Record the details of books borrowed by a Borrower
Data items:	Borrower Name
	Borrower Address
	Accession Numbers of books
	Date of Loan

Required:	Profile of a Borrower's current loans and reservations
Comment:	To improve control and customer service
Data items:	Borrower Name
	Borrower Status
	Borrower Address
	Accession Numbers of books on loan
	Individual loan dates for those books
	Accession Numbers of books currently reserved
	Individual dates for those reservations

Transaction 4

Required:	Input details of books returned
Comment:	Record books returned by the Borrower
Data items:	Borrower Name
	Borrower Address
	Accession Numbers of returned books

Transaction 5

Required: Deletion of Borrower
Comment: Delete a Borrower record
Data items: Borrower Name
                   Borrower Address

Transaction 6

Required: Deletion of an Acquisition
Comment: Delete an Acquisition record
Data items: Accession Number
                   Title
                   Author(s)
                   ISBN

Transaction 7

Required: Input a book reservation
Comment: Record a reservation
Data items: Borrower Name
                   Borrower Address
                   Reserved books: ISBN
                                         Title
                                         Author(s)
                   Date of reservation

Required: Output a standard letter requesting book return
Comment: If the book is not in stock the current Borrower of the
                   book will be sent a letter demanding its return
Data items: Borrower Name
                   Borrower Address
                   Reserved book: ISBN
                   Title
                   Author(s)
                   Date of letter (Request Date)

Required: Reservation Delays Report
Comment: To list out all those Borrowers who have received
                   requests for the return of a book but who have not
                   complied within seven days of the Request Date
Data items: Borrower Name

Borrower Address
Requested Book: Title
                     Author(s)
                     ISBN
                     Request Date

Required: Letter notifying receipt of reservation
Comment: Letter to the Borrower who has reserved the book informing him that it is has been received
Data items: Borrower Name
Borrower Address
ISBN
Title
Author(s)
Reservation Date
Notification Date

Required: Uncollected Reservations Report
Comment: A report showing all those Borrowers who have made reservations but who have not collected them within seven days of the Notification Date
Data items: Borrower Name
Borrower Address
Reserved Books: ISBN
                     Author(s)
                     Title
                     Date of Reservation

Required: Last Reminder letter
Comment: To inform Borrowers who have not returned books within seven days of the Request Date that their borrowing rights have been suspended
Data items: Borrower Name
Borrower Address
ISBN
Title
Author(s)
Request Date

Transaction 8

Required: Input a reservation deletion

Comment: Some Borrowers cancel their reservations due to delays
Data items: Borrower Name
             Borrower Address
             ISBN
             Title
             Author(s)
             Reservation Date

Transaction 9

Required: Update Current Price
Comment: Permits current valuation of Stock
Data items: Title
             Author(s)
             ISBN
             Current Price

Transaction 10

Required: Notification of Overdue Loans
Comment: To inform Borrowers that their books are now overdue
             and should be returned to the library
Data items: Borrower Name
             Borrower Number
             Accession Numbers
             Titles
             Author(s)

2 Designing the Data Flows

2.1 INTRODUCTION

The main objective of an information system is to produce data to support the operations or decision-making of the enterprise. Data flows from sources are the routes by which data is captured while data flows to sinks represent the outputs of the system. Consequently a consideration of data flows appears to be an appropriate starting point for the design of a system.

A prototyping approach to information system development will generally mean that the design process is interwoven with the actual construction of the system (see Chapter 1 of *Introducing Systems Analysis*). However, iterative systems design still requires a suitable starting point. New system inputs (eg forms and screens which collect data) and outputs (eg displays and printed reports) are the real deliverables of a computer system and, as far as many users are concerned, are the main criteria for judging a proposed system. The Analyst will therefore often undertake some initial design of the inputs and outputs before embarking on the design of data storage or processes required to facilitate these data flows. A screen painting tool or the report generator of a fourth generation language may be used to effectively produce a mock-up of what the system will produce.

This chapter describes the process of designing input and output data flows. The process itself may be represented by means of a data flow diagram (see Figure 2.1). The design approach requires an initial decision on which of the required processes will be computer-based and which will be undertaken manually. Several possible system boundaries may be defined in discussion with users and subsequently evaluated as to

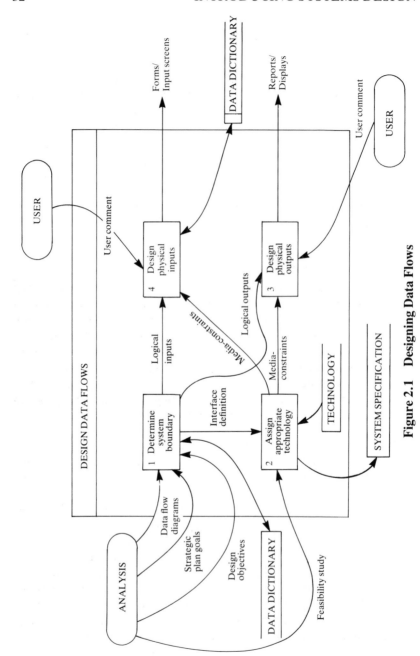

Figure 2.1   Designing Data Flows

how well they each meet the system objectives and the constraints of the system environment.

After agreeing the proposed boundary of computerisation, the most appropriate technology must be selected for capturing the required data, transforming it and for reporting the required output to users. This will demand detailed form and report design as well as the development of an appropriate human–computer interface. The latter is a particularly difficult area where the foundation laid by thorough analysis work and early design may be undermined, particularly if the user has no further opportunity to contribute to the design task. Designing and documenting the human–computer dialogue will be described in the next chapter.

2.2 THE ACTIVITY OF DESIGN

The increased availability of fourth generation software with screen painters, report generators and dialogue developers promises increased flexibility in this time-consuming and contentious aspect of design. Suggested input screens and output reports can be created relatively quickly and layouts and procedures can be discussed with users who are able to view and comment upon the 'real thing', rather than a paper image. Furthermore, significant improvements in programmer productivity are possible by automatically generating the format of inputs and outputs from the contents of the data dictionary.

However, despite the advantages offered by this iterative approach to input and output design it must be recognised that the design of forms, reports and transient screen displays remains one of the most creative tasks that the Analyst is required to do. These are the most visible deliverables of a computer-based information system and so it is essential that skill and thought are applied to the design of required forms, reports and displays. Users of systems will not care whether the internal mechanism of the computer processing is extraordinarily clever if the way in which they are expected to enter the data is difficult or awkward and if the reports are difficult to use. The effectiveness of many systems, computer based and manual, has been sabotaged at the outset by the poor design of forms to collect the data required (Garbage In – Garbage Out) and the poor presentation of information produced by the system.

2.3   TOP-DOWN SYSTEM DESIGN

The top-down approach to systems *analysis* began by examining the business objectives specified in the corporate Strategic Plan. These were then refined into specific system objectives which gave suggested targets for improvements. The operational arrangements for supporting these systems were investigated and their logical equivalents established. One of these logical models – the data flow diagram – can provide an appropriate 'top' level for design. It is used to explore and determine the scope of the system before progressing to the detailed design of individual inputs, outputs, databases, processes and controls.

2.3.1 Giving People Computing Power

Designing a system in a top-down manner begins by determining which processes are to be undertaken within the new computer system and which are not. This is shown as process 1 in Figure 2.1.

In spite of the extensive use made of computers in business, many users are still concerned that their tasks may be performed by the computer and thus make their skills less valuable to their employers and to society in general. The frequency of industrial disputes when such technology is introduced is a reflection of this concern. Eason (1984) argues that the slow adoption of information technology in many areas of business is caused by the worries of users concerning the impact of computerisation. They may be concerned about the possibility of actually losing their job or the prospect of extensive change in their responsibilities. Users frequently fear the need for retraining for new skills and the possible changes in formality at work.

Even the balance of power in the workforce may be altered when a new system is introduced. One of the authors of this book was involved in a project in a first time user company where a potential operator had to take tranquillisers before she could face the prospect of a software demonstration. Happily the same person is now in complete charge of the company's computer system having been fully trained and involved in the introduction of the new system.

The design of a business information system and the way it is to be integrated into the organisation will determine the type of operating procedures required and significantly affect users' working lives. Job design is an influential factor in the overall success of an information system. It can motivate people to use a new system to the benefit of the organisation and themselves. Alternatively, poor job design can lead to anxiety, mistrust, boredom and other de-motivating factors that reduce the employee's commitment to both the system and the organisation. Some opportunities in job design include:

- *Job enlargement*; ensure that the person has the responsibility to complete the tasks assigned to him. This may be achieved by giving the jobholder a 'customer' to whom he or she is responsible for accepting orders for work and for delivering the finished work on completion. Typists working in general typing pools are less satisfied than those who work for a particular person in the organisation where a document can be seen through from initial preparation to final printing.

- *Job rotation*; variety is important to most jobholders and each person should be given the opportunity to carry out different tasks. In some systems the rotation of jobs is also a measure of control undertaken to reduce the risks of a breach of security.

- *Job enrichment*; giving an operator more responsibility or more functions to perform may enrich an otherwise impoverished job. It may be achieved by giving responsibility for quality control, dealing with customers or the maintenance of the system itself. Minimising the undesirable or meaningless aspects of a job may also be achieved by looking for opportunities for automation or spreading the responsibility for such tasks.

- *Job design participation*; nobody knows the pitfalls and intricacies of a job as well as the jobholder. Participation in the shaping and definition of new jobs required in the system is beneficial and helps ensure an early identification with the eventual success of the system.

- *Work groups*; participation in a team encourages a sense of responsibility, belonging and obligation to the other members of the team. A group may wish to elect their own leader or supervisor and divide and rotate the responsibilities themselves. Giving people direct feedback from the results of a job ensures that a person knows whether he or she is succeeding or failing.

For job design to work well the designer must consider the job descriptions and relationships identified in the early stages of systems analysis. These can be used to identify job opportunities as well as highlighting likely changes in function, status and reporting arrangements that will result from the proposed design. These changes, or the threat and rumour of such changes, are certain to cause anxiety amongst the current jobholders who will begin to resist change through undermining confidence in both the system and the system developer. Consequently job change and job design must be actively managed by the designer and not be left to chance. An individual training strategy for each person affected by the system change must be drawn up and implemented. This strategy may be as wide-ranging as total re-skilling for a post on offer elsewhere in the organisation.

The designer must also be careful not to unwittingly impose his or her own job expectations upon others. Not all employees wish to have their tasks 'enriched' or 'enlarged'. Some people are not motivated by the interest of the job but by the money it provides. Mumford has suggested a job satisfaction inventory where employees are quizzed about their job expectations and needs. These can then be matched to tasks required in the system. Employees who prefer to undertake repetitive work without supervision and responsibility can be allocated these sorts of tasks in the newly designed system. The payment of technology bonuses should also be considered. Most people would wish to see the enrichment of their jobs filtering through to the pay packet!

2.3.2 Determining the System Boundary

The starting point for top-down systems design is the strategic plan and a set of levelled data flow diagrams. This latter hierarchical model has been previously constructed in a logical manner to represent the information system in terms of data flows, transformations of that data, and what data needs to be stored and output to achieve its objectives. It is not constructed in a way which is constrained by the present sequence or location of the current operations, nor is it limited by the possible implementation environment. The Analyst will not have embodied any assumptions about *how* the system is to work, such as which tasks will be computerised or whether a central or distributed computer facility is more suitable. (See also Chapter 6 of the companion text, *Introducing Systems Analysis.*)

A data flow diagram is a process-oriented model of the system which is further supported by a data dictionary containing the detailed definitions of the processes, flows and stores shown on the diagram. A continuous line may be superimposed on the data flow diagram to represent the boundary of the computer system. Placing this boundary is a relatively difficult task. If it is located in an inappropriate position then the objectives of the system may not be met, or alternatively it may lead to a solution that is too complex. A consideration of the type of processes shown in the diagram can help define an appropriate boundary.

Heuristic and Algorithmic Processes

Decisions about the position of the system boundary are initially made by closely examining the data flow diagram in a top-down, level by level, process by process manner, proceeding from the data sources to the data sinks. The purpose of this is to consider the appropriateness and potential benefits of computerising each process. This is assessed in terms of its contribution to the objectives of the business as well as its economical, technical and operational feasibility in the light of the current circumstances of the organisation.

One of the most significant factors determining the location of the process is likely to be whether it is heuristic or algorithmic. Heuristic processes are those which require a person's discretion and judgement when they are undertaken. These decisions typically include alternative goals and perhaps several routes to achieving these goals. Dealing with people in a negotiating or consultative manner is often associated with these processes.

For example, the proposed system at InfoSys may demand an evaluation of the market for the texts available from the Mail Order Book Club. Those responsible for this market research activity make discretionary decisions and plans. They may be assisted by the production of mailshot statistics and an examination of past and present orders. However, there are no firm rules for identifying a future book club best-seller, it is largely an intuitive 'gut reaction' combined with an element of risk. The computer system can be used to support the marketing decisions but not to make them. Heuristic processes are currently best allocated to human participants in the system, although the development of knowledge-based or expert systems which aid this type of problem-solving are becoming more accessible.

In contrast, algorithmic processes have a set of specified rules which always produce an agreed solution. These typically require the simple collection, manipulation, storing, and reporting of data to be used in other processes. Computers are very good at performing such tasks and consequently these processes are prime candidates for inclusion within the computer system boundary. For example, the calculation of net pay from gross pay, the addition of all invoice amounts, the forecast of next month's sales using time series analysis are all algorithmic processes. Human beings are usually quite poor at such tasks and hence jobs that contain extensive rule-following are usually subjected to cross-checks and re-calculation.

Other factors affecting whether processes are included or excluded from the computer system are the interwoven problems of economic, technical and operational feasibility (see Chapter 3 of *Introducing Systems Analysis*). For example, the technological capability and expertise to support a very ambitious, all-embracing design may exist but this possibility may be rejected because it may not be operationally acceptable in the organisation at the present time. It is clearly technologically possible to include all the processes of the Mail Order Book Club order processing system (Figure 2.2), including full automation of the picking of books for orders, within the boundary of a proposed design. This could be achieved by the selection of books from shelves by robots traversing defined routes through a warehouse, similar to the systems employed by some mail order companies. However, when economic and operational constraints are considered this option is likely to be rejected. The capital investment required for such a solution would not be cost effective for a small organisation. The scope of other proposed designs may also be limited by operational factors such as the availability of expertise within the organisation or the rigidity of departmental boundaries.

The Human–computer Boundary

The line representing the human–computer boundary is drawn on the data flow diagram to surround the logical data processes in the proposed area of computerisation. The intersection of data flows and the boundary line determines the position of the human–computer interface and this will be discussed in the next chapter.

The boundary line drawn on the top-level data flow diagram may provide a very graphical way of discussing the scope of the system with senior managers and representatives of users. Indeed a series of boundaries may be presented offering different costs and benefits. It is

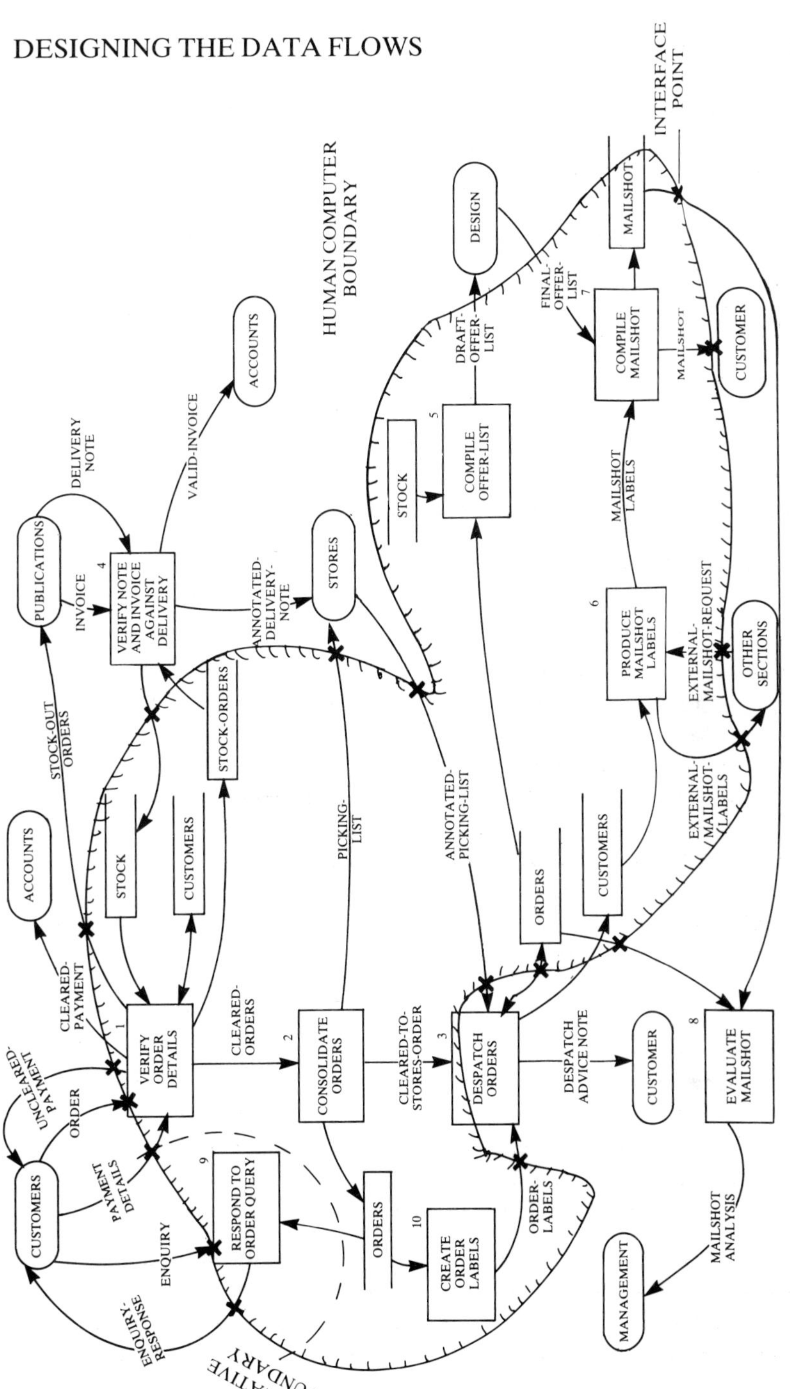

Figure 2.2 Mail Order Book Club Level 0 Data Flow Diagram

DATA DICTIONARY   **PROCESS**

Process Name: VERIFY ORDER DETAILS
System Name: Mail Order Book Club

Description: Accepts orders for books from club
members, verifies the order with stock & member
details and passes cleared orders for consolidation

Inputs	Logic summary	Outputs
ORDER	GET ORDER	CLEARED-ORDER
PAYMENT	GET PAYMENT	STOCK-OUT-ORDERS
STOCK	IF PAYMENT NOT CLEARED	CLEARED-PAYMENT
ISBN	SEND UNCLEARED PAYMENT	MEMBERSHIP
TITLE	ELSE (CLEARED PAYMENT)	REQUEST
AUTHOR	IF NEW MEMBER	
CUSTOMER	SEND MEMBERSHIP REQUEST	
MEMBER NO:	ELSE (EXISTING CUSTOMER)	
MEMBER-NAME	GET STOCK DETAILS	
ADDRESS	IF STOCK REQ > STOCK IN HAND	
	DESPATCH STOCK OUT REPORT	
	ELSE (STOCK LEVEL OK)	
	CLEARED ORDER	
	ENDIF	
	ENDIF	
	ENDIF	

Author: BW   **Date: 7/10/87**

Figure 2.3   Data Dictionary Entry for the Process 'Verify Order Details'

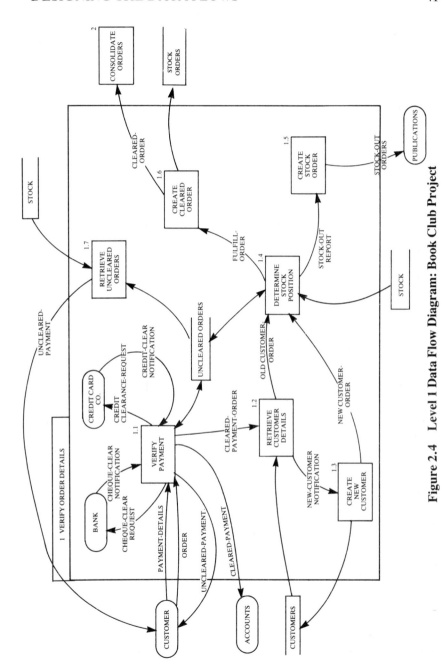

Figure 2.4   Level 1 Data Flow Diagram: Book Club Project

quite acceptable at this level for the line to cut through a process showing that only part of it is automated. In these instances the lower level data flow diagrams and their supporting data dictionary entries should be examined to locate the exact division of human and computer processes. If this is not possible then the data flow diagram must be decomposed even further. Processes where the distinction between automated and manual parts is unclear are unacceptable. Light hashing may be used to indicate the computer side of the boundary line.

Figure 2.2 illustrates a possible system boundary (shown by the hashed line) for the Mail Order Book Club order processing system. The feasibility of automating each of the ten high level processes should be considered in turn, from the technical, economic and operational standpoint. For the purposes of illustration two processes are considered in greater detail. The process 'Verify Order Details' is defined in the data dictionary entry in Figure 2.3 and shown in greater detail in the lower level data flow diagram in Figure 2.4. Examination of Figure 2.2 indicates there are strong arguments for at least partial inclusion of process 1 within the computer system boundary as the rules can be clearly defined. Consideration of the lower level data flow diagram indicates the options are:

- wait until the payment accompanying an order has been cleared before entering the order details (ie exclude process 1.1 Verify Payment from the system boundary);

- enter the order and payment details when received and cancel the order if the payment is not cleared (ie include the process 1.1 Verify Payment within the system boundary).

Further investigation reveals that a very low proportion of orders received each day are not cleared for payment and so recording the order details data at an early stage in the system causes few amendments for uncleared payments. It is clearly possible to rigorously define the criteria for order verification, and data entry is also likely to be very straightforward. The application is also likely to be operationally feasible because all orders are received by one office (and no plans exist for other office locations) and the anticipated volume can be easily entered within the time available (a maximum of 90 orders per day are expected).

In contrast, the process 'Respond to Order Query' appears to offer a variety of possibilities. For example, the company may wish to generate computer-produced letters or use stored information on book club transactions to answer any order queries. Alternatively, they may prefer to retain customer queries as a purely manual activity, believing that personal contact is essential. In the long run the scope of such computerisation will depend upon the following factors:

- the number of queries (the more frequently they arise the greater the time taken up in replies);

- the type of query (detailed responses may require access to stored information);

- the medium of the query (phone or letter);

- the required response time for the query (immediate responses may need to be computer-produced).

Once the initial location of the boundary has been agreed then a careful check has to be made on the use of stored data by the processes. Both manual and computer-based processes may require access to the same stored data. Therefore, it is likely to be beneficial to extend the boundary to avoid duplication of stored data, excessive system interaction and possible contention for access to the system. This decision will depend, for example, upon whether the manual system needs to access the most up-to-date records of orders or whether a reply

Input Data Flows	Output Data Flows
Payment	Uncleared-payment
Order	Cleared-payment
Stock-delivered	Stock-out-orders
External-mailshot-request	**Stock-order-details**
Annotated-picking-list	Draft-offer-list
Final-offer-list	Mailshot
Despatched-to-customer	External-mailshot-labels
Enquiry	**Order-details**
Orders-cleared-to-stores	Enquiry-response
Order-labels	

Figure 2.5 InfoSys Mail Order Book Club: Logical Inputs and Outputs

can be based on an earlier version of the data contained in an output
report.

2.4   IDENTIFYING INPUTS AND OUTPUTS

Determining the position of the system boundary enables the Analyst to
identify the logical inputs and outputs of the system (see Figure 2.1).
Figure 2.5 lists the data flows which intersect the system boundary and
so define the human–computer interface. The data structures of the data
flows crossing the boundary in an inward direction form the logical
specification of the required system inputs. Similarly, the data structures
of the outward data flows form the logical specification of the system
outputs.

Further details concerning the volumes and frequency of the data
flows will be found in the data dictionary entries supporting the data
flow diagram. The Analyst uses this information to decide on the most
appropriate type of input operation (whether it is to be on-line or a
batch process) and to assign the most effective data capture technique.

Logical data flows (in the outward direction) cross the agreed system
boundary and will specify the contents of displays and reports for the
user as well as direct communication with other systems. Figure 2.5
shows that the system produces outputs such as labels for order
despatching, picking lists for stores, and stock-out information for the
publishers. These have been listed from the data flow 'payment' in a
clockwise direction. The data dictionary entries for these data flows will
show the data structures and data elements which will appear in the
outputs. This may be further supported by an outline report layout
undertaken in the analysis phase. The data flows printed in bold are data
flows moving to or from a data store. These were not previously named
in the diagram (Figure 2.2) but clearly this is a system input or output
and so a process will be required to capture the data or generate the
output. In this way the drawing of the system boundary will further
refine the layout and detail of the data flow diagram.

Each of the input and output data flows defines the human–computer
interface (see Chapter 3). The internal data flows indicate the need to
pass data between internal processes and will normally correspond to
the passing of parameters between programs. This will be discussed in
detail in Chapter 6.

2.5 ASSIGNING APPROPRIATE TECHNOLOGY

Detailed examination of input and output data flows in the data dictionary and data flow diagram will reveal the technical requirements needed to support effective input and output. The configuration must reflect:

- the number and complexity of different data flows;

- the timing of data flows;

- the response time required by users;

- the location of data flows;

- the type of users and their skill level.

With this information the Analyst can make broad decisions about the computer hardware in four main areas: data capture, data processing, data storage and data reporting.

Processing Load

The overall sizing of the required processing power of the system and the functionality of its workstations will be affected by the number and complexity of the processes invoked by data flows. The Analyst will examine the data flow diagrams, the entity-relationship model and the entity life history considering such factors as:

- The volume and frequencies of events requiring data inputs. A need for handling thousands of enquiries per hour will require different technology to one in which similar enquiries are infrequent. Hardware must be able to achieve the specified throughput of data flows from data capture to information reporting.

- The number of simultaneous tasks required. A need to simultaneously handle enquiries, input new transactions and output reports demands much more power than a dedicated single task system. The Analyst must determine the desired concurrency of activities.

- The number and location of users entering and retrieving data. Remote users may require on-line access to the data or be satisfied with a printed report which does not reflect the current values of the data. Data entry may also be seasonal (entering examination results).

Input Device	Example Application
Traditional QWERTY keyboard	Word processing
Numeric keypad	Manufacturing production lines
Optical character or mark recognition device	Multiple choice examinations
Badge and bar scanner	Security systems
Kimball tag reader	Stock control systems in retail garment industry
Light pen	Library book issue systems
Touch-sensitive screen	Some bank cash tellers
Mouse	Personal or graphics applications
Voice and vision	Electronic conferencing and security systems

Figure 2.6   Applications of Data Capture Devices

– Overall transaction response times. Some inputs will need to be acted upon and processed immediately (ie in transaction mode) but for others a delayed response after accumulation of similar inputs (ie in batch mode) will suffice.

– System availability and enquiry response time. The technology selected must ensure that the requirements of all users can be satisfied without unnecessary delay. Seasonal variations in response requirements must also be acknowledged.

2.6   DATA INPUT

There are many ways of capturing the data for a system. The most traditional mechanism is the keyboard. However, technological advances continue to add to the range of possible input devices. Figure 2.6 is a table of input devices with examples of applications.

The selection of an appropriate input method will be guided by:

- *What type of data is being input?* The nature and format of the data required by the system is important. For example, alphanumeric data may be entered by keyboard or optical character readers but voice transmission of such data may be too error-prone.

- *How often is data captured?* The volumes and frequency of input are also important. For instance, large, frequent sets of data giving account debits and credits may require input directly via magnetic strip or optical character reading. Entering this data in any other way may be both time-consuming and expensive.

- *In what circumstances?* The user and environmental constraints will limit the choice. A numeric keyboard may be used for logging data in dirty, dusty building sites. A user may be unwilling to develop keyboard skills and hence demand the use of a mouse controlled interface.

  Technological constraints must also be considered. For example, the need to receive data through physical links with other, established computer systems.

The following guidelines may assist the Analyst in the evaluation of alternatives.

Seek to minimise data transcription. Every time that data is transcribed or copied the chance of error or delay is increased. Most transcriptions demand routines to trap erroneous input either through repeated data entry (data verification), software checking of data contents (data validation) or both. Direct entry of data overcomes transcription problems.

Seek to minimise data transmission. Every transmission, whether by word of mouth, post or telephone, incurs cost, delay and an increased chance of error.

Seek to minimise the amount of data recorded. The input of many systems can be predicted in advance. A request, for example, for the payment of water rates can pre-print or code data about the user's name, address, postal code, property reference and payment required.

The only data required from the customer is the payment of the bill! *Turnaround* documents will contain the information that is already known (often presented in an appropriate OCR font) and leave space for the completion of the remaining unknown values.

Once logical input requirements have been established and an input technology assigned then detailed form design can commence. Design is likely to encompass:

i)   data collection forms for the users and operators of the system;
ii) input screen design;
iii) the design of direct capture documents such as OMR and OCR forms.

Many of the detailed considerations of input form design are also important in output presentation and are discussed in depth in the next section.

2.7   OUTPUT DESIGN

Information may be output to the user through a variety of devices. The most common technology used is a monochrome or colour visual display screen for transient display of information, or printers (character, line and laser) for permanent 'hard copy' output. Some systems need the output of graphical information and therefore require the use of high resolution visual display units or plotters. Voice, music and video are also candidate technologies for applications such as office automation and electronic conferencing.

Once again the following questions can be asked by the Analyst:

– *What type of information is being output?* The nature and format of the information being produced. For example, periodic management reports may need to be printed for consideration at board meetings and so hard copy output from a high quality printer is required. Responses to ad hoc queries may normally be required via a screen with the facility to make occasional hard copy from a fast dot matrix printer. A further example is the Profit and Loss Report which may initially be required in draft format but later needs to be produced in quality print for the company's external auditors.

The information contained in Figure 2.7 does not need to be

```
30/08/85        BIAS  Q-ERY:Reporter :   Quoin Demo Ltd         Page  3
User 1          ==========================================

BALANCE SHEET
=============

Fixed Assets
------------
    Capital Vehicles            9700.00
    Capital Plant               3868.44
    Capital Office Equipment    3589.98
    Capital Computer             488.95
                               --------
        Total fixed assets                      17647.37

Current Assets
--------------
    Stock                       2450.00
    Work in Progress           16426.68
                               --------
                                           18876.68

    Sales Ledger Balances
    Mr H Dickenson                82.54
    J Dempsey Ltd                  8.97
    Pro & Crastin Ltd          21000.00
    Steetwise PLC               7687.20
    Trewin, Pike & Klogg        4201.41
                               --------
    Total sales ledger debtors              32980.12

    Prepayments                  750.00
                               --------
                                             750.00

    Cash
    Holiday Stamp Stock A/C      234.25-
    Bank Current A/C          32407.16-
    Cash (Wages)                371.31-
    Petty Cash                   30.38
                               --------
                                           32982.34-

        Total current assets                19624.46

        TOTAL ASSETS                        37271.83


30/08/85        BIAS  Q-ERY:Reporter :   Quoin Demo Ltd         Page  4
User 1          ==========================================

LESS
Creditors
---------
    Purchase Ledger Balances
    Brightside & Low              24.15-
    W Craig                      140.30-
    Down & Featherstone           30.88-
    Ford & Slatter                37.80-
    LMS Roads                    142.79-
    Magnum Ltd                   112.45-
    Proof & Spirit                 6.33-
    Rankin & Cool Ltd             14.73-
    A Tattersall & Co             11.56-
    Wadsworth & Co               452.88-
                                --------
        Total Purchase Ledger Creditors        973.87-

    Inland Revenue              3332.55-
    HM Customs & Excise         1098.60
                               --------
                                            2233.95-

    Provisions                  1172.07-
                               --------
                                            1172.07-
                                           --------
                                            4379.89-
                                           =========
                                           32891.94
                                           =========

Financed by Long Term Creditors
-------------------------------
    I M Aboss Capital A/C       4787.73-
    Bonclays Trust plc         10000.00-
    Car Loan                    5895.97-
                               --------
                                           20683.70-

Net Profit (+ve = loss) per P&L A/C        12208.24-
                                           --------
                                           32891.94-
                                           =========
```

Figure 2.7   Sample Balance Sheet

generated in a high standard of presentation since it is not the final product and will be further amended by the user.

– *How much information is output and how often?* The volumes and frequency of output are also important in the selection of the output device. For example, a printed stock report produced at the start of the trading period may be sufficient for certain users. However, immediate display of the most recent information about stock levels may be required by an order clerk who is responsible for accepting and allocating stock to customer orders. An historic order report does not provide the information needed for the clerk to do his job successfully.

The frequency of information requirement is particularly important in a car park display. Limited but continuously updated information of the current number of spaces available may be displayed to the prospective customers waiting in a queue. In this case, it would clearly be of little use to refer to a printed report of spaces available at a previous time.

– *In what circumstances?* User and environmental constraints also influence the selection of the output device. Blind people will require special consideration and sound or touch devices may be needed. Factory operatives may need information which cannot be inadvertently destroyed by the processes in which they are involved. The Analyst may consider video recording display screens which could be rerun to access this information. Technological constraints are the final consideration. The location of the information requirement may demand output devices that have certain security features, are tolerant to dirt and dust or which are mobile and can be wheeled freely around the factory floor.

2.7.1 Designing Computer Reports and Displays

The point has already been made that the logical content of all data flows (inputs and outputs) which intersect the boundary may be derived from the data flow diagram and its associated data dictionary entries. Consequently, these models are therefore the most appropriate starting point for the detailed design activity. Whilst many authors would consider designing forms, reports and screens to still be more of an art than a science, some significant design factors should be kept in mind. These design factors and the principal features of a report are illustrated in Figure 2.8.

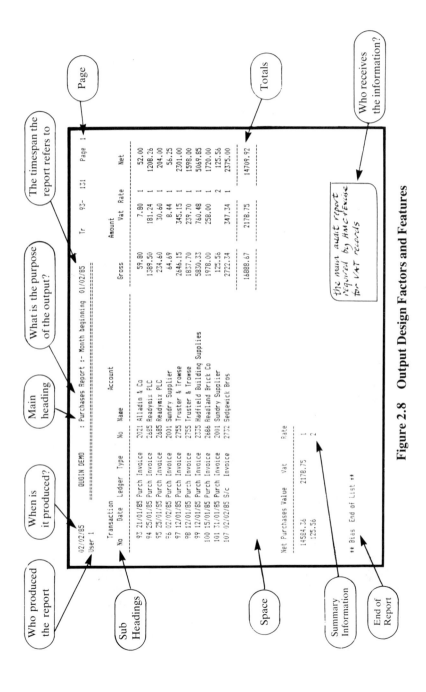

Figure 2.8   Output Design Factors and Features

– *Who receives the information?* All messages need to match the needs of the anticipated user. Hence the Analyst must research the skills and knowledge level of all likely users and determine an appropriate vocabulary for the report. In a recent system the term 'not called off' was commonly used within the company but not by the customers who were to receive a copy of certain reports. Consequently, the term 'no delivery instructions received' was the column heading presented on the report.

– *What is the purpose of the information?* There are many types of report which might be required for different purposes by the users of the system, e.g. a report may form the paper record of data being deleted from the system or be used as a turnaround document which will collect further data to be entered at a later time. A more detailed list of report types is given later in this chapter.

– *When and how often is the information required?* It may be produced on demand, daily, weekly, monthly or perhaps only annually. Timeliness of information is very important since the value of information is rapidly lost if it is produced later than the need to act on it. Consider the use of a report giving details of the profitability of a contract which can only be produced six months after the completion of that contract. The information has no real value to the management of the contract as they cannot alter their actions in the light of the knowledge that they are losing money. Reports need to be as up-to-date as possible and supplied to management while they can still act on the information.

– *What is the best format for supplying the information?* Paper reports and documents are still important to many people. Deeds and contracts are still necessarily found in hard copy. The Analyst will consider the quality required and the cost of producing the result. In some instances the requirements may justify the costs of special preprinted stationery. There are many alternative formats to computer listing paper or preprinted forms, eg punched cards (shop tags), microfiche, plastic identity cards (eg exhibition cards), screen displays, audio output and direct data transmission. The choice is a matter of feasibility – economic, technical, operational – and the Analyst must clearly determine the requirements and evaluate the options.

```
Borrower No: LP P07620174                    29 July 1988

                                             Due back
0115400568 2 548   Mystery Aboard            15-07-88
0711200599 1 993   The Book of France        28-08-88
0415700278 1 887   Get by in France          28-08-88
```

Figure 2.9   On-demand Library Book Request

```
QR16 Rel 2.15        Job Expenditure Details         30/08/85 [1]

Job No   172 97 Nicholson Rd + 2 Others    Job Reference
Client   1731                              Contract Value
                                           Estimated Cost
   Last Trans 22/08/85   Complete          Surv Val (      )
                         Rel Date          Cost O/s (      )
Cost MTD                 Retention
Cost Total    38082.99   Invoiced   49108.00  Margin 28.95% * 11025.01


   Nominal     MTD        Details               Total
      1                Materials              22163.62
      2                Labour                 15898.37
      3                Labour Only Subcontractors
      4                Domestic Subcontractors    21.00
      5                Nominated Subcontractors
      6                Overheads
      7                Plant Hire
      8                Waste Disposal
      9                Spare
```
Do you want a breakdown of expenditure (Y/N) [P]

Figure 2.10   Query Job Cost Details

```
30/08/85                    BIAS  Q-ERY:Reporter :      Quoin Demo Ltd
User  1                     ====================================================
```

[file PRLS.DAT Rel 1.03] negative = credit positive = debit

TRADING ACCOUNT
===============
Revenue

```
        Sales Extensions & New Work        35820.30-
        Sales Maintenance                  24157.84-
        Sales Special Projects             31262.22-
                                          ------------
                                                          91240.36-
```

Stock

```
        Stock Movement this period         15035.12
                                          ------------
                                                       15035.12
                                                      ------------
                Summary of income                                 76205.24-
```

Expenditure

```
        Materials                          25443.58
        Labour                             13357.18
        Labour Only Subcontractors         10746.37
        Domestic Subcontractors              786.78
        Nominated Subcontractors             287.50
        Overheads                             75.07
        Plant Hire                          1116.34
        Waste Disposal                       364.00
        Holiday Stamps Allocated             984.40
                                          ------------
                                                       53161.22

        NHI Employers                       1728.72
                                          ------------
                                                        1728.72
                                                      ------------
                Summary of expenditure                             54889.94
                                                                  ------------
                **** Gross Profit *****                            21315.30-
                                                                  ============
```

Figure 2.11a   A Trading Account

30/08/85   BIAS Q-ERY:Reporter :   Quoin Demo Ltd
User 1   ==

PROFIT & LOSS ACCOUNT
=====================
Revenue

        Gross profit brought down ****   21315.30-
        Discount Received   377.28-

                                                      377.28-
                                                    ----
                Summary of revenue   21692.58-

Expenditure

        Discount Allowed   1.59
        Bank Charges   114.17
        Interest Charges   613.34
        Staff salaries   2426.72
        Vehicle Leases   1055.25
        Vehicle Repairs & Sundries   1027.14
        Vehicle Fuel & Repairs   2131.50
        Rent   240.00
        Rates   170.62
        Stationery & Sundries   146.79
        Advertising   171.88
        Telephones   319.98
        General Insurances   512.80
        Accountancy Fees   400.00
        Repairs & Maintenance   152.56

                                                     9484.34
        Depreciation

                Summary of expenditure   9484.34

                NET PROFIT (+ve = loss)   12208.24-
                                                             ==========

              Figure 2.11b   A Profit and Loss Account

Not all reports will be explicitly shown on the data flow diagram and so it is useful to briefly review a number of report types which are likely to be found in most systems.

- *On-demand reports.* These are usually produced to satisfy ad hoc queries about data stored in the system. For example, a library member may go to the issue desk and request a listing of all the books he currently has on loan. Figure 2.9 is an example of an on-demand report which meets the needs of the library member who has forgotten which books have been borrowed. Figure 2.10 is an example from a job costing system in which a building contractor has requested how much money has been spent on a particular project so far.

- *Summary reports.* Some reports only give the totals from the detailed listings of individual data records. For example, the Trading Account shown in Figure 2.11a and the Profit and Loss Account in Figure 2.11b contain summarised information about the income and expenditure transactions for a particular period of time. An Aged Debtor Report is also a summary of the outstanding amounts owed by the customers of a company. The data is grouped in a predetermined way and summarised for an overall picture. Such reports may be produced at specific intervals and so may not be up-to-date when used near the due date of the next generation.

- *Exception reports.* These reports assist decision-making by including only data items which are extraordinary in some way. Their purpose is to prompt some action or procedure. Many data values can be considered normal, acceptable or predictable and the inclusion of such values in a report only confuses the recipient. Exception reports only show data items which have exceeded a limit (below a stock re-order level), or are unexpected in a way that demands investigation or action. For example an Outstanding Debtor Report (Figure 2.12) shows all the invoices which are due and have not been paid within the normal period of business credit.

- *Internal reports.* Some reports contain detailed information but are not used outside the organisation and so the promotion of the company image is not important. Some outputs act as files for answering queries by those who cannot access the data directly, for example, a price list. The production of such internal reports

```
30/08/85  Quoin Demo Ltd : Outstanding Debtors Invoices :- Month beginning 01/09/85  Ac  1000- 1999   Page 1
User 1  ================================================================================================
```

A/c No	A/c Name	Tr No	Ref	Date	Type	Gross	Paid/Used	Outstanding	Balance Due
1155	Mr H Dickenson	472	tg	13/06/85	Sal Inv	1443.25	1360.71	82.54	82.54
1157	J Dempsey Ltd	487	tg	18/06/85	Sal Inv	334.42	325.45	8.97	8.97
1615	Pro & Crastin Ltd	1410	KL	01/09/85	Sal Inv	21000.00		21000.00	21000.00
1732	Steetwise PLC	143	OPEN	30/04/85	Sal Inv	364.02		364.02	
		488	tg	18/06/85	Sal Inv	7870.60	3700.00	4170.60	
		491	tg	18/06/85	Sal Inv	5405.00	5298.50	106.50	
		1347	MLW	13/09/85	Sal Inv	3013.88		3013.88	
		1359	MLW	19/09/85	Sal Inv	32.20		32.20	7687.20
1774	Trewin, Pike & Klogg	727	tg	09/07/85	Sal Inv	1025.11		1025.11	
		1166	MLW	23/08/85	Sal Inv	2093.00		2093.00	
		1169	MLW	29/08/85	Sal Inv	1083.30		1083.30	4201.41

```
                                                       TOTAL AMOUNT OUTSTANDING   32980.12
                                                                                =========
```

** Bias   End of List **

Figure 2.12   An Outstanding Debtor Report

```
    QUOIN DEMO                    Weekly          Pay Period  44    Payment Due  09/02/85        1
-------------------------------------------------------------------------------------------------
Processed      8    Excluded      3    Starters    0   Leavers        0
-------------------------------------------------------------------------------------------------
PAYROLL COSTS
            Payslip   Cash                737.65
                      Giro                 92.38
                      Cheque                            830.03  Total take home
                      ----------------------------------        ----------------------------
            HMP           0.00 SAYE        11.00
            SSP           0.00 Co Order     0.00
            Co Sick       0.00 Loan Repay   0.00
            New Loan      0.00
            Bonus        17.00 Union        1.00
            Travel       21.00 Goods Bt     0.00
            Fares        35.00 Cleaning     0.00
            Tools        49.00              0.00
            sundries      0.00              0.00
                          0.00              0.00
                          0.00              0.00
                          0.00              0.00
                          0.00              0.00   12.00  Total deductions
                      ----------------------------------        ----------------------------

                      PAYE                            100.81-
                                                              ----------------------------
                      NHI ees                          66.58
                      NHI ers        71.78
                      NHI rebate      0.00                          NHI Total    138.36


                                               ----------  ----------------------------
                                                   807.80  TOTAL GROSS PAY

            HOLIDAY       Cost                           Qty     Stamp       Value
            Hol Stamps   32.80                            4      8.50        34.00


            Hol Fund      8.00   40.80                                        8.00
-------------------------------------------------------------------------------------------------
            TOTAL EMPLOYERS COST   112.58        920.38  TOTAL PAYROLL COST    42.00


COIN ANALYSIS
        £20      33     660.00
        £10       4      40.00
        £5        2      10.00
        £1       23      23.00
        .50p      6       3.00
        .20p      5       1.00
        .10p      3       .30
        .05p      4       .20
        .02p      7       .14
        .01p      1       .01
-------------------------------------------------------------------------------------------------
            Total         737.65
```

Figure 2.13   Coin Analysis Report

frequently triggers further operational processes. For instance, the Coin Analysis shown in Figure 2.13 will give the wages clerk the information for the requisition of coins from the bank.

– *External documents.* System outputs such as customer invoices and rate demands are generated from the internal data but are used outside the organisation. In such cases it is difficult to ask the recipient whether the design is understandable and usable. Figure

MARKS & SPENCER
CHARGECARD

PO Box 210, Chester X, CH99 1DS. Telephone: 0244 681681

STATEMENT

Statement date:
11th Jan 89

Credit limit:
£1000

APR 34.5 %

Please quote your account no. in all correspondence:-

Date	Reference	Description	Amount	Balance
11 Dec88		Balance Brought Forward		0.00
12 Dec88		Leicester	70.48	70.48
16 Dec88		Leicester	12.84	83.32
17 Dec88		Leicester	35.47	118.79
27 Dec88		Leicester	5.99	124.78
28 Dec88		Leicester	14.99	139.77
3 Jan89		Payment Received Thank You	77.46CR	62.31

HOME FURNISHINGS SPRING EVENT! Look out for lower prices on a large selection of home furnishings & furniture. And, of course, the Marks & Spencer End of Season Sale continues in all our stores. So don't forget to use your Account when shopping for yourself or the home.	Present Balance **£62.31** Minimum Payment **£10.00** To reach your Account by:— **5 Feb89**

Figure 2.14   A Balance Forward Statement

2.14 is a computer-generated statement produced to communicate the details of outstanding invoices to a customer.

– *Archival documents.* Some reports are produced when the appropriate data is no longer required on the system. For example, the details of a dead person's medical records may be output on paper or microfiche for research purposes. Similarly, reports of historical financial transactions may be required for company taxation purposes. Figure 2.15 is an example of a report which records on paper the transactions deleted when a file is periodically reorganised.

The layout of outputs can be made on special paper charts or directly onto a screen using some form of screen painting and formatting software. The latter is much more effective, as the user can quickly appreciate the contents and aesthetics of the displayed information because it is in the medium which will be used in the final system. It also permits easier amendment of layouts which is particularly useful if the user is present and able to discuss fine details of position and vocabulary. The extensive formatting facilities of spreadsheets make them ideal for the presentation of mock-up layouts.

In this chapter we are confined to a paper-based design of a report – shown in Figure 2.16. It has many good features and some where improvements could be made. We shall use it to illustrate the elements which an Analyst will consider in the presentation and layout of a report.

Contents

The information content of the reports and screens are recorded in the data dictionary. Information needs to have special qualities for it to be valuable. It should be timely, relevant, accurate and unbiased. There is little point to the provision of information if it is too late to be acted upon to the benefit of the organisation. A common fault is to give the user too much information, particularly on routine reports, simply because the data is available. Care must be taken not to add useless or meaningless data comparisons to the logical data requirements. Consultation with the people who will use the output will ensure that this does not occur. Certain other data items may be added to reflect statutory requirements, company standards (terms of trading) or the scope of distribution.

```
   30/08/85                    Quoin Demo Ltd    : Washday Deletions      Delete Date ( 01/07/85      Page  7
     User 1                               ===========================================

Tr No   Ref   Cheque  Cr Ac  Dr Ac   Type        Net        Vat    Dsc/Pd/Usd  Job        Net      Description
------  ------  ------  ------  ------  ----------  ----------  ----------  ----------  --------  ----------  ----------------------------
  268 tg      451760    451     52 S A/c Trf      99.42                                           99.42   NHI ER
  269 tg               1157    270 S Payment     378.35                                          378.35   Pmt on 000116
  270 tg               1730    270 S Payment     925.75                                          925.75   Pmt on 000121
  271 tg               1732    270 S Payment     630.20                                          630.20   Pmt on 000117
  272 tg               1732    270 S Payment     492.20                                          492.20   Pmt on 000125
  273 tg                 62   1870 S Invoice     201.50    30.23 1    231.73     100              201.50   Sales Materials
  274 tg                 62   1157 S Invoice     200.00    30.00 1    230.00     100              200.00   Sales Materials
  275 tg                 61   1732 S Invoice    5523.00   828.45 1   6351.45     189             5523.00   Sales Rehabilitation
  276 tg               1870    270 S Payment     231.73                                          231.73   Pmt on 000273
  277 tg                273    270 S A/c Trf     489.00                                          489.00
  278 tg               1732    270 S Payment     253.00                                          253.00   Pmt on 000119  Inv 1757
  279 tg               1871    270 S Payment    4000.00                                         4000.00   Pmt on 000165  Inv 1767
  280 0226  N          2126      1 P Invoice     111.26    16.69 1    127.95     100 1           111.26   Materials
  281 0419  N          2126      1 P Invoice     260.97    39.15 1    300.12     100 1           260.97   Materials
  282 0413  N          2126      1 P Invoice     182.77    27.42 1    210.19     182 1              .92   Materials
                                                                                197 1           155.70   Materials
                                                                                189 1            26.15   Materials

  283 0420  N          2126      1 P Invoice     196.20    29.43 1    225.63     100 1           196.20   Materials
  284 0473  N          2126      1 P Invoice       4.50      .68 1      5.18     100 1             4.50   Materials
  285 0221  N          2364      1 P Invoice     201.60    30.24 1    231.84     197 1           201.60   Materials
  286 013307 N         2222    157 P Invoice       7.00     1.05 1      8.05                       7.00   Vehicle Repairs & Sundries
  287 30392  N         2023      1 P Invoice      11.22     1.64 1     12.86     189 1            11.22   Materials
  288 30662  N         2023      1 P Invoice      20.78     3.04 1     23.82     189 1            20.78   Materials
  289 30912  N         2023      1 P Invoice      11.82     1.73 1     13.55     170 1            11.82   Materials
  290 30927  N         2023      1 P Invoice       8.38     1.23 1      9.61     189 1             8.38   Materials
  291 30741  N         2023      1 P Invoice       3.98      .58 1      4.56     189 1             3.98   Materials
  292 30988  N         2023      1 P Invoice      93.08    13.61 1    106.69     197 1            93.08   Materials
  293 30858  N         2023      1 P Invoice     119.89    17.53 1    137.42     197 1           119.89   Materials
  294 30865  N         2023      1 P Invoice      15.13     2.21 1     17.34     170 1            15.13   Materials
  295 31151  N         2023      1 P Invoice      11.83     1.73 1     13.56     191 1            11.83   Materials
  296 31142  N         2023      1 P Invoice      55.85     8.17 1     64.02     197 1            55.85   Materials
  297 31412  N         2023      1 P Invoice      32.67     4.78 1     37.45     191 1            32.67   Materials
  298 142556 N         2124      1 P Invoice       9.97      .68 2     10.65     170 1             9.97   Materials
  299 142663 N         2124      1 P Invoice      53.23     7.98 1     61.21     183 1            53.23   Materials
  300 142748 N         2124      1 P Invoice        .74      .11 1       .85     189 1              .74   Materials
  301 142829 N         2124      1 P Invoice       4.21      .62 1      4.83     195 1             4.21   Materials
  302 142847 N         2124      1 P Invoice      13.26     1.94 1     15.20     170 1            13.26   Materials
  303 142938 N         2124      1 P Invoice      28.78     4.29 1     33.07     189 1            28.78   Materials
  304 142953 N         2124      1 P Invoice       2.15      .32 1      2.47     189 1             2.15   Materials
  305 25527  N         2242      1 P Invoice      19.90     2.98 1     22.88     191 1            19.90   Materials
  306 3107   N         2262      7 P Invoice      11.00     1.65 1     12.65     170 1            11.00   Plant Hire
  307 463273 N         2375      1 P Invoice     143.59    20.46 1    164.05     189 1           143.59   Materials
  308 490453 N         2127      4 P Invoice       6.71     1.00 1      7.71     197 4             6.71   Bona Fide Subcontractors
  309 Pay08W                      J Job Tfr                                      191 2           112.31   P08W Hr  40/      Exp      LAB
  310 Pay08W                      J Job Tfr                                      197 1           142.36   P08W Hr  40/    4 Exp      BRI
                                                                                197 2           123.36   P08W Hr  40/    4 Exp      LAB
                                                                                197 6           187.76   P08W Hr  40/    4 Exp      OVE
```

Figure 2.15   Archival Report

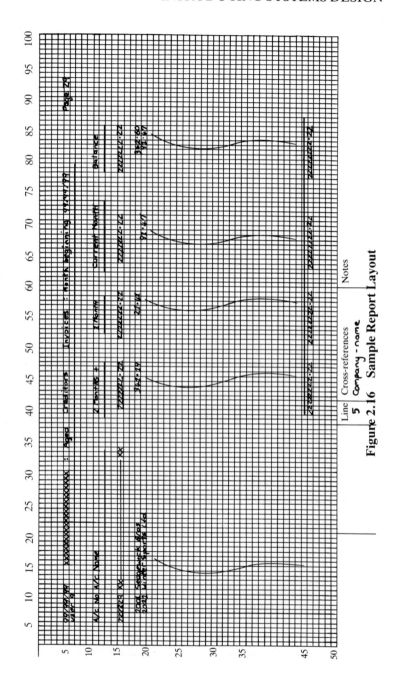

Figure 2.16   Sample Report Layout

There are two types of data items on any report. *Fixed data items* consist of headings, descriptions of data items and instructions for the user. A report will be referred to on many occasions during its useful life in the system and will therefore require unique identification. Headings need to be bold and may contain some sort of logo to conform to house rules of documentation. Figure 2.16 shows fixed data items in the form of the heading 'Aged Creditors Invoices' and the company name. However, this does not uniquely identify the report since its contents would differ depending upon the date it was produced. The date (line 5, column 5–13) and the period to which the report refers (line 1, column 93–102) are *variable data items*.

Variable items are data values retrieved or computed from the stored or input data. Some variable data items may be derived from other data items as the system produces the report, eg the subtotals (line 46, columns 48–59, 63–73, 80–90) and grand total (line 46, column 99–109). Page numbers are also required for lengthy reports and are reset for each occasion the report is run.

Order

Information generally has to be presented in some specified order, for example numerical, chronological or alphabetical. This sequence allows easy searching and browsing, particularly if the report extends over several pages.

Reading lengthy listings is easier if the importance of the data items is reflected in the order of presentation. A report showing debtors in declining size of debt is more immediate than one given in alphabetical order. Readability and understanding will be enhanced if a report is marked with clearly identifiable blocks of data, separated by some space for emphasis. A new block of data will correspond to a change in the value of a key data item. It may also be separated by a sub-total for the preceding block. The unprinted space also enhances the quality of communication. The reader should compare the two reports shown in Figures 2.11 and 2.15 from this perspective.

Figure 2.16 contains data on the sums of money owed by a company's creditors. It is presented in ascending order of the account number. Alphabetical name order and descending value of balance are two possible alternatives which should be considered. There is sometimes an unwitting tendency for designers to produce reports in an order that reflects the system's convenience, not the user's. The most important derived item is the balance of each account on the date of the report, and this is presented to the far right of the report where its position makes it noticeable to the reader.

Presentation and Layout

Some simple guidelines for presentation and layout will assist in the design of effective inputs and outputs.

Keep Familiarity and Consistency

Information should always be presented in a consistent and accessible way. Familiarity of style and format will promote quicker acceptance of a new report and less misunderstanding of the information content. Related reports should have a similar format so that key information can always be found in the same location on the form. Communication is enhanced by the adoption of a 'house style' for such aspects as headings, typeface and logos.

Use Alignment and Space Wisely

Alignment of both fixed and variable data will contribute to ease of understanding and use. Thus numeric strings should be aligned at their decimal points, as in the data values in columns 48–59, 63–73, 80–90, and 100–110 (line 14). Below, some example data illustrates the assistance such conventions have in making reports readable.

$$
\begin{array}{rcl}
362.60 & \text{NOT} & 362.60 \\
91.47 & & 91.47 \\
17,587.94 & & 17,587.94
\end{array}
$$

The convention for left alignment of alphabetic strings is illustrated in the data field containing account name (line 17–19, columns 12–42).

Sedgewick Bros	NOT	Sedgewick Bros
Winter Sports Ltd		Winter Sports Ltd
Teddington PLC		Teddington PLC

Negative numerical data always presents a problem and should be aligned to the right by using a suffix not a prefix.

1548.24–OR (1548.24)   NOT   −   1548.24 or −1548.24

Space is also very important and a clearly presented report will have variable space between columns to break it into logical segments. Several lines should be left between headings, data and totals (lines 40–44 are left blank before the totals are printed). Most reported information will require manual filing. The layout should take into account the manner in which it is to be filed and space allowed accordingly at the top or the left hand side of the page. The purpose of such care is to prevent data being lost through holes being punched in the printed data or hidden in binder margins.

Use Informative Headings

A report form or display always requires a title which can be repeated on all subsequent pages of the document. The pages should also be numbered to allow easy reference or the re-collation of a dropped report! Meaningful column headings are often difficult to fit in, but it is wise not to abbreviate them excessively and so leave their interpretation in doubt. Figure 2.16 uses the heading 'A/c' as the commonly understood abbreviation for Account. The use of the full column name would unbalance and dominate the data in the column below. Laser printing facilities used in association with desktop publishing may be able to overcome this problem by varying the size and style of printed characters for headings.

Other Issues

Input and output forms should display elements of:

- *Structure*. A hierarchical structure will provide both understanding and guidance to the user. Abbot (1983) likened the structure of a form to that of a conversation (Figure 2.17). It consists of a main body of questions but has supporting information and trivia such as signature and dates. Questions should be grouped naturally in blocks to preserve their meaning and the order of the blocks and the questions within them should reflect their relative importance and use. The most frequently answered questions should come first and mandatory questions should precede optional ones.

- *Definition*. Most input and output is likely to require sup- plementary definition. Some forms attempt this by giving instruc- tions and explanations on a separate sheet and hope that it remains attached during the duration of the form's use. Others place all supporting notes either at the beginning or the end of the document and so reference is made through clumsy page turning and searching. The most appropriate place for supporting information is just before the relevant question or display. However, this may cause repetition and an unattractive layout.

Borders and colour can be used to emphasise the structure and importance of some data items. However, colour may be lost in the printout (if no colour printer or plotter is available) or in the reproduction.

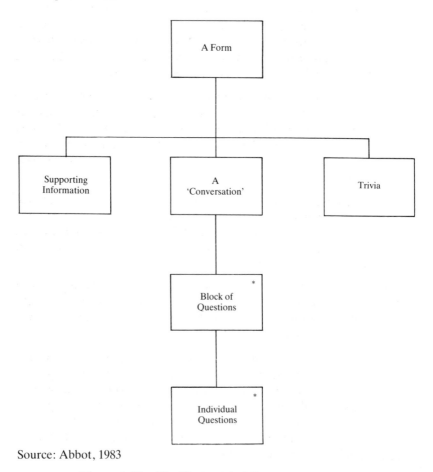

Source: Abbot, 1983

Figure 2.17   The Hierarchical Structure of a Form

2.8   INFOSYS: DESIGNING THE DATA FLOWS

Figure 2.18 shows the level 1 data flow diagram for the seminar booking system at InfoSys. A suggested boundary for the computer system has been sketched onto the model. The process 'Evaluate Seminar Success' had been excluded from automation as it clearly involves discretionary procedures which are determined by criteria relevant at the time. Management may be able to effectively use a range of computer-generated reports and queries on such variables as those seminars which have been well attended, those which have not been popular and the most popular venues and times of year for particular seminar types. But future trends in computing, government policies and anticipated competition from other companies in the same market will also strongly influence the nature of the seminar plans. Consequently, its heuristic nature has led it to be excluded from the computer system.

InfoSys also wish to maintain a friendly, flexible and knowledgeable contact with all past, present and future delegates who make enquiries in any form. This process is also felt to be most successfully undertaken manually although the stored data in the system will be at the disposal of the person handling the query. Accommodation is also arranged outside the computer system.

The remaining processes which deal with initial vetting of applications, recording details of delegates and accommodation requirements, generation of booking confirmations and delegate lists and handling of cancellations, are considered to be sufficiently rule-based to allow their inclusion in the system boundary.

The Analyst must ensure that the computerisation of these processes will effectively contribute to the achievement of targets set within the Strategic Plan. The list of inputs and outputs which therefore require detailed design is given in Figure 2.19.

The data flow Seminar-confirmation is a major output of the proposed system and is hence a suitable example for illustrating the design process in more detail. This output must clearly be produced on hard copy since it has to be sent to the applicant by post. A computer-generated printed copy of the seminar booking confirmation is suggested, copies of which can also be used to inform Accounts of the transaction and Accommodation of booking requirements.

The data structures contained in the Seminar-booking-confirmation

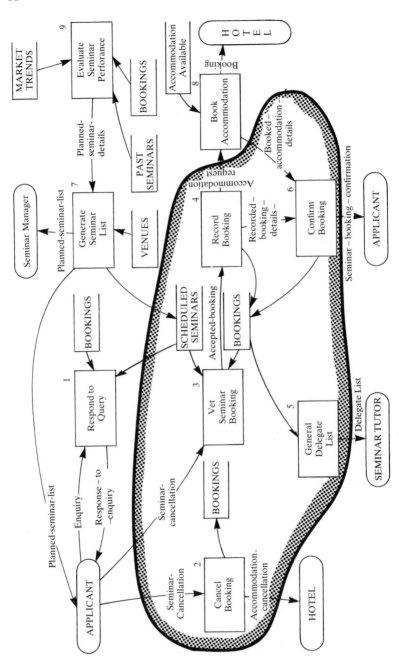

Figure 2.18   Seminar Booking System Data Flow Diagram

Inputs	Outputs
Seminar-booking-details Seminar-cancellation Seminar-programme	Seminar-confirmation Delegate-list Seminar-query Booking-query Seminar-attendance

Figure 2.19   Seminar Booking System

has been logically defined in the data dictionary. This includes the following:

Date-confirmation-sent
Booking-number

Delegate-details
  Delegate-name
  Delegate-address

Seminar-details *(1–6)
  Seminar-number
  Commencement-date
  Finish-date
  Title
  Venue
  [No-nights-accommodation]

{Payment-acknowledgement}

The expected volume of this data flow is 12500 per year (50 bookings per day for 50 weeks), to be produced in batch mode at the end of the day in time for the evening post. This will demand a high quality fast printer, as analysis has suggested that a maximum of 90 multi-part seminar booking confirmations (many with continuation sheets) will need to be printed, sealed in an envelope and despatched daily.

Figure 2.20 is a possible layout design for the example. It requires the use of special headed continuous stationery with the COMMUNIQUE logo to enhance its image. Each additional seminar booking made at the same time is confirmed on a separate sheet. The delegates may then separate the sheets for their own use.

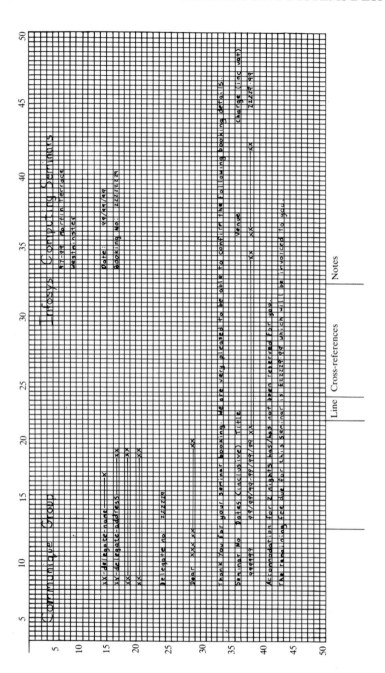

Figure 2.20   Seminar Booking Confirmation

2.9 SUMMARY

This chapter has stated that input and output design is a suitable starting point for the whole design task. It has suggested that:

- Inputs and outputs can be identified directly from the system boundary imposed on the data flow diagram. The location of this boundary will be guided by the nature of each process as well as the feasibility of the technological solution. Decisions about job design and allocation will also affect the boundary and hence influence the inputs and outputs.

- The agreed boundary will naturally define the logical inputs and outputs at the points where data flows from sources and flows to sinks cross the system boundary. The supporting data dictionary entries of these flows will define the *logical* contents of the inputs and outputs.

- An appropriate technology must be allocated to inputs and outputs taking into account system constraints, volumes and economic feasibility.

- The detailed design of inputs and outputs must be undertaken. This chapter has concentrated on output design because many outputs are not explicitly shown on the data flow diagram. Furthermore, these outputs may not immediately suggest themselves to users or developers. However, input design also shares many of the aesthetic difficulties associated with output layout.

2.10 EXERCISES

The following questions refer to the Library case study introduced in Chapter 1.

1 Impose and justify a system boundary on the data flow diagram of the library system. List all inputs and outputs shown explicitly on the diagram.

2 Allocate appropriate technology to each of these inputs and outputs. Explain how the choice of this technology adheres to the guidelines offered in this chapter.

3 List the reports available from the system together with their classification (archival, exception, etc). Construct report layouts

Please do not write in the blue shaded areas
Please write clearly in **BLACK INK**
and **CAPITAL LETTERS**

1

👤 Your details

V10

1 Full name of vehicle keeper

Mr/Mrs/Ms/Miss _____

Company name *if applicable* _____

Date Stamp

2 **Address** *including postcode* _____

_____

_____

_____

🚗 Vehicle details

3 **Registration mark of vehicle** | _____ | 2

3
VC

4 **Taxation class of licence required** _____

If bicycle or tricycle, give cylinder capacity _____ (cc)

If hackney, give seating capacity excluding driver _____ (seats)

If showman's haulage or general haulage, give unladen weight _____ (kg)

5 **Make and model** _____

4
prefix

serial number

📇 Licence details

6 **State whether the licence is to run for 6 or 12 months** _____ (months)

7 **State date of expiry or surrender of last licence** _____ 19___

If you don't know this date because you first had the vehicle without a licence, give the *exact* date you got the vehicle _____ 19___

8 **State date from which the new licence is to run**

*This must be the **first** day of the month in which you want the licence to start*

First day of _____ 19___

9 **Answer this question if there is a break between the dates at 7 and 8 above.**
Has the vehicle been kept (eg parked) or used on a public road at any time between these dates (other than for a pre-arranged compulsory vehicle test)? Answer YES or NO _____
Keeping or using an unlicensed vehicle on a public road is an offence which could result in a penalty of £400 or five times the annual rate of duty, whichever is the greater.

5

o/u payments

6
period

expiry month

☐
SR

☐
V5 changes

☐
V62 noted

✍️ Declaration

I declare that I have checked the information given in this application and that to the best of my knowledge it is correct.
The maximum penalty for making a false declaration is £2000 or 2 years' imprisonment.

I enclose *the payment of £*_____ *and the other documents required*

Signature _____ Date _____

*If you are signing for a partnership,
limited company or other legal entity, give your position in the firm*

Printed in the UK for HMSO. Dd8318497. 1.87.

V10 Rev. Oct. 86.

Figure 2.21 Vehicle Licence Application Form

showing the contents and appearance of three of the reports on your list. Explain the rationale behind the design of each of these reports highlighting particularly significant features.

4 Discuss the likely organisational effects of the proposed project and their implications for employees. What job design opportunities do you foresee?

The following two questions do not refer to the case study.

5 Figure 2.21 shows a form produced by the Department of Transport. State what you consider to be:

- the purpose of this form;

- how well if fulfils this purpose.

6 Investigate the Participative System Design approach of Land and Mumford. A suggested starting point is:

Mumford E, Defining system requirements to meet business needs: a case study example, *The Computer Journal* 28(2), 1985 pp 97–104.

Mumford E, Land K, Hawgood J, A participative approach to the design of computer systems. *Impact on Society* 25(3), 1978 pp 235–253.

3 Designing Dialogues

Chapter 2 gave some guidance on the task of designing of inward and outward data flows, highlighting the *reports* which provide information for the users who undertake business tasks and the *forms* which capture the required raw data for this output. The logical contents of these system inputs and outputs were identified from where the data flows crossed the agreed system boundary. The Analyst now needs to define the computer procedures to capture data and display and print output. This is the task of human–computer interface design, a task which includes designing screen displays and dialogues or conversations to link them together (Schott and Olson, 1988).

This chapter will discuss the importance of the effective design of the human–computer interface and sets out criteria against which a dialogue design may be evaluated. A user-centred, structured approach to dialogue design is introduced, and complementary techniques for documenting this dynamic element of a system are presented. These techniques are the menu tree, the logical dialogue outline and the screen layout chart.

3.1 WHAT IS A HUMAN–COMPUTER DIALOGUE?

A human–computer dialogue may be defined as:

'an exchange of information governed by agreed conventions which takes place between a computer-based system and its users via an interactive terminal·' (Coats and Vlaeminke, 1988)

A dialogue consists of a set of procedures for the exchange of information between the user and the computer. The appropriate commands and responses provide the mechanism for executing the

75

processes provided by the system and required by the user. The structure of the dialogue will control the interaction between the user and computer and determine how information is presented and received. A dialogue may vary in this degree of control from user-initiated (where the user is in command), to computer-initiated (where the user simply responds to the requests of the system).

In general a dialogue needs to:

- determine what task/process the user requires the system to undertake;

- obtain the data input from the user and make this available in a suitable format to the required computer task/process;

- command the computer task/process to be performed;

- receive data output from the computer task/process and present it to the user in the appropriate format.

Conventions for undertaking these tasks are as important in a human–computer dialogue as they are in an everyday conversation. Participants in a conversation must normally use the same language, take turns to speak, listen whilst the other person speaks, and respond to information supplied by the other. These conventions enable everyday conversations between humans to be effective and generally lead to the required actions resulting from clearly stated instructions or commands. However, if instructions are ambiguous, mumbled, or incomplete then the message becomes garbled and the resulting actions incorrect and unpredictable. The same principles of clarity are required of a human–computer dialogue – ambiguity and incompleteness will lead to the wrong processes being invoked.

3.2 WHY IS DIALOGUE DESIGN IMPORTANT?

Computer systems are important tools which assist the performance of many critical tasks in the management and operation of the enterprise. The human–computer dialogue is the vehicle by which this assistance takes place. To most users the dialogue *is the system*! Ambiguities and difficulties in the dialogue cause problems in training and operation and lead to systems underperforming. For example, a clerk who has problems entering data because of poor screen design is likely to make more transcription errors. Similarly, a manager who wishes to display the latest sales forecasts may be frustrated by problems in obtaining that information (through poor menu design) and confused by the results that appear (due to a complicated screen layout). The clerk will have to tolerate such poor design features but will perform the task inefficiently. However, the manager is a discretionary user of the system and the lack of his support and use of the system will reduce the chances of achieving a successful implementation.

To be effective a dialogue has to be both *functional* and *usable*.

Functionality is concerned with ensuring that all the required data has a mechanism for input and output. Hence dialogues have been designed for each interface defined in the data flow diagram and each dialogue is complete in that it captures or displays all the data required in the input or output. Hence the system is correct and complete.

Usability should reinforce functionality. Operators of the system should be given a dialogue that is:

- Natural.

- Consistent.

- Not redundant.

- Supportive.

- Flexible.

This should ensure that the system is convenient to use. Such convenience should help ensure correctness. The issues of usability are examined in more detail in the next section.

It must also be recognised that the dialogue is only part of the interface. Ergonomists (see Shackel, 1986) have also found that physical discomfort at the workstation will lead to a system being less usable. Such discomfort may result from poor colour co-ordination, poor keyboard feel and functionality, problems of inadequate lighting, intrusive noise and poor physical layout. All these factors may result in an underperforming, underachieving user. (See Cakir, Hart and Stewart, 1978 for a comprehensive review of ergonomic issues.)

3.3 CRITERIA FOR A 'GOOD' DIALOGUE DESIGN

Coats and Vlaeminke (1988) assess the merits of dialogues according to five general criteria. They suggest that a 'good' dialogue has the qualities described below.

Natural

An effective dialogue does not cause the user to significantly alter his or her approach to the task in order to interact with the computer system. A dialogue should use the vocabulary of the user in preference to one that reflects the operation of the system. Coats and Vlaeminke give a good example of this:

> 'A designer might consider the task to be 'updating the expense file', but if the users call it 'posting P47s' that is how the dialogue should refer to it.'

Similarly, is *Zap* a particularly appropriate command for clearing a spreadsheet? (SuperCalc.)

Naturalness can also be reflected in the order in which a dialogue requests the entry of information. This should acknowledge the order in which data becomes available to the user and so not require any preceding sorting or rearrangement of data.

Consistent

Expectations about the way that the system will perform and react are important. Arbitrary changes in phrasing, format and layout cause frustration and anxiety. For example, a user will reasonably expect a dialogue to display help and error messages in the same area of the screen no matter which part of the system is currently being used. Furthermore, users often take their knowledge from one application to another and expect related systems to behave in a similar manner. Many difficulties have been caused by commands such as 'quit' and 'exit' which have different consequences in different systems. Obviously the design cannot be consistent with all other systems in existence, but consistency with common conventions and industry standard practices is advisable.

Recently, pressure has been exerted to accept the adoption of a common user access (see Adie, 1988) in all systems developed for the next generation of personal computer hardware. This requires future dialogue designs to conform to defined standards in features of the interface such as the use of panels for menu, entry, logos and function keys.

However, even if such pressure for standardisation is unsuccessful, it is important that inconsistencies do not creep into the system design. One particularly successful spreadsheet refers to a range of cells as an Entry in certain functions and a Block in others.

Not Redundant

The principle of requesting the user to input the minimum data necessary for the required operation of the system was introduced in the previous chapter. The absence of superfluous information should save input time and reduce error rates. The data flow model should ensure that redundant data does not appear in the design. Default values (where the expected response is provided by the system for the user's confirmation), should be used wherever possible to reduce the actual keystrokes required. Derived data should always be produced by the system, not by the operator.

Supportive

The amount of assistance the dialogue provides for the user of the system is also very important. Many systems provide help facilities which are designed to aid the operator undertake an operation or correct an error. Such assistance should not be provided indiscriminately. The possibility of turning help facilities on and off will assist the new user still learning the system, the infrequent user who simply needs reminding, and the frequent, experienced, operator who will prefer not to have the screen filled with explanatory messages. Help screens should be relevant and sensitive to the context of the difficulty. Unfortunately, the provision of sophisticated help facilities imposes a significant development burden and consequently many help screens are simply reiterations of pages of the user manual.

Supportive confirmations are particularly important where the input is destined to cause significant changes in the system – create a record, delete a file, etc. For example:

Customer Code: **132**

Customer Name: J Bland
                23 Redhill Road
                Leicester

Is this correct (Y/N): N

Reporting operational errors is normally achieved by displaying appropriate messages at particular points in the dialogue. These error messages need to state exactly what is wrong and also give specific instruction in the corrective action necessary. For example:

Opening entries do not balance

Credit £123.90 to a Sundries account

Flexible

Finally a dialogue should be able to cater for or tolerate different levels of user knowledge and performance. There is usually more than one way to perform a task and hence dialogues must be designed to accept variations in the way a user converses with it. Much research is concerned with developing tools for adaptive dialogues which are sensitive to the needs of various users and recognise changes in skill levels and competence.

3.4 A STRUCTURED USER-CENTRED APPROACH TO DIALOGUE DESIGN

The following approach to the design of human–computer dialogues is based on the principles set down by Martin (1973) and developed further by Hebditch (1979) and more recently discussed by Coats and Vlaeminke (1988). For illustrative purposes the transaction for entering the order details in the Mail Order Book Club system will be considered stage by stage.

3.4.1 Determine the Purpose of the Dialogue

A dialogue may be required for many types of transaction. For example, users may need to input data for a process, make enquiries on stored data, produce management reports or invoke housekeeping routines. A dialogue may also require several input data flows in order to undertake a specific processing function. The dialogue should therefore be organised and structured in a form appropriate to the task and frame of reference of the user. This requires the Analyst to identify and order the logical segments of the process for the purposes of the human-computer dialogue.

Transaction 1 needs a dialogue to enter the details of the order received from a valid Book Club member itemising the book titles required this period and the payment which accompanies the order. Data is transcribed from an order form regularly sent to members with details of special offers and standard items for sale. Figure 2.4 is repeated as Figure 3.1 and will remind the reader of the relevant section of the data flow diagram.

3.4.2 Understand the User Profiles

Users vary in their frequency of system use as well as in their general level of competence and experience. Casual users will need more assistance from the dialogue than experienced users who will be annoyed or inhibited by excessive prompts and explanations.

The user of the 'Verify Order Details' dialogue will be an experienced order clerk who will be given appropriate training. The majority of the tasks in the clerk's job specification will be computer-oriented (such as answering queries and maintaining records) and hence frequent use can be expected.

3.4.3 Determine the Dialogue Style

There are four main ways of structuring the dialogue.

Menus

Menus present a selection of the possible options at certain stages in the dialogue (see Figure 3.2). Users select a particular option by giving the appropriate letter or number, or by selecting an icon with a keyboard highlight or a mouse. Many systems use permanently displayed or 'pull down' menus within a dialogue. Figure 3.3 shows a menu which has been pulled down and superimposed on another menu of system file icons.

The main advantage of this style of interface is that it requires few keyboard skills and hence is ideal for the inexperienced or infrequent user. It is also applicable to circumstances where no specialised knowledge or training can be given or assumed. Error rates with menu dialogues are generally low and the system is effective even if the user is frequently interrupted or distracted.

However, menus may be intolerably slow for experienced users. For example, a single transaction such as entering invoice details, may demand several menu selections as the user travels down the menu

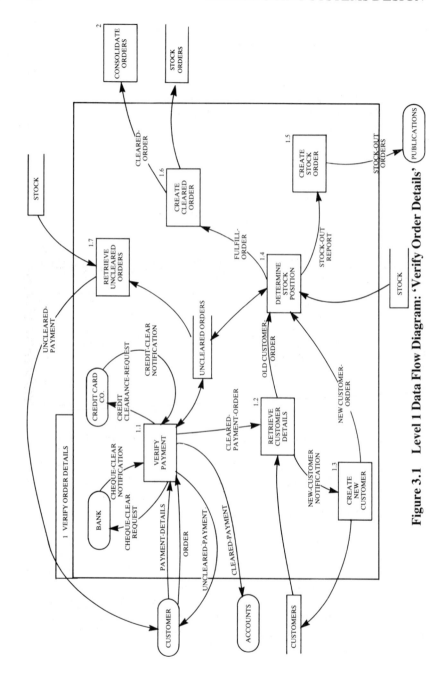

Figure 3.1   Level 1 Data Flow Diagram: 'Verify Order Details'

Mail Order Book Club	Main Menu	15/12/87

1 Maintain Member Details   6 Enter Despatch Details
2 Maintain Book Details   7 Print Labels
3 Compile Offer List   8 Print Management Reports
4 Special Offer Orders   9 Housekeeping Functions
5 Standard Orders   0 Exit

Enter option required [?]

Figure 3.2   A Menu Screen

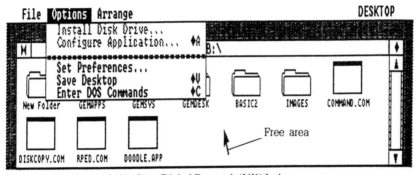

Reproduced with permission from Digital Research (UK) Ltd

Figure 3.3   Pull Down Menu from the Amstrad PC 1640 Manual

hierarchy and several more to return to the original menu position. Consequently, the design of the menus should offer flexible paths around the system and so provide short-cuts to normal routes. This can cut down the irritation of experienced users.

Menus also demand that the system inputs can be explicitly predicted and that the range of predictions is relatively small. Menu screens should probably be restricted to about 7–10 choices with further menus called from some (perhaps all) of these options. We have seen screens which offer 23 options, some of which lead down to menus of a similar size. It is also unwise to exceed more than three levels of menu. Excessively deep menus lead to users becoming confused about their current position in the system.

Menus are not an appropriate choice of dialogue structure for the order entry transaction where a large number of possible books may be selected for a particular order. However, the Club compiles and issues a special offer order form to all its members and a pull-down menu may be constructed to display the selection of all the current month's offers. Figure 3.4 shows the possible use of this dialogue structure for the entry of such special offer orders.

```
Mail Order Book Club   Special Offer Order Entry        15/12/87


Member number: [540128]        Mrs D Simpson
                               156 Thornton Way
                               West Lynham
                               Suffolk

Special Offer Menu

Item      Title                        Author             Offer Price

1  Introducing Systems Analysis        Skidmore and Wroe      9.50
2  Design of Man-Computer Dialogues    J Martin              20.00
3  Business Computing                  S Skidmore            10.00
4  The Small Business Handbook         B Wilson               7.50
5  A Guide to DB2                      C Date                15.00

-----------------------------------------------------------------------

Select item required (1–5 or 0 for exit) [?]
```

Figure 3.4   Special Offer Order Entry Screen: Menu Mode

Form Filling

Organisations use many clerical forms for ordering goods, completing applications, making proposals, etc. A similar principle is used in the 'form-filling' dialogue where input data is entered onto screens that resemble a form. Areas of the screen are protected from input and the cursor is placed at relevant points to indicate where and in what order the data is to be entered. This is illustrated in Figure 3.5.

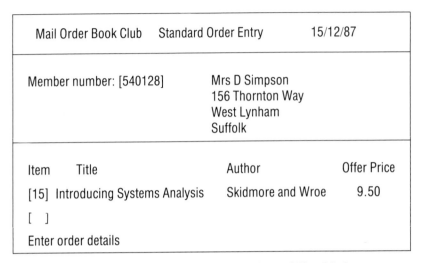

Mail Order Book Club   Standard Order Entry   15/12/87
Member number: [540128]   Mrs D Simpson 156 Thornton Way West Lynham Suffolk
Item   Title   Author   Offer Price [15] Introducing Systems Analysis   Skidmore and Wroe   9.50 [   ] Enter order details

Figure 3.5   Order Entry Screen: Form-filling Mode

Completion of forms is a familiar activity to many employees and systems can often be designed to match proposed or existing clerical forms. This familiarity reduces the need for training. Furthermore, a relatively large amount of data can be entered on one screen and the values of this data do not have to be predicted by the dialogue.

The form-filling technique can be recommended for all levels of user for both entering and displaying data. Certain principles of design can enhance the method:

- The data entry progresses left to right and top to bottom. This reflects the natural entry of a clerical form.

- Entry fields should be clearly delimited (note the use of brackets in Figure 3.5) to distinguish them from displayed or retrieved data.

- The form should collect information *available* at that time. It should not try to encompass data that is input at different stages or times.

- Default values should be used wherever possible. Data already available on the system should be retrieved, not re-entered.

Form filling is particularly appropriate where the dialogue demands the entry of a large number of fairly standard data items. The validation of these items may take place during input or after a batch (usually a screenful) of data has been entered. The former demands access to data files and this may slow down the entry process. The latter requires a simple and unambiguous editing facility so that users can quickly skip to fields that need re-entering.

Command Language

In menu and form-filling modes the user has responded to a computer-initiated dialogue. However, command or direct language is user-initiated. Commands or codes which should be known to the system are directly entered from the keyboard. The system has not tried to predict these commands in any way. Figure 3.6 is an example of direct command input by the user of an Amstrad 1640 personal computer running under MS-DOS. The command lines are emboldened.

```
A>dir b:
chapter 1.txt   chapter2.txt   chapter3.txt   chapter3.bak

A>diskcomp a: b:
Insert FIRST diskette in drive A:
Insert SECOND diskette in drive B:
Press any key when ready. . .

Comparing 40 tracks
9 sectors per track, 2 side(s)

Compare OK

Compare another diskette (Y/N)?

A>
```

Figure 3.6   Command Language Dialogue

Command language offers little support to the user but it does provide a precise, concise dialogue that allows a considerable degree of flexibility and control. Dialogue familiarity depends on learning a wide range of commands which must be regularly rehearsed if they are not to fall into disuse, or even worse, misuse! For example does:

pip b:=a:rest.txt

copy the file rest.txt from Drive A to B or vice-versa? High error rates are often associated with command dialogues but this can be reduced if the syntax is easy to recall and consistent with other systems. Operating systems are usually command driven and display a certain perversity in their command words (see Figure 3.7).

Operating system	Command name	Root word
UNIX	rm	remove
VMS	del	delete
Harris	el	eliminate
CP/M	era	erase
OS/360	decatalog	decatalog

Figure 3.7   Operating System Command Names

The importance of consistency is re-emphasised by Gwei and Foxley (1987) who point out that many users with computer experience try out command names from their previous systems. Commands are also more convenient if they can be entered in a shortened form, for example:

DISP instead of DISPLAY

STRU instead of STRUCTURE

In general, command language is the least supportive dialogue structure and is most appropriate to experienced and frequent users.

Natural Language

The use of natural language is a relatively recent trend in dialogue design. Such dialogues are currently limited in both syntax and vocabulary and the style is generally very formal. In the order entry dialogue shown in Figure 3.8 the question and answer structure uses the system as the initiator of the conversation and the user responds in a natural-like language. However, in many database query languages the user is able to interrogate the system data with a limited range of syntax, as shown in the example SQL query in Figure 3.9.

In practice, all the dialogue types will probably be used with different parts of the system. A menu structure will probably be most appropriate where the range of inputs is relatively small and all possible inputs have to be explicitly displayed. Forms are particularly suitable for input of a large set of data values taken from standard operational transactions –

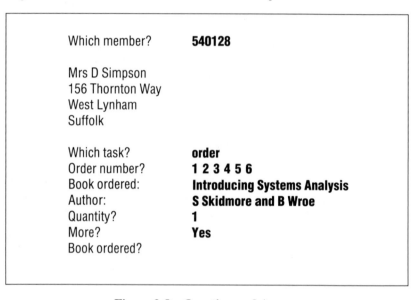

```
Which member?        540128

Mrs D Simpson
156 Thornton Way
West Lynham
Suffolk

Which task?          order
Order number?        1 2 3 4 5 6
Book ordered:        Introducing Systems Analysis
Author:              S Skidmore and B Wroe
Quantity?            1
More?                Yes
Book ordered?
```

Figure 3.8   Question and Answer

```
SELECT BOOK-ISBN, TITLE

FROM BOOKSTOCK

WHERE AUTHOR-NAME = "Skidmore"

AND PUB-DATE > 1986

ORDER BY BOOK-ISBN;
```

Figure 3.9   SQL Query Example

such as time sheets, invoices, down-time notifications, etc. Command language is appropriate where only a few input values will be required for each process and these values are taken from a limited set of easily recalled commands. Question and answer dialogues are suitable for applications where the range of input values is too great for a menu structure, too complex for command language, or where the next question depends upon the answer to the current one.

3.4.4 Design the Screen Layout

Many of the design guidelines discussed in the previous chapter for report layouts are also very relevant to the design of dialogue screens. However, a number of other particular issues have also to be considered.

What Supportive Information is Required?

The input of certain data items will demand that a confirmatory data value is retrieved from a file. An example has already been given where Customer Code was confirmed by the display of Name and Address. These supporting messages should be sufficient to convince the operator that the correct record has been retrieved but not too comprehensive that they crowd the screen with unnecessary data.

Error and warning messages also need to be identified and located in a consistent and prominent position on the screen.

How Should the Information be Displayed?

Presentation of displayed information is as important as it is on printed reports. In input screens, the physical grouping of data items must match the need for easy data entry or later audit. For example, the most convenient entry of the book order line details is in the sequence in which it appears on the member order form rather than in the sequence of the book file. Requiring a user to sort the data before input will lead to poor acceptance of the system and add to the input time.

It must be recalled that consistency in the positioning of the information on the screen is also important since it reduces the training time and adds to the fluency of a dialogue. All screens within an application system should be consistent and reflect the same house style and conventions for positioning help, error and warning messages.

Avoid screen clutter. Figure 3.10 shows such a screen which obscures the information presented on it.

Coded data items should only be used where the screen is frequently used by a trained operator, otherwise the full description of the items should be used to avoid misunderstanding.

```
 Find [          ] Next [          ] Add [          ] Delete [          ] Amend [          ]

                     ::::  CUSTOMER INFORMATION   ::::    12/10/88    User 4

 Customer No:9999999              Sales Area:              XXXXXXXX

   Name            : XXXXXXXXXXXXXXXXXXXX Discount                % 99v99
   Address 1       : XXXXXXXXXXXXXXXXXXXX Settlement date          99/99/99
   Address 2       : XXXXXXXXXXXXXXXXXXXX Last transaction date    99/99/99
   Address 3       : XXXXXXXXXXXXXXXXXXXX Last transaction no        999999
   Address 4       : XXXXXXXXXXXXXXXXXXXX

   Current balance owing        -9999999v99 Turnover this mth     -9999999v99
                                            Turnover this yr      -9999999v99

   Trans £   Trans date   Description                    Amount      New Balance
   9999999  99/99/99  XXXXXXXXXXXXXXXXXXXXXXXXXXXXXX –9999999V99 –9999999v99
   9999999  99/99/99  XXXXXXXXXXXXXXXXXXXXXXXXXXXXXX –9999999V99 –9999999v99
   9999999  99/99/99  XXXXXXXXXXXXXXXXXXXXXXXXXXXXXX –9999999V99 –9999999v99
   9999999  99/99/99  XXXXXXXXXXXXXXXXXXXXXXXXXXXXXX –9999999V99 –9999999v99
   9999999  99/99/99  XXXXXXXXXXXXXXXXXXXXXXXXXXXXXX –9999999V99 –9999999v99
   Help line:    ::::: message :::::          Error message:    ::::: message  :::::::
```

Figure 3.10   A Cluttered, Unstructured Screen Layout

Captions for data items are required to assist the user in identifying the exact meaning of the input or output. These need to be clear and distinct from the data items themselves. Figure 3.10 shows examples of positioning the caption both too close and too distant from the data item it identifies.

Which Screen Features Should be Used to Highlight Information?

Visual display terminals have a wide range of features which may be used to make the human–computer dialogue more effective. These include:

Colour

Inverse video

Graphical icons

Blinking

Character Size

Character Intensity

Character Style

Sound

The convention of using both upper and lower case characters also adds dimension to the information displayed.

Finally, the structural elements of a conversation, such as introductions, confirmation of understanding, indications of non-understanding and farewells will be required in the human–computer dialogue. The screen layout will require heading information to introduce the purpose of the dialogue and instruct the user how to proceed and leave the conversation.

3.4.5   Document the Dialogue Design

It is difficult to show the dynamic nature of dialogues in a static paper model. The content of a screen varies as it is completed by the user entering data or as it is unfolded to display information. However, a number of documentation models are available.

The Menu Tree

A hierarchical menu tree structure is often used to show how the processes of a system are linked together. The contents of the menu tree are likely to correspond to the processes (add a customer record, produce aged debtors report, etc) of the data flow diagram. The user enters the system at the top of a menu tree and is presented with a list of options or further menus available. By selecting from each menu the user is guided down through the system until the required process appears on the menu offered.

The menu tree is a very simple document which can help users and operators become fluent with the overall structure of the application. Many menu trees are pinned on the walls of user departments where they provide easy reference. Figure 3.11 shows such a menu structure for the order processing systems at the Mail Order Book Club.

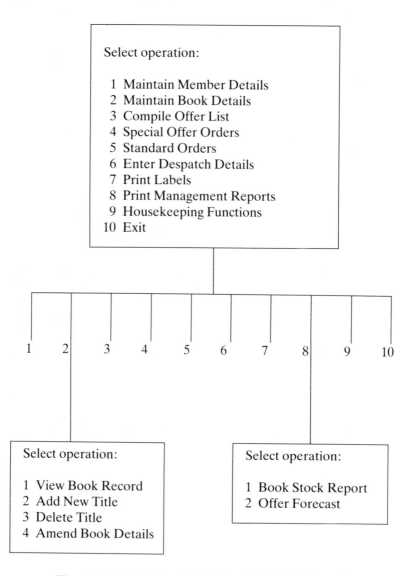

**Figure 3.11   InfoSys Mail Order Book Club Menu Tree
Showing Representative Examples of Sub-menus**

Logical Dialogue Outline

Once the overview of the system is designed, the Analyst can proceed with documenting the component system dialogues. A logical dialogue outline will show the links between input and output screens and document a user's route through the dialogue. Downs, et al (1987) have described the use of this technique within the context of the steps involved in the SSADM (Structured Systems Analysis and Design Method) methodology.

A logical dialogue outline is constructed in a columnar fashion using the symbols shown in Figure 3.12 to present the sequence of control through the screens of the dialogue. Symbols used are similar to those of a system flowchart (see Chapter 5 of *Introducing Systems Analysis*). Additional symbols include a triangle to show the position of a user decision point, from which different dialogue routes radiate. Control can also be transferred to other dialogues by using a lozenge shaped symbol. Flow lines can be annotated to show routes after a decision is made and may also be numbered for identification purposes.

The columns of the logical dialogue outline are used to position the user decisions, record the data items involved (these are taken from the data flow lines entering and leaving the processes of the DFD), the logical screen(s) required, processing comments and any cross referencing which is necessary. For each on-line transaction the Analyst charts the normal routes of the user dialogue through the logical screens with each logical screen giving a brief description of its purpose. A number of logical screens are likely to make up one *physical screen* with the logical screen representing different states of the physical one. For example 'Enter Customer Number' and 'Display Customer Details' are two logical screens but the dialogue is likely to take place on one physical screen.

The flow of the dialogue can now be reviewed by the user, and details of error handling and security routines added. Figures 3.13a and 3.13b show a logical dialogue outline for the transaction which enters the member order.

Screen Layout Charts

The data item details of the dialogue are drafted onto screen layout charts or 'mock-up' screens using software painting facilities. In this

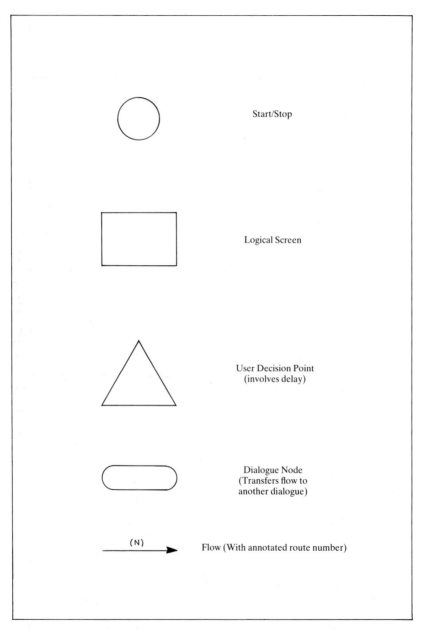

Figure 3.12   Logical Dialogue Design Symbols

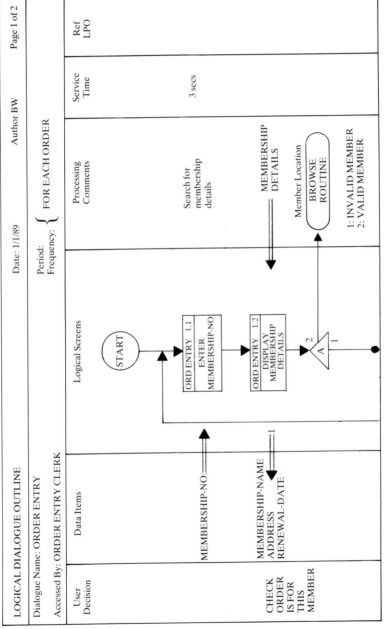

Figure 3.13a   Logical Dialogue Outline

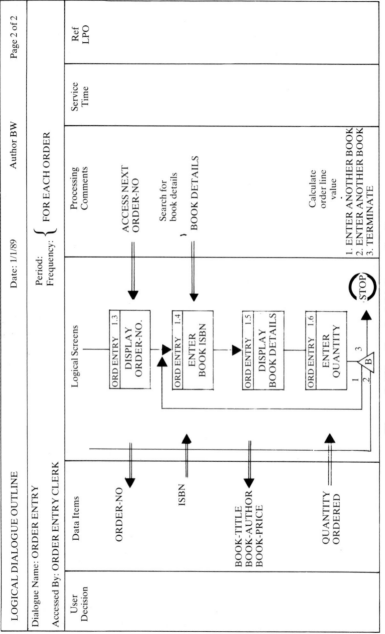

Figure 3.13b   Logical Dialogue Outline

chapter we are limited to paper for designing the physical dialogue. Screen layout charts, such as the one shown in Figure 3.14 serve as system documentation but the design may have to be altered when it is transferred to the screen and its aesthetic qualities become clearer.

3.4.6   Build a Prototype Dialogue

The point has already been made that for many users the interface *is* the system. The design process should recognise this and ensure that dialogues are continually improved and tested through a thorough user and system review.

A prototype can be constructed as a paper and pencil simulation. The logical dialogue outline supported by the menu tree and screen and report layouts is a manual simulation of the interface. The user can 'walk through' the dialogue by starting at the menu map, entering the logical dialogue outline and examining the outputs that result on layout charts. This can be supported by a series of overhead slides which show screen features such as highlighting, colour and inverse video.

Many fourth generation languages have screen painting facilities. It can be a relatively simple task to quickly build a series of screens which the user will need in completing a particular task. Screen painters enable the users and Analyst to collaborate in modifying the layout and contents of the screen to get a closer match between the facilities and aesthetics of the dialogue and the users' needs. Dummy menus can also be constructed to link these screens. The prototyping of inputs and outputs is discussed in more detail in Chapter 6.

The testing sessions of a prototype interface may be recorded by a video camera. The film of the interaction is then studied by the design team who are concerned with analysing the success of the interface. The dialogue may be altered to take into account common errors and omissions. A single demonstration of a system does not reveal many operational difficulties. The designers also benefit from the critical examination of their assumptions about the user, the system and the environment.

3.4.7   Check Response Criteria

Response time is the interval between the user signalling the end of an input (the entry of a customer code) and the display of a response from

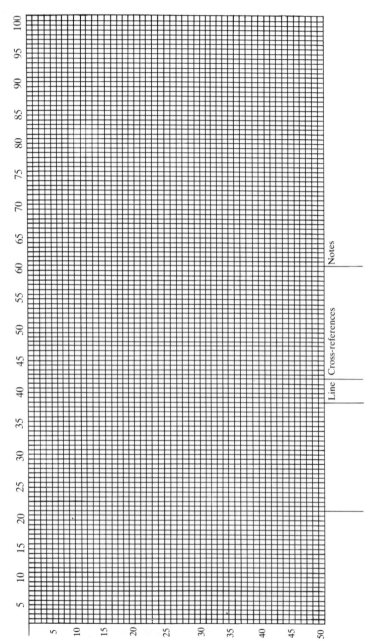

Figure 3.14   Screen Layout Chart

the system (retrieval of customer details). Response times must reflect the requirements of the system which will have been identified in analysis and recorded in the service time column of the logical dialogue outline. Response times that do not meet the required criteria must be investigated. However, it is likely that the problem lies in software and hardware performance rather than in the structure of the dialogue.

3.4.8 Establish Security and Integrity Procedures

The human–computer interface is a possible source of a breach of system security and integrity. Computer systems should always be designed to protect the users from both the system and from themselves. This is considered in detail in the next chapter.

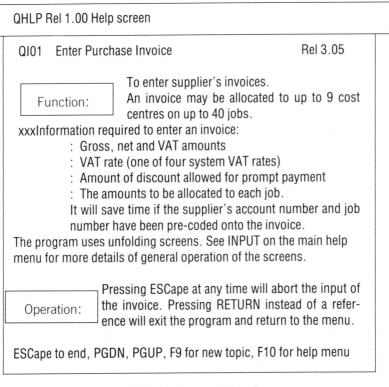

Figure 3.15 A General Help Screen

3.4.9   Provide On-line Help and Training

The general principles of help facilities have already been discussed. However, progressive assistance can also be given through accessing data already on the system. An example of this is where a user at one point in a dialogue (input supplier invoice) is expected to recall knowledge of record keys (account numbers). The system can be designed to accept the first letter of the name and search the database to retrieve all the record numbers which have a supplier name starting with this letter. The user is then able to select the one required and proceed with the dialogue.

Figures 3.15 to 3.17 illustrate this progressive help feature. The first screen (Figure 3.15) is a general instruction screen which serves as an on-line page from the manual. Figure 3.16 shows the input screen at a point where the user needs help in finding which supplier code to enter. Figure 3.17 illustrates the window of helpful data (ie the supplier codes and corresponding names which may be browsed through until the required supplier is found). The system will then return the user to the point at which the dialogue was temporarily left, but with the selected data now entered.

```
QI01 Rel 1.01 Input a Purchase Invoice                    02/02/85   User 1
Reference   CRM123   Date          2/ 2/85                    Hold     N
            Supplier                [       ]

            Invoice Net
                  Vat           Rate (1-4)          %
                        -----------
                  Gross         Discount            %

Line     Remaining                            Total

         Net amount
         Nominal

         Description
```

Figure 3.16   On-line Help: Before Image (Supplier Code Required)

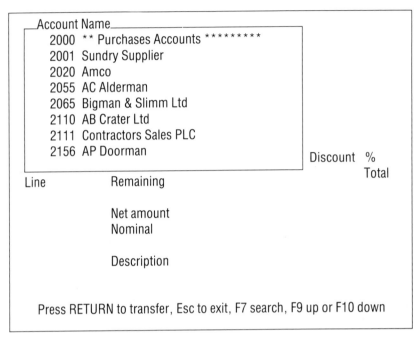

Figure 3.17 On-line Help: After Image (with Window of Supplier Data)

3.5 INFOSYS: DESIGNING THE DIALOGUES

The Seminar Booking System at InfoSys is an on-line system which depends upon quick response to enquiries about the titles and dates of scheduled seminars. Booking transactions are recorded onto the system at the time of input but a batch process of printing the daily booking confirmations has been specified to reduce system demands by the printer.

The on-line transactions required to support the processes enclosed by the human–computer boundary have been organised in a hierarchical structure illustrated in the menu tree shown in Figure 3.18. The menu is given in skeleton form.

The screen layout chart and the logical dialogue outline for the input dialogue of the transaction 'record a booking' are given in Figures 3.19a, 3.19b and 3.20. Drawing the logical dialogue design chart raises a number of design issues which need resolving. For example, if the next

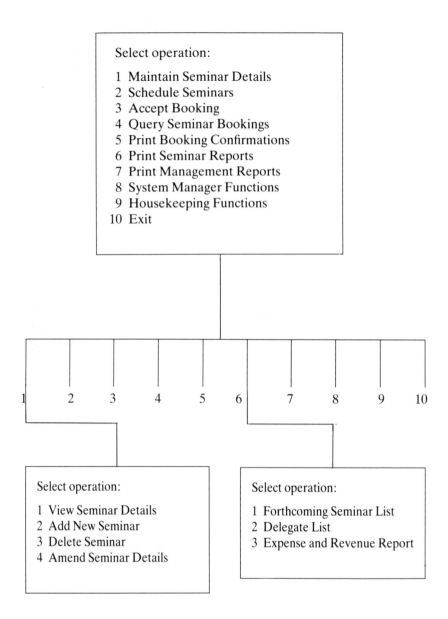

**Figure 3.18   InfoSys Seminar Bookings System Menu Tree
Showing Representative Sub-menus**

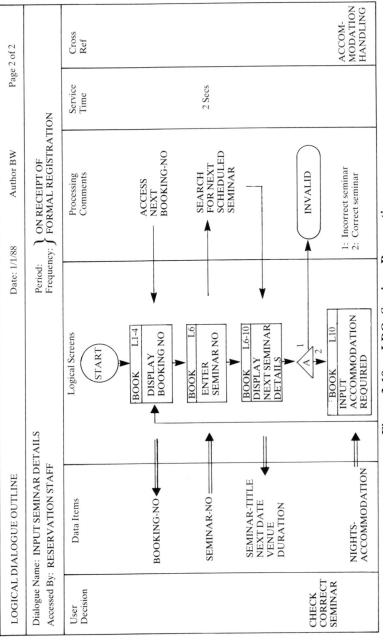

Figure 3.19a   LDO: Seminar Reservation

LOGICAL DIALOGUE OUTLINE

Date: 1/1/88   Author BW   Page 2 of 2

Dialogue Name: INPUT SEMINAR DETAILS
Accessed By: RESERVATION STAFF

Period:
Frequency: } ON RECEIPT OF FORMAL REGISTRATION

User Decision	Data Items	Logical Screens	Processing Comments	Service Time	Cross Ref
		START			
	BOOKING-NO	BOOK L1-4 DISPLAY BOOKING NO	ACCESS NEXT BOOKING-NO		
	SEMINAR-NO	BOOK L6 ENTER SEMINAR NO	SEARCH FOR NEXT SCHEDULED SEMINAR	2 Secs	
	SEMINAR-TITLE NEXT SEMINAR DATE VENUE DURATION	BOOK L6-10 DISPLAY NEXT SEMINAR DETAILS			
CHECK CORRECT SEMINAR		A 1 2	INVALID		
	NIGHTS-ACCOMMODATION	BOOK L10 INPUT ACCOMMODATION REQUIRED	1: Incorrect seminar 2: Correct seminar		ACCOMMODATION HANDLING

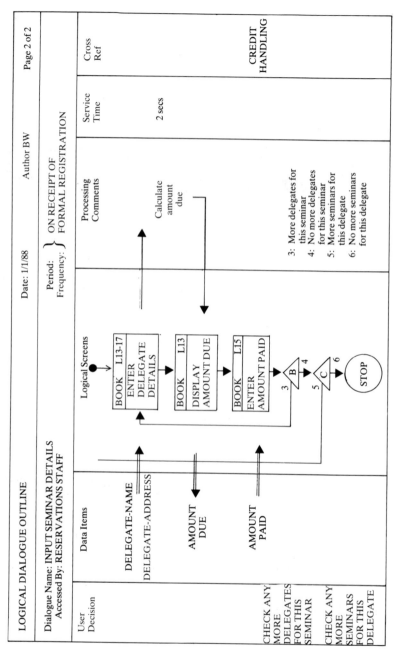

Figure 3.19b   LDO: Seminar Reservation

seminar scheduled is full, should the system automatically search for the next presentation of that seminar type? The exercise of simulating the dialogue on paper will bring many such difficulties to the attention of the Analyst, who might construct alternative views for the user to consider and select.

Record a Booking

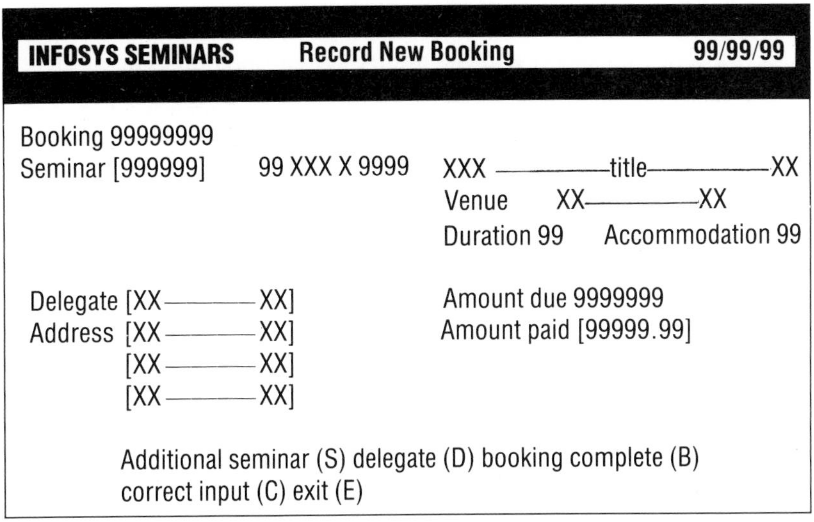

INFOSYS SEMINARS	**Record New Booking**	**99/99/99**

Booking 99999999
Seminar [999999]　　99 XXX X 9999　　XXX ———————title———————XX
　　　　　　　　　　　　　　　　　　　Venue　　XX————————XX
　　　　　　　　　　　　　　　　　　　Duration 99　　Accommodation 99

Delegate [XX———————XX]　　　　Amount due 9999999
Address　[XX———————XX]　　　　Amount paid [99999.99]
　　　　　[XX———————XX]
　　　　　[XX———————XX]

　　　Additional seminar (S) delegate (D) booking complete (B)
　　　correct input (C) exit (E)

Figure 3.20　Booking Screen Layout

3.6　SUMMARY

The inputs and outputs of the system all demand an interface between the operator and the system. This is the human–computer interface and it consists of screens linked together by dialogues and conversations. This chapter has:

- Specified that the dialogue should be both functional and usable. Functionality is concerned with ensuring that the dialogue is correct and complete; usability is concerned with the convenience of the interface. Convenience should reinforce correctness.

- Suggested five criteria for good dialogue design. These are that the dialogue should be natural, consistent, not redundant, supportive and flexible.

– Presented a structured, user-centred approach to dialogue design.

– Introduced three models for documenting dialogue design. These were the menu tree, the logical dialogue outlines and the screen layout charts.

3.7 EXERCISES

The following questions refer to the library case study.

1 It has been decided that the library system should be menu driven. Design the menus of the system and document them using a menu tree.

2 Select three parts of the system where you believe that the dialogue should be respectively:

- *Form fill*. Design an appropriate form for this application and document it using a screen layout chart.

- *Question and answer*. Design an appropriate dialogue and document it using a logical design outline.

- *Command driven*. Give examples of the command values and justify why this dialogue type should be used in this instance.

3 Draw a logical dialogue outline for the making of a reservation.

The following questions do not refer to the case study.

4 Design and document a dialogue to query the status of an order received by the Mail Order Book Club.

5 Examine the logical dialogue outline of Figure 3.13:

- Specify the contents and position of the error messages.

- Consider how the dialogue could be made more adaptable to the user.

6 List the good and bad features of the screen shown in Figure 3.10. Redesign the screen layout to improve the overall appearance. More than one screen may be used if preferred.

7 Examine an application software package and assess its:

- naturalness;
- consistency;
- flexibility;
- supportiveness.

4 Systems Controls

4.1 INTRODUCTION

Controls have to be implemented in all stages of systems development. They are particularly critical in input design (to prevent Garbage In – Garbage Out) but such operational controls must not be unduly stressed at the cost of those in other phases of system development. This chapter begins by identifying the areas of risk using the 'onion skin' approach suggested by Wong (1977) which provides a framework for systematically identifying computer-related risks (see Figure 4.1). Controls to prevent and detect errors and incursions are presented in subsequent sections of the chapter.

The Data Protection Act (1984) is perhaps the most significant piece of legislation to affect system developers. It lays down standards and requirements for computer systems which are enforceable through law, and carry penalties if they are not adhered to. The final sections of this chapter examine the Act and its implications for systems development.

4.2 AREAS OF RISK

Wong's model (see Figure 4.1) identifies risks due to:

Corporate Objectives

These risks occur where the computer installation is affiliated to a company whose objectives do not command general approval. This may be due to a number of factors such as pollution, warfare contracts, personal injustice or political animosity.

Economic Factors

Trade problems and recession may create a number of circumstances

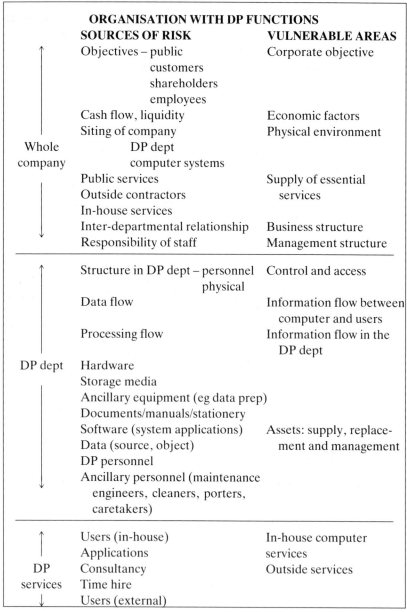

ORGANISATION WITH DP FUNCTIONS

SOURCES OF RISK	VULNERABLE AREAS

Whole company

SOURCES OF RISK	VULNERABLE AREAS
Objectives – public 　　　customers 　　　shareholders 　　　employees	Corporate objective
Cash flow, liquidity	Economic factors
Siting of company 　　　DP dept 　　　computer systems	Physical environment
Public services Outside contractors In-house services	Supply of essential 　services
Inter-departmental relationship	Business structure
Responsibility of staff	Management structure

DP dept

SOURCES OF RISK	VULNERABLE AREAS
Structure in DP dept – personnel 　　　　　　　　　　physical	Control and access
Data flow	Information flow between 　computer and users
Processing flow	Information flow in the 　DP dept
Hardware Storage media Ancillary equipment (eg data prep) Documents/manuals/stationery Software (system applications) Data (source, object) DP personnel Ancillary personnel (maintenance 　engineers, cleaners, porters, 　caretakers)	Assets: supply, replace- 　ment and management

DP services

SOURCES OF RISK	VULNERABLE AREAS
Users (in-house) Applications	In-house computer services
Consultancy Time hire Users (external)	Outside services

Source: K K Wong, 1977

Figure 4.1　The 'Onion Skin' Approach to the Systematic Identification of Computer Related Risks

which affect the security of the computer department. Economic issues will be important both to the individual (who may be suffering personal money problems) and to the group involved in organised collective bargaining. Precautions will also have to be taken to secure continuity of supply and maintenance of computer equipment.

Physical Environment

Typical problems are fire, floods, pollution and explosions. Other risks may include air crashes (if the computer centre is built near an airport), road accidents and vandalism. Wong feels that:

> 'Of the many problems which threaten the computer operation, those affecting the physical environment are perhaps the easiest to comprehend and for which to organise safeguards.'

Supply of Essential Services

Essential services include water, heat, gas, and most crucially, power. Loss of these facilities may either be deliberate (due to an industrial dispute) or accidental (a dog chewing through a power cable). Whatever the reason, a back-up generator is essential if computer operations must continue. Security problems may also result from breakdown of communication lines or wire tapping.

Business Structure

This will encompass fraud, industrial action and boycotts by user departments. It will also include circumstances where the management structure too easily permits fraudulent activity which can be blamed on 'computer errors'.

A large number of fraud cases are permitted, perhaps encouraged, by lack of attention to management reporting structures. Careful consideration of organisational arrangements is essential. Adequate reporting and auditing controls must be established in a structure that recognises a proper segregation of duties.

The risks identified so far are relevant to the whole company. However, there are also significant security problems within the data processing section itself. These may arise from:

Staff Relations

Wong states that 'Demotivated staff are unlikely to obtain satisfaction from their jobs, and may well believe that they are inadequately rewarded or receive insufficient praise for their efforts ...'. This may lead them into temptation, attempting to by-pass the security system either as a challenge, or for financial gain.

Information Flow

This encompasses the flow of data from the DP department to the user and also within the computer section itself. This will include the disclosure or misuse of confidential information, perhaps for blackmail, by users and DP staff acting in collusion. Risks within the DP department include negligence, accidents and a lack of discipline in the development of systems.

Risks from the Supply, Replacement and Management of Computer Resources

Wong includes the following risks in this category:

- faulty equipment, stationery and software;

- breakdown of hardware, software and systems;

- arson, theft and sabotage;

- business interruption;

- misplacement or destruction of data, programs, etc;

- out-of-date program and system documentation;

- sickness and injury to senior staff;

- industrial action and blackmail;

- misappropriation of computer resources;

- data corruption and decay of storage media.

Risks from Supplying or Receiving Computer Services

These arise from the moral and legal liabilities associated with offering services to both internal and external users. Such risks are particularly significant in offering services to external customers. Thus organisations selling DP services might have the following problems:

- mis-routeing of output;

- poor delivery of services;

- liabilities associated with late delivery and/or poor performance;

- contractual risks;

- staff misconduct;

- professional errors and omissions on consultancy assignments.

Thus security risks occur at a number of levels and the current extent of computer fraud is difficult to quantify. Some commentators feel that it is underestimated whilst others believe that the whole problem is inflated out of its true proportion. Norman comments that:

'The vast majority of all computer insecurity incidents can be traced back to application programs. Most computer goofs are application program errors, either in program specification or writing. Most reported 'computer fraud' has been achieved either by writing (rarely) fraudulent programs or by exploiting (commonly) loopholes deliberately or accidently left in programs'. (Norman, 1983.)

Developing software controls that identify errors and unauthorised access is an important task and such controls are examined in detail in the following section. However, having acknowledged this, it must also be stated that many lapses of physical security have also been recorded. Norman lists a catalogue of incidents identified by Lewis Security Systems. Three examples are listed below and they serve to demonstrate that computer security is perhaps not taken as seriously as it should be.

Case 1

The report of an open side door to a secure computer centre. This was used to pop outside for fresh air, although 'we are air-conditioned.'

Case 2

The case of an alert guard who noticed a visitor wearing a wrongly coloured badge, stopped the man, and immediately issued him with the correctly coloured badge for that area, without any interrogation.

Case 3

The computer complex with three computer halls protected by eleven locked doors each with a card lock. All eleven locks were jammed or distorted but 'we have not had them repaired because the large number of temporary staff on shifts would necessitate our issuing them all with cards.' *All cases* (Norman, 1983).

4.3 THE SCOPE OF AUDIT

The last section illustrated how security risks exist at many different levels and how a security policy is required that recognises this. This section examines some to these controls in greater detail. The term 'auditing' is used to cover all such controls, although some of the checks discussed here might be implemented by personnel who would not consider themselves to be auditors in the conventional sense.

It has been suggested (Thomas and Douglas, 1981) that the overall work of the computer auditor should encompass:

- ascertaining the systems and reviewing the organisational and operational controls of the computer department;

- ascertaining and reviewing application systems which are under development or being run;

- carrying out audits of live data and results for systems in use;

- carrying out an efficiency and effectiveness audit.

They suggest three levels of control:

Organisational

This covers an overall review of general principles, management and organisation. Tasks might include:

- an investigation into how system developments are established, controlled and resourced;

- a review of whether there are adequate controls and division of duties in the specification, development, testing and incorporation of program amendments;

- an inspection of operating logs to see if they are properly maintained, scrutinised and filed.

Application Review

This will consist of a general review of each separate application or procedure. Tasks might include:

- a consideration of the feasibility study report to see whether it meets the defined terms of reference;

- an inspection of the development timetable to see whether it is realistic and fits in with corporate plans;

- an evaluation of the planned training strategy to see whether it is both reasonable and realistic;

- an inspection of system costings and the method adopted to 'charge' these costs to users and as assessment of the principle and fairness of such charging arrangements.

Detailed Review

This examines each part, routine and program in the ystem. It should consider such questions as:

- What checks are carried out on individual documents, and are these checks laid down in the manuals? Are such checks properly made and are they adequate?

- Is there any validation carried out during data preparation, and if so, is the correction of errors properly controlled?

- How is the confidentiality of information preserved, and how is the correct circulation of output ensured? What controls exist to stop unauthorised copies of data from being produced?

- Are there adequate on-line recovery and back-up procedures, so that the requirements of the system can always be met?

Thus auditing has a wide scope and is not purely concerned with compliance to establish accounting and financial procedures. This range of activity may not be ercognised by the organisation, or indeed by the auditors themselves:

'. . auditing has been linked with the accounting function, and on the whole has not extended its scope to become interested in compliance or security within the data processing area.' (Chambers, 1986.)

4.4   CONTROL OF SPECIFICATION AND DEVELOPMENT

The auditor should be able to both participate in and critically evaluate the specification models produced in the project. It is essential that audit is considered at every stage of the system development cycle and not just tagged on at the end as a series of operational controls. Such participation will ensure that checks are both relevant and timely. It should also mean that the auditor has a detailed and complete picture of the system which has been built up over a long period of time. The task of auditing a system 'cold' is really quite daunting.

1   Initial System Proposal

The auditor will be concerned with such issues as:

- A review of the terms of reference to see if they are unambiguous and adequate for the task at hand. Sloppily defined terms of reference can lead to project difficulties and disagreements between the parties involved.

- The inspection of the timetable for the project, itemising the different stages and the resources needed. Project plans may be put together too hastily and without sufficient attention paid to the staff and computer resources required. Furthermore, there may be a tendency to underestimate requirements either because of genuine optimism or in the belief that 'this will get the project approved'. The auditor should scrutinise plans carefully and may also be responsible for the establishment of standards for project proposal documentation.

2   Audit of the Outline Proposal

At this stage the auditor will be able to make more specific recommendations. These will involve:

- A review of the adequacy of the internal controls and checks through the system. At this stage these will not be specified in detail but the auditor will be looking for evidence that controls have been considered and that these appear to be both relevant and valuable.

- An assessment of the likelihood of the stated objectives of the system being achieved within the agreed timescales and resource constraints. It is accepted that many computer projects over-run both in time and money. These factors have to be reviewed so that changes in plans are justified, understood and sanctioned.

3 Audit of the Detailed Models

It is at this stage that the auditor will be able to look at the system in greater detail. He will be able to assess more accurately the chance of project success and the resources that will be involved. Furthermore, he will be able to consider the detailed audit checks that are planned and evaluate their relevance and completeness. Detailed tasks might include:

- An assessment of the clerical activities scheduled for the new system and the quality of staff to be used for those tasks. It is sadly true that many system developers do not give sufficient consideration to the clerical activities that surround their computer system.

- That adequate control procedures and checks are written into the system at each stage, and that some sort of checking can be performed independently of the computer system. These controls need to be scrutinised and evaluated. All parts of the system need to be examined to see if there are circumstances where the auditor feels there should be checks, but none appear to be planned.

4 Audit of Programming and Program Testing

The auditor will have checked the system specification and will also evaluate the final delivered system. Therefore, he might consider that no audit is required in the program development stages. Some auditors might like to check program code but it is probably more sensible to restrict controls to program development standards and documentation. In general, standards are a good way of imposing controls and so the auditor should be actively involved in their definition.

5 Auditing System Implementation

This will involve the planning of the system delivery, including documentation and training. Suggested tasks could encompass an examination of the manuals provided, ensuring that they are complete, up-to-date, and relevant to the users or operators that they are intended for. Back-up and emergency procedures should also be detailed.

The manuals should be written in an appropriate language and, most importantly be *correct for the current state of the system*. Manuals which do not reflect the present system configuration are both confusing and potentially damaging. The user expects the screens and report formats produced by the system to be the same as those that appear in their manual. When they do not do so, they become both confused and doubtful, and their confidence in the delivered system is reduced.

6   Audit of System Testing

The auditor must be convinced that the systems have been tested properly and in accordance with defined standards. He may request active participation in the system tests and help check out printed reports and forms. He may also use this opportunity to test out the checks that he has suggested or authorised by entering invalid data. Once the system has been delivered the auditor should be an important member of any post-implementation review. At this stage he will be reviewing the controls of the system to ensure that they are both adequate *and* that they are being adhered to. This will include the maintenance of back-up copies, files and documentation, which must be open to his inspection.

4.5   THE CONTROL OF DATA

It has been stressed that audit and security have much wider scope than purely operational controls. They are as much concerned with corporate responsibilities and management structures as with the correct input, output and processing of data. The wide ranging nature of control should be recognised in the definition and scope of the auditor's tasks.

However, it must still be said that most documented errors are caused by accident: the wrong input of data, incorrectly defined processing, misinterpreted output. These are due to genuine mistakes, mis-keying and misunderstandings. It is the task of the system developer to design systems that minimise the chance of such errors reaching processing or system outputs. Controls will be required on data at all stages of its collection, processing, storage and retrieval. Data should be accurate and complete at all times, and its manipulation both authorised and legitimate. It is important to recognise that the necessary controls will be implemented in the clerical procedures of the system as well as in the software itself.

Clerical Controls

It may be possible to implement *control* totals that are summed both manually and automatically. These totals are compared and if they agree then the data is assumed to have been entered correctly and the batch can be posted for processing. Such totals are particularly common in accounting systems where the accuracy of data is paramount. Addition may be on inappropriate fields such as account numbers and the nominal codes entered on the batch. These are useful accuracy checks but clearly they have no particular significance. These meaningless sums are often termed *hash totals*.

Clerical controls are also of importance where source documents are posted around sections or buildings. It is very easy for forms or returns to be 'lost in transit' with the result that certain transactions, such as employee payments, do not take place. Movement control is usually enforced by the completion of *batch control documents* that give sufficient information for the recipient to check for the completeness of contents. Typical of data on a control sheet would be:

- *Serial number of the batch*. To check whether this follows the last received batch of documents. Has a whole batch gone missing in the post?

- *Count of batch contents*. The number of forms that should be in the batch.

- *Serial numbers of forms*. The serial numbers or number range(s) of the enclosed forms.

Such checks will be a part of the input system described in Chapter 2. A large data processing centre will have a section dedicated to data control, responsible for checking input data, enforcing input schedules, locating errors, organising and validating output, etc. They will also wish to impose standards of good house-keeping so that disks are properly and clearly labelled, unused files deleted, proper control documentation established and maintained. This is often sadly missing in microcomputer installations where disks go unlabelled (or labels never changed), hard disks become cluttered with obliquely named files which no-one can recall creating, let alone naming, and back-up procedures ignored because "we haven't got enough spare disks".

Software Controls

The source for most of these checks will be a data element data dictionary definition. These will permit the formulation of a whole range of controls performed by the *software itself*. Thus the system is used to trap input errors using the skill and knowledge of the system's developer. Typical of these checks are:

Format checks. That data always conforms to the specified format. Thus a product code designated as two letters followed by four numbers is always entered this way. Invalid entries such as A2341 or AS231 are rejected.

Range checks. The data has to lie within certain values. These may be set globally (eg Property Reference Code must be between 100 and 200) or may be more selective to identify uncommon occurrences. Thus, if 90% of all Property Reference Codes are between 100 and 110, then legitimate, but infrequent codes may trigger a request for operator checking.

'You have entered code 121. This is a Warehouse. Please confirm that this code is correct. . . .'

Sequence checks. Used to test that transactions which are supposed to be in a certain order are actually arranged in this way. Thomas and Douglas (1981) comment that:

'Although well-known, this check is not applied in systems as widely as it could be. Coupled with the issue of sequentially prenumbered stationery, where stationery control is exercised, this check can provide control over a number of aspects of the non-computer part of the system.'

Consistency checks. Two data items may be related in some way. Thus 'maternity leave' is always associated with sex = 'female'. Many such relationships exist and should be exploited to the full. It should stop some of the more ludicrous errors like those quoted in Warner and Stone of one air*man* discharged on the grounds of pregnancy, and the award of a flying badge to a carpenter (Warner and Stone, 1970).

Record and item counts. Counting the items (how many invoices that have been entered) represents a simpler but less reliable alternative to *control and hash totals*.

Flag fields. The inclusion of flag fields that record whether a certain state or process has taken place. These are essentially included in the file definition for *control purposes only*. Thus, if a salary field has been up-dated the flag is set to a value which traps all subsequent attempts to access the salary information. It can be viewed as a switch that is set once and prevents any subsequent activity until it is re-set.

Code design. It may be feasible to implement a code design which has elements of self-checking. Thus the first facet of the code (say the first three numbers) may be split off and certain checks performed. Included amongst these might be consistency checks against other parts of the code.

'If the first three numbers of the code are less than 100 check that the fourth number is not greater than 7.'

This code was part of one used for supply requisitioning. The first three numbers were employee codes. Those with a code beginning with less than 100 could not order more than £7(000) worth of goods.

A code is helped by the addition of a check digit. This represents a number added to the end of the code which permits the rest of the code to be checked for transcription, transposition and random errors. One of the most common methods of allocating a check digit is the modulus 11 algorithm. This is best illustrated by example.

A company uses product numbers of six digits, 345213 is a typical example. It wishes to incorporate a check digit into the code in an attempt to reduce the number of clerical input errors. This will thus make a new seven digit code.

The method of calculation is as follows:

Number		3	4	5	2	1	3
Multiplier		6	5	4	3	2	1
Product		18	20	20	6	2	3
Sum of Products				69			
Divide by Modulus 11	6 remainder 3						

The remainder is added to the code to make the new one:

3452133

Every time this code is entered by the operator the software undertakes a modulus 11 check to validate the check digit. If the last entered figure is 3 *and* the rest of the code is correct then the input is permitted. The value of this can be demonstrated by the effect of a simple transposition error.

Number		3	5	4	2	1	3	3
Multiplier		6	5	4	3	2	1	
Product		18	25	16	6	2	3	
Sum of products				70				
Divide by modulus 11	6 remainder 4							

The check digit is incorrect and so an error has been made in the entry.

It should be recognised that all these checks should be applied together. The erroneous input 3542133 may have survived format and range checks only to be tripped up by the check digit. However, the latter is not a coding panacea. Thomas and Douglas point out that it will not prevent the mistake of a user who has a list of valid and verifiable numbers and applies the wrong one by mistake. They suggest that 'a check digit system always has some value, but the auditor should assess how much reliance should be placed on it' (Thomas and Douglas, 1981).

4.6   AUDITING TECHNIQUES

Test Data Method

In this method, the auditor prepares some dummy data and passes it through the system. The effect of this data is predicted in advance: how it will be presented in reports, the effect of processes on it, which data items should be rejected or questioned, etc. These predictions are then compared with the results from the system run and any discrepancies are investigated. In many respects it is like *system testing* (see Chapter 7), but in this instance it is undertaken by an external observer – an auditor and not the system developer.

Test data may be constructed to examine the processing of normal, unusual and ridiculous figures. These figures must be carefully controlled within the system, so that legitimate transactions are not sparked off by them. There are many, perhaps apocryphal stories, of vanloads of goods touring the European mainland looking for fictitious addresses entered by auditors as part of the test data. In such instances the dummy nature of the data had not been recognised and as a result the usual administrative arrangements had been set in motion.

This latter problem can be overcome by establishing areas of the system which are specifically for audit testing purposes. Thus a firm may set up a customer, a department or an account specifically allocated to audit. This section of the system works like all the rest but the usual physical consequences of the processing are withheld. This so-called integrated test facility is usually feasible where the system has been designed with audit as one of its main design objectives. The weakness of this approach is ensuring that the dummy audit sections are actually working the same as the rest of the system and have not been singled out for special, legitimate processing!

Chambers (1986) states that the test data method may be used to good effect in the following circumstances:

1 Test input data controls, including data validation.

2 Test processing logic and controls.

3 To test computation of such values as discounts, payslips, VAT and commission.

4 To test related manual controls.

He feels that it is a useful audit tool but that it is very time-consuming and only gives a snapshot of the system's activities. It only deals with dummy data and so 'it cannot be said to directly contribute to the verification of balance sheet and operating statement items, or any other items'. The external auditor will be more concerned with verification and so he is more interested in an auditing technique which permits him to interrogate real data. This will not only give the verification he requires, but also provide an insight into the system's controls. Direct access is provided by Audit Enquiry programs.

Audit Enquiry Programs

These packages vary widely in sophistication but they are primarily used to examine files, retrieve data and produce requested reports. They permit the auditor to access the system files and data directly, and to make the required tests and enquiries on the actual operational figures. Chambers feels that such packages help the auditor in five ways.

1 They compensate for the loss of visual evidence. The records may be read almost as if they were their physical equivalents.

2 Data may be extracted for further audit investigation. Thus problems and inconsistencies may be pursued through subsequent enquiries. In this way the audit enquiry program is a much more sensitive tool than the test data approach.

3 They provide independent verification of the values, details and analysis of the presented data. The test data method cannot do this because it cannot use the real figures.

4 Complex calculations may be conducted faster, more accurately and more completely than with clerical audit procedures.

5 'They allow identification of items which do not comply with the laid down system rules or which, while complying, seem unreasonable.'

An example of the use of an audit enquiry package and guidelines for their selection is given elsewhere (Chambers, 1986).

Audit: The Operating System

The Operating System may be a useful source of audit information. Most Operating Systems maintain *operational logs* that record what use has been made of the system. In many practical instances it has been the Operating System which has provided important clues about fraudulent activity. Pointers have included statistics about use, aborted attempts to log into certain files, high activity on files at unusual times and overuse of certain terminals.

In a useful review of the audit facilities of a selection of mainframe Operating Systems (Douglas, 1984) Sandra Bennett describes the Burroughs System Log, and lists the utilities which are available to interrogate it. These include an 'analyser' which can print all or part of either the current or previous logs.

'The utility provides facilities for printing information relating to periods of time, particular jobs or particular types of messages. One of these options will print a list of security violations. Another option will provide information on hardware faults . . .'.

4.7 AUDIT: SOME FURTHER CONSIDERATIONS

Special difficulties may be encountered in auditing certain types of configuration. This will be illustrated by considering two particular problem areas – on-line processing and microcomputers.

Audit of On-line Systems

Many of the controls outlined earlier can only be sensibly applied to *batch* systems. In most instances they depend upon the existence of a physical document which can be used to verify the transaction. However, this is unlikely to be true of on-line systems where data is entered straight onto the system without any intervening form or paper document. The problems this can cause led to Hooper (quoted in Chambers, 1986) claiming that:

'Where on-line systems are concerned the matter of audit trails becomes more important than ever because the use of visual display input terminals is like writing in invisible ink.'

This creates the major problem of ensuring that the user can only gain access to authorised data and that he can only make the changes which are permitted. This requires a systematic approach to allocating security passwords and levels, and supporting these with appropriate application and system software. This is easier said than done! Even Operating Systems, which are generally the result of considerable software effort, may be breached by knowledgeable users.

Case 1

Computing (23 March, 1978) described how students at Thames Polytechnic were asked to break the security routines on a DEC System 10. Three students succeeded, breaking into a file that contained their examination marks and amended their results.

Case 2

A programmer breached a rival software company's security to locate and display the code of a proprietary software package. (Norman, 1983.)

Many Operating System developers have tried to offer flexibility in their software by giving more optional security facilities. These are useful when the computer section *know they exist, know how to use them* and, as importantly, *know when to use them*. However, such flexibility can lead to more opportunity for fraudulent activity. Bennett, in her review of the Burroughs Master Control Program (MCP) reveals that:

'It is possible to compile and run the MCP with both the system log and the job log required options set off. Burroughs do not recommend this, but it is possible.' (Douglas, 1984.)

Thus Operating Systems may not possess (either through omission or choice) adequate audit features. This is even more true of application software, particularly where audit and security has been given relatively low priority in the system design.

Thomas and Douglas list 21 checks that the auditor should make on the access controls of on-line systems. Four representative examples are given below:

– There is a limit to the number of false attempts permitted when trying to gain access from a terminal. After this limit has been passed, the terminal is locked out from the centre until the activity has been investigated.

– There is a logging system which records the use and work of the terminals, and summarises the nature of the valid use of each terminal and itemises its misuse.

– Passwords are used at different levels and for different operations such as access to the system, enquiry, input and update. A user may be issued with more than one password.

– There is a limit set on the amount of time that a terminal can be actively continuous, and after that time it is required to repeat the 'sign-on' procedure. This limit should be monitored, reviewed and enforced. (Thomas and Douglas, 1981)

Thus, the complexity of developing and operating an on-line system poses additional audit problems which have to be considered and overcome.

Martin, in his consideration of accuracy controls in real-time systems (Martin, 1973) suggests that transaction checks naturally become more significant because batches do not exist. He places great emphasis on the role of interface design in reducing erroneous entries, providing 'eight vital aspects' in the 'battle for accuracy on real-time systems'.

1 The psychological considerations in dialogue design must be planned so as to minimise the probability of terminal operator errors.

2 The dialogue must be structured in such a way as to catch as many errors as possible.

3 The system must be planned so as to facilitate immediate correction of errors caught.

4 The real-time error-detection process must be backed up with off-line file inspection and, if applicable, balancing routines.

5 Self-checking operations must be built into both the real-time dialogue and the linkage of this dialogue to the file-inspection routines.

6 Transactions and posting procedures must be devised so that transaction balances and file balances can be taken where they are useful.

7 Procedures must be worked out to bridge all periods of system failure and recovery in such a way that errors are not introduced here.

8 Careful controls must be devised to prevent unauthorised persons from modifying the files or making entries at terminals. (Martin, 1973)

This list is significant for two main reasons. Firstly, it recognises the importance of dialogue design almost a decade before it became fashionable. The growth of on-line systems has led to the interface becoming much more important and hence the developer should be at ease with different interface types and principles of good practice (see Chapters 2 and 3). It has become a major weapon in error detection.

Secondly, the list demonstrates the interaction of interface, input and control design. These three facets should reinforce each other. A well designed screen is devalued if it permits the entry of erroneous data, while validated data items on a friendly screen are reduced in impact if they are irrelevant or incomplete.

Audit of Microcomputers

Many microcomputer implementations use packaged software. The auditor must evaluate the audit features of competing packages and so contribute to the eventual selection of an appropriate product. Features of importance include:

– The provision of a complete and adequate audit trail.

– Data validation facilities, particularly in input control.

- An assessment of the product's documentation.

- Password levels and flexibility. Password maintenance and security. How easy is it to find out the allocated passwords and change them?

The Operating System is one of the most fundamental sources of audit information. Mainframe computers maintain detailed logs as a matter of course (unless they are turned off!) and have often provided the information required to trap unauthorised activity. Microcomputers usually have only very rudimentary logging facilities, if any at all! The log might only detail the name of the file, its size, and the date and time that it was last accessed. One suggestion is that 'a manual log be maintained in an agreed form. The auditor should review the type of logging system in operation, and should carry out random checks on the log to ensure that programs were run as scheduled, and they only accessed permitted files.' (Thomas and Douglas, 1981.)

This may seem good sense, but it does appear to be rather optimistic. It is unusual for many users to know what files are on a disk, let alone details of the last amendments and updates. The security and audit shortcomings of microcomputer operating systems are likely to continue reducing the chance of performing an effective microcomputer system audit.

4.8   DATA PROTECTION LEGISLATION

A number of attempts were made to introduce data protection legislation in the 1960s. These were mainly Private Member's Bills and stood little chance of reaching the Statute Book. In 1970 an official Committee, under the chairmanship of Kenneth Younger, was established to consider privacy intrusions. They were, however, restricted to examining the private sector, a limit that caused some concern.

The Younger Committee took evidence as well as undertaking a limited amount of field research. Lindop (in Bourne and Benyon, 1983) describes how people were asked:

"If there was freely available in your public library a list in which all the properties in the various streets in your town were listed in numerical order, and against each number there was the full name of those people who lived there, would you regard that as an invasion of personal privacy?"

Thirty-five percent of the respondents said "yes" and, moreover, "there ought to be a law against it".

This was, in fact, a description of the electoral register which is available in public libraries in the United Kingdom. Not only was it not recognised as such in the Younger fieldwork, but 35% of the people questioned saw it as a significant privacy threat.

The Younger Committee made a series of recommendations and the Government reacted to these by producing a White Paper on the subject in 1975 – three and a half years after the Younger Commission had reported! This paper also established a Data Protection Committee to advise the Government on legislative requirements. The Chairman was Sir Norman Lindop and his committee reported in December 1978. His work was largely lost in the change of government in 1979 (from Labour to Conservative) and the subsequent White Paper of 1982 did not borrow many of its principles. The Data Protection Authority proposed by the Lindop Committee was replaced by a Registrar appointed by the Crown. Similarly, statutory codes of practice, favoured by Lindop, were rejected as impractical as they would impose 'an unacceptable burden on resources'. It was the 1982 paper that formed the basis of the subsequent Data Protection Act considered in the following section.

However, before looking at the Act in more detail it must be acknowledged that pressure for the Data Protection legislation came from three sources.

Council of Europe Convention

The Council of Europe (which has no connection with the EEC) drew up a voluntary charter which individual countries could agree to if they so wished. This agreement is established by signing the Convention and then passing national legislation that enshrines the principles of the charter. When five countries have ratified the Convention by passing appropriate laws, then its terms became mandatory on all ratifying countries. The United Kingdom signed the Convention in 1981 but its failure to develop national legislation meant that it ran the risk of economic discrimination. Ratifying countries might oppose the export of data to a country that did not have data protection legislation. This point is recognised by the UK Data Protection Registrar who explained that one of the concerns of the 1984 Data Protection Act was to counter problems:

'arising from the possibility of damage to our international trade
which might occur if the United Kingdom were not to ratify the
'Council of Europe Convention for the Protection of Individuals
with regard to Automatic Processing of Personal Data'. Countries
ratifying this Convention might place restrictions on the transfer of
personal data to countries which have not ratified it.'

The Data Protection Act, 1984. Guideline No 1

UK Industry

There was great concern that trading losses might result from the lack of
legislation. Non-European countries were also beginning to enact laws
that specifically disallowed the export of data to countries that did not
have adequate data protection legislation. This was of particular
significance to multinational companies and one large corporation cited
it as their main reason for considering the re-location of their
headquarters to a European country which had already implemented
the requirements of the Council of Europe Convention. Certainly *The
Times* saw industry pressure as a significant issue:

'Commerce – not liberty is the motive power behind the Government's legislation in the field of data protection. Fear of losing
markets, not the desire to defend individual privacy against
computer driven intrusions colours the clauses of the Data
Protection Bill. . . .'

Source: *The Times* 12 February, 1983

Human Rights and Professional Groups

Civil liberty pressure groups, especially the National Campaign for Civil
Liberties (NCCL) were active in the fight for adequate legislation.
However, there has been little apparent concern from the public at
large, despite a number of well-researched TV documentaries that
recounted a series of harrowing tales. Indeed, Norman Lindop once
commented that "what we needed at the time was a jolly good scandal
to give us some political leverage."

Despite this indifference the Data Protection Registrar feels that
individual privacy is an important concern of the Data Protection Act.
He sees it as dealing with the problems:

'arising from the threat which the mis-use of the power of

computing equipment might pose to individuals. This concern derives from the ability of computing systems to store vast amounts of data, to manipulate data at high speed and, with associated communications systems, to give access to data from locations far from the site where the data are stored.'

Data Protection Act, 1984. Guideline No 1

4.9   DATA PROTECTION ACT 1984

The Data Protection Act received its Royal Assent on July 12, 1984. It applies to automatically processed personal data, giving rights to individuals to access data held about them and to seek compensation for loss or damage caused by the misuse of personal data. The Act is enforced by the Data Protection Registrar.

Definitions

The Act uses a number of definitions.

Data means information recorded in a form in which it can be processed by equipment operating automatically in response to instructions given for that purpose.

Personal data means data consisting of information which relates to a living individual who can be identified from that information, including any expression of opinion about the individual but not any indication of the intentions of the data user in respect of that individual. Identification may be direct (through names) or through codes.

The word 'automatic' is important. The Act excludes manual records. In some respects this could be interpreted as an incentive to de-computerise sensitive information. For example, coded records which identify individuals could be maintained on a system where one field is used to point to a manual file reference containing controversial statements. Data subjects would have access to the computer-held data but not (under the terms of the Act) to the manual data to which the computer system refers. The absence of a complementary 'Freedom of Information Act' permits the exploitation of this loophole.

Data Subject means an individual who is the subject of personal data. A company is not an individual unless that company is a Sole Trader.

Data User means a person who holds data and/or controls the contents and use of the data. A data user is able to register the details of his data with the Data Protection Registrar and to have these placed on the Data Protection Register.

A data subject is, given certain exemptions and conditions, able to examine what personal data is being held about him by the data user. The subject may then ask for a copy of such data.

Principles

The Data Protection Act is framed within the spirit of the following Principles:

1 The information to be contained in personal data shall be obtained, and personal data shall be processed, fairly and lawfully.

2 Personal data shall be held only for one or more specified and lawful purposes. These specific purposes are listed on the Register.

3 Personal data held for any purpose or purposes shall not be used or disclosed in any manner incompatible with that purpose or those purposes.

4 Personal data held for any purpose or purposes shall be adequate, relevant and not excessive in relation to that purpose or those purposes.

   The role of the data dictionary in reinforcing this Principle is worth stressing. The compilation of the dictionary should ensure that the role of every data item in the system can be explained and justified.

5 Personal data shall be accurate and, where necessary, kept up-to-date. Accurate means correct and not misleading as to any matter of fact. Personal data received from a third party is viewed as accurate if both of the following conditions apply:

   • The data and any information extracted from it are marked as received data.

   • If the individual the data relates to has told the user that he considers the data to be inaccurate, then this has been recorded with the data.

   The design implications of these two requirements necessitates some thought. It appears necessary to add two fields to systems, one denoting the source of the data and, if it is received, another acknowledging the accuracy of that data from the data subject.

6 Personal data held for any purpose or purposes shall not be kept for longer that is necessary for that purpose or purposes.

7 An individual shall be entitled:

  a) at reasonable intervals and without undue delay or expense to:

    – be informed by any data user whether he holds personal data of which that individual is the subject, and

    – to access any such data held by a data user; and

  b) where appropriate, to have such data corrected or erased.

Thus the data subject becomes, in effect, another user of the system whose requirements must be taken into consideration in third level design (see Chapter 5).

8 Appropriate security measures shall be taken against unauthorised access to, or alteration, disclosure or destruction of, personal data and against accidental loss or destruction of personal data.

Thus some of the security measures mentioned earlier in this chapter become required by law rather than being just advisory.

Rights of Individuals

The data subject has right of access to data held about him or herself. This is in accordance with one of the Principles of Data Protection and is laid down in detail in the Act itself. An individual shall be entitled to:

  a) be informed by any data user whether the data held by him includes personal data of which that individual is a data subject; and

  b) be supplied by any data user with a copy of the information constituting any such personal data held by him.

The request from the data subject for such information must be made in writing and be accompanied by the required fee.

The Courts may order data users to pay compensation for damage or distress suffered by data subjects as a result of:

- loss of data;
- destruction of data without the authority of the data subject;
- disclosure of, or access to, data without the authority of the data subject;
- inaccurate data.

Exemptions

The data subject does not have rights of access to the data if it is held for certain circumstances or for certain purposes or reasons. Briefly, these are:

1 Data held for:

    "the prevention or detection of crime"

    "the apprehension or prosecution of offenders"

    "the assessment or collection of any tax or duty".

2 Data held by a government department, supplied by a third party, in connection with the making of judicial appointments. This covers the appointment of judges but not of jurors.

3 Data to which legal professional privilege (as between lawyer and client) could be claimed.

4 Data held solely for statistical or research purposes. This is on condition that the data is not used for any other purpose and that results do not identify particular data subjects.

5 Data whose disclosure is prohibited by law where the Secretary of State decides that this prohibition should override the subject access provisions in the interests of the data subject or any other individual and makes an order conferring exemption.

6 Data covered by the Consumer Credit Act 1974.

7 Data held solely for recovery or 'back-up'.

8 Data held by regulatory bodies discharging statutory functions in connection with the protection of the public against dishonesty, incompetence or malpractice in financial matters.

The Secretary of State may also make Orders exempting from subject access provisions or modifying these provisions in relation to:

9 Data concerning physical or mental health or social work.

The exemptions above apply to *subject access*. Certain systems are excluded from the act *as a whole*. These include:

- Personal data which is required to be exempt for the purpose of safeguarding national security. A certificate is required to support the exemption signed by a Cabinet Minister, the Attorney General or the Lord Advocate.

- Personal data held for the purposes of payroll, pensions or accounts. (This exemption is lost if the payroll is also used for personnel management.)

- Data held by an individual 'concerned only with the management of his personal, family or household affairs or held by him only for recreational purposes.'

- Data held by an unincorporated members' club and relating only to members.

- Data consisting only of names and addresses and used only for the distribution of articles or information.

Neither of the preceding two exemptions applies unless the data subject has been asked whether he objects to the personal data being held, and has not objected. The exemption for distribution lists only applies if the system consists only of data items necessary or distribution. The exemption is lost if more that just name and address is held.

4.10 DESIGN IMPLICATIONS OF THE ACT

The Data Protection Registrar acknowledged the partial nature of the Act in his first Guideline.

The Act lays down a framework of law within which its purpose can be achieved. This approach has two consequences:

- there will inevitably be uncertainty about the application of the Act in particular circumstances;

- some uncertainties may only be definitely resolved following decisions by the Data Protection Registrar, the Data Protection Tribunal or the Courts.

Furthermore, it now appears that blanket exceptions will not be granted. The exception of data held for the 'prevention or detection of crime' should not give the police the right to refuse access to any data that they hold. In the case of the police 'they might be entitled to refuse access to their modus operandi files or their files of suspected persons, but not to the criminal records, which refer to crimes which have already resulted in prosecution.' (Elbra, 1984)

Thus the Data Protection Act has to settle down and its scope determined through case law. Attention will also have to be increasingly focused on the *software* implications of the Act. At the time of writing most firms are concerned with the administrative burden of the Act: filling in forms, appointing responsible staff, circulating information, etc. However, noises are already being made about the cost of implementing system changes so that software complies with the requirements of the Act. Jeff Pipe, assistant city treasurer of Birmingham City Council, described the provisional figure of £13m in overall costs to local authorities to implement the legal requirements of the Act as 'laughable' (*Computing* September 13, 1984). The same article describes just one of the software requirements of the legislation.

'to resist a charge of holding incorrect data on your file you have to indicate whether the data was supplied by the data subject or by a third party. Computer files will have to be amended to include that indicator.'

However, despite current uncertainty over the software implications of the Act, there are certain design tasks that are definitely required. Briefly, these are:

1 An initial survey of applications must be undertaken, establishing whether registration is necessary and, if it is, producing the information required for registration. This may be a large undertaking, particularly identifying applications developed on microcomputers outside the control of data processing management. This survey must also determine whether the standards and procedures of applications are rigorous enough to comply with the requirements of the Act.

2 Ensuring continuous compliance with the Act. Applications must remain within their stated scope. New applications and extensions and maintenance to current systems must be investigated and, if

necessary, registered. It is a criminal offence to operate outside the terms of the register entry.

Furthermore, each register entry is only for a maximum of three years. It must be renewed within six months of the date it is due to expire. Failure to renew an entry will require a fresh application for registration.

3 One of the Data Protection Principles explicitly recognises the necessity of physical security.

'Appropriate security measures shall be taken against unauthorised access to, or alteration, disclosure or destruction of, personal data and against accidental loss or destruction of personal data.'

Thus it is important that security requirements are understood and enforced.

4 Developing administrative procedures, controls and enquiry routines for data subjects. The data subject becomes another user of the system and this should be reflected in system design.

5 Ensuring that correct clerical procedures support the computer applications.

'Staff at all levels in an organisation play an important role in ensuring the organisation's compliance with the legislation. They may be personally liable for offences committed under the Act, as well as responsible for committing the organisation.' (Peat, Marwick, 1984)

6 Establishing a system for administering subject accesses and the cost and fees for such an access.

4.11 CONTROLS AT INFOSYS

Two specific examples of controls are examined in this section. The first looks at the software controls that could be attached to a particular input of the seminars section. The second is the completion of the data protection registration forms for the company.

Input Control

Figure 4.2 is the registration form for a particular conference. A number

(13) **Automating Systems Development**

(14) **14-16 APRIL 1987** (15)

The conference runs from midday Tuesday 14 April to midday Thursday 16th April 1987.

Registration Form

Please return this form no
later than 16th March, 1987 (16)

It is essential that this registration form be completed by all delegates, including authors and co-authors.
Please use a separate form or copy for each application.

Please tick boxes
to indicate requirements

Conference Fee (including lunch, refreshments & evening meal)

RESIDENTIAL ☐ £295.00 (1)

NON-RESIDENTIAL ☐ £230.00 (2)

Accommodation

Evening prior to the course
Monday 13 April: Evening Meal (3) ☐ £ 6.00
Bed & Breakfast (4) ☐ £14.00

*I enclose a cheque made payable to INFOSYS LTD
enclose an order for: (5)
TOTAL £...................

Signed .... Date .... (7)

Name (BLOCK CAPITALS PLEASE) .... (6)

Prof/Dr/Mr/Mrs/Miss* .... (8) Position .... (9)

Employer .... (10)

Address to which correspondence should be sent: .... (11)

....

.... Tel No. .... (12)

*Delete as appropriate

Figure 4.2 Sample Registration Form (Data Items Numbered)

of checks can be made when the information on this document is entered into the system.

For example:

– Completeness check on items 1 and 2. One of these should be completed.

– Check total on item 5. This should be the addition of items 1, 3 and 4. If item 2 is selected, then items 3 and 4 should be disallowed.

– Check on completion of items 6–12.

– Consistency check between the date of item 16 and the receipt date of the application (or the date shown in item 7 if this is deemed to be more appropriate).

Data Protection Act: Application for Registration

Figure 4.3 is the registration application for the Seminars section. The Form DPR–1 is in two separate parts. Part A records information about the applicant and other details covering the whole application. This includes such information as company name and address, contact name, company registration number, period of registration, etc. This is not shown on Figure 4.3.

Part B is the application for the registration of a particular purpose and one part B must be completed for each purpose that is to be registered. Figure 4.3 is the application for the Seminars section. A few additional notes may aid the clarity of the entries.

Section B2. InfoSys is taking part in a monitoring campaign run by the Equal Opportunities Commission. This requires the recording of sex (C011 – already needed for bedroom allocation) and ethnic origin (C114).

Section B3. Certain courses are run under the aegis of the Department of Employment. Personal details of a sample of course members must be disclosed to the Department so that it can validate course accessibility.

Individual applicants are checked for credit-worthiness with their banks or with reputable credit monitoring agencies.

InfoSys intends to sell their databank of past, current and potential course members to other agencies (D374, 377, 380, 381).

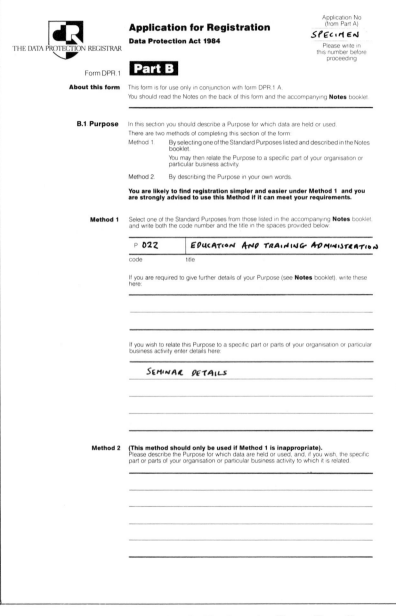

Application for Registration

Data Protection Act 1984

THE DATA PROTECTION REGISTRAR

Application No
(from Part A)

SPECIMEN

Please write in
this number before
proceeding

Form DPR.1 **Part B**

About this form This form is for use only in conjunction with form DPR.1 A.

You should read the Notes on the back of this form and the accompanying **Notes** booklet.

B.1 Purpose In this section you should describe a Purpose for which data are held or used.

There are two methods of completing this section of the form:

Method 1. By selecting one of the Standard Purposes listed and described in the Notes booklet.

You may then relate the Purpose to a specific part of your organisation or particular business activity.

Method 2. By describing the Purpose in your own words.

You are likely to find registration simpler and easier under Method 1 and you are strongly advised to use this Method if it can meet your requirements.

Method 1 Select one of the Standard Purposes from those listed in the accompanying **Notes** booklet, and write both the code number and the title in the spaces provided below:

P **022**   **EDUCATION AND TRAINING ADMINISTRATION**

code   title

If you are required to give further details of your Purpose (see **Notes** booklet), write these here:

If you wish to relate this Purpose to a specific part or parts of your organisation or particular business activity enter details here:

SEMINAR DETAILS

Method 2 **(This method should only be used if Method 1 is inappropriate).**
Please describe the Purpose for which data are held or used, and, if you wish, the specific part or parts of your organisation or particular business activity to which it is related.

Figure 4.3 Application for Registration Form (Page 1)

B.2 Description of Personal Data — Data Subjects

SPECIMEN

In this section you should describe the types of individual **(Data Subjects)** about whom personal data are to be held for the Purpose described in section B.1. Do this by ticking the appropriate boxes below.

Data Subject	Code	Current	Past	Potential
Employees, trainees, voluntary workers	S001			
Employees of associated companies, organisations	S002			
Employees of other organisations	S003	✓	✓	
Recipients, customers or clients for goods or services (direct or indirect)	S004	✓	✓	✓
Suppliers of goods or services (direct or indirect)	S005			
Claimants, beneficiaries, payees	S006			
Account holders	S007			
Share and stock holders	S008			
Partners, directors, other senior officers	S009			
Employers	S010			
Competitors	S011			
Business or other contacts	S012			
Advisors, consultants, professional and other experts	S013	✓	✓	✓
Agents, other intermediaries	S014			
Trustees	S015			
Members, supporters of a club, society, institution	S016			
Assignees, guarantors, other parties with legitimate contractual or business interest	S017			
Donors and lenders	S018			
Complainants	S019			
Witnesses	S020			
Offenders and suspected offenders	S021			
Tenants	S022			
Landlords, owners of property	S023			
Correspondents and enquirers	S024	✓		
Survey respondents, other persons assisting research	S025			
Patients	S026			
Self-employed persons	S027			
Unemployed persons	S028			
Retired persons	S029			
Students	S030			
Minors	S031			
Applicants for permits, licences, registration	S032			
Taxpayers, ratepayers	S033			
Licence holders	S034			
Vehicle keepers	S035			
Elected representatives, other holders of public office	S036			
Authors, publishers, editors, artists, other creators	S037		✓	
Immigrants, foreign nationals	S038			
Relatives, dependants, friends, neighbours, referees, associates, contacts of any of those ticked above	S039			
Members of the public	S040			

If you wish, you may write additional descriptions of Data Subjects here; start each description on a new line:

2

Figure 4.3   Application for Registration Form (Page 2)

B.2 Description of Personal Data – Data Classes   *SPECIMEN*

In this section, you should describe the **Classes** of personal data to be held for the Purpose described in B.1. Do this by ticking the appropriate boxes below. You should refer to the **Notes** booklet for examples of data items which might be covered by each Class.

Identification Data

					Details of Transactions		
Personal identifiers	**C001**	☑	Professional expertise	**C054** ☐	Goods, services provided to the data subject	**C091**	☐
Financial identifiers	**C002**	☑	Membership of committees	**C055** ☐	Goods, services obtained from the data subject	**C092**	☐
Identifiers issued by public bodies	**C003**	☐	Publications	**C056** ☐	Financial transactions	**C093**	☐
Personal Characteristics			Student record	**C057** ☐	Compensation	**C094**	☐
Personal details	**C011**	☑	Student financial records	**C058** ☑	**Business Information**		
Physical description	**C012**	☐	**Employment Details**		Business activities of the data subject	**C101**	☑
Habits	**C013**	☑	Current employment	**C061** ☑	Agreements, contracts	**C102**	☐
Personality, character	**C014**	☐	Recruitment details	**C062** ☐	Trading licences held	**C103**	☐
Family Circumstances			Termination details	**C063** ☐	**Health & Other Classes**		
Current marriage or partnership	**C021**	☐	Career history	**C064** ☐	Physical health record	**C111**	☐
Marital history	**C022**	☐	Work record	**C065** ☐	Mental health record	**C112**	☐
Details of other family, household members	**C023**	☐	Health & safety record	**C066** ☐	Disabilities, infirmities	**C113**	☐
Other social contacts	**C024**	☐	Trade union, staff association membership	**C067** ☐	Dietary, other special health requirements	**C114**	☑
Social Circumstances			Payments, deductions	**C068** ☐	Sexual life	**C115**	☐
Accommodation or housing	**C031**	☐	Property held by employee	**C069** ☐	Racial, ethnic origin	**C116**	☑
Property, possessions	**C032**	☐	Work management details	**C070** ☐	Motoring convictions	**C117**	☐
Immigration status	**C033**	☐	Work assessment details	**C071** ☐	Other convictions	**C118**	☐
Travel, movement details	**C034**	☐	Training record	**C072** ☐	Criminal intelligence	**C119**	☐
Leisure activities, interests	**C035**	☐	Security details	**C073** ☐	Political opinions	**C120**	☐
Lifestyle	**C036**	☐	**Financial Details**		Political party membership	**C121**	☐
Membership of voluntary, charitable bodies	**C037**	☐	Income, assets, investments	**C081** ☐	Support for pressure groups	**C122**	☐
Public offices held	**C038**	☐	Liabilities, outgoings	**C082** ☐	Religious beliefs	**C123**	☐
Licences, permits held	**C039**	☐	Creditworthiness	**C083** ☐	Other beliefs	**C124**	☐
Complaint, incident, accident details	**C040**	☐	Loans, mortgages, credits	**C084** ☐	**Miscellaneous Information**		
Court, tribunal, inquiry proceedings	**C041**	☐	Allowances, benefits, grants	**C085** ☐	References to manual files, records	**C131**	☐
Education, Skills, Profession			Insurance details	**C086** ☐	Uncategorised information	**C132**	☐
Academic record	**C051**	☐	Pension details	**C087** ☐			
Qualifications and skills	**C052**	☑					
Membership of professional bodies	**C053**	☑					

If you wish, you may describe additional Classes of data here; start each description on a new line:

C002 : CREDIT CARD NUMBERS ONLY

C011 : SEX ONLY (FOR BEDROOM ALLOCATION)

C013 : SMOKING / NON-SMOKING

3

Figure 4.3   Application for Registration Form (Page 3)

B.3 Sources and Disclosures

SPECIMEN

In this section, you should describe:

In column A — The sources from which you intend or may wish to obtain any of the data you have described in section B.2
In column B — The person or persons to whom you intend or may wish to disclose these data.

Do this by ticking the appropriate boxes below.

Individuals or Organisations directly associated with the Data Subjects

		A. Source	B. Disclosure
The Data Subjects themselves	D101	☑	☑
Family, relatives, guardians, trustees	D102	☐	☐
Other members of their households, friends, neighbours	D103	☐	☐
Employers — past, current or prospective	D104	☑	☑
Employees, agents	D105	☐	☐
Colleagues, business associates	D106	☐	☐

		A. Source	B. Disclosure
Legal representatives	D107	☐	☐
Financial representatives	D108	☐	☐
Doctors, Dentists, other health advisers	D109	☐	☐
Social, spiritual, welfare, advice workers	D110	☐	☐
Other professional advisers	D111	☐	☐
Landlords	D112	☐	☐

Others — please specify here:

☐ ☐

☐ ☐

Individuals or Organisations directly associated with the Data User

		A. Source	B. Disclosure
Members, including shareholders	D201	☐	☐
Other companies in the same group	D202	☐	☐
Employees, agents	D203	☐	☑
Recipients, customers, clients for goods or services	D204	☐	☑

		A. Source	B. Disclosure
Claimants, beneficiaries, assignees, payees	D205	☐	☐
Suppliers, providers of goods or services	D206	☐	☐
Persons making an enquiry or complaint	D207	☐	☑
Tenants	D208	☐	☐

Others — please specify here:

☐ ☐

☐ ☐

Organisations or Individuals (General Description)

Central Government

		A. Source	B. Disclosure
Inland Revenue	D301	☐	☐
Customs & Excise	D302	☐	☐
Driver & Vehicle Licensing Centre (DVLC)	D303	☐	☐
Department of Education & Science (DES)	D304	☐	☐
Department of Health & Social Security (DHSS)	D305	☐	☐
Department of Employment	D306	☐	☑
Home Office	D307	☐	☐
Ministry of Defence, including armed forces	D308	☐	☐
Other central government, including Scottish, Welsh & Northern Ireland Offices*	D309		

Local Government

		A. Source	B. Disclosure
Education department	D321	☐	☐
Housing department	D322	☐	☐
Social Services department	D323	☐	☐
Electoral registration, Assessment, Valuation departments	D324	☐	☐
Other local government*	D325		

Other Public Bodies

Other public bodies not elsewhere specified*	D331	
Foreign governments or authorities*	D332	

Continued

4

Figure 4.3 Application for Registration Form (Page 4)

B.3 Sources and Disclosures *Continued*

SPECIMEN

Justice		A. Source	B. Disclosure
Police forces	**D341**	☐	☐
Prosecuting authorities	**D342**	☐	☐
Other statutory law enforcement agencies, investigating bodies *	**D343**	☐	☐
The courts	**D344**	☐	☐
Judges, magistrates	**D345**	☐	☐
Prison service	**D346**	☐	☐
Probation service	**D347**	☐	☐

Health & Social Welfare

		A. Source	B. Disclosure
Health authorities, family practitioner committees	**D351**	☐	☐
Hospitals, nursing homes	**D352**	☐	☐
Registered medical practitioners	**D353**	☐	☐
Registered dental practitioners	**D354**	☐	☐
Nurses, midwives, health visitors	**D355**	☐	☐
Other health care agencies, practitioners *	**D356**		
Social welfare agencies, practitioners *	**D357**		

Other		A. Source	B. Disclosure
Public utilities	**D361**	☐	☐
Banks	**D362**	☐	☑
Building societies	**D363**	☐	☐
Insurance companies	**D364**	☐	☐
Other financial organisations *	**D365**		
Accountants & auditors	**D366**	☐	☐
Lawyers	**D367**	☐	☐
Credit reference agencies	**D368**	☐	☑
Debt collection, tracing agencies	**D369**		
Employment, recruitment agencies	**D370**	☐	☑
Private detective agencies, security organisations	**D371**	☐	☐
Trade, employers associations	**D372**	☐	☐
Trade unions, staff associations	**D373**	☐	☐
Professional bodies	**D374**	☐	☑
Voluntary, charitable, religious organisations or associations	**D375**	☐	☐
Political organisations	**D376**	☐	☐
Education or training establishments, examining bodies	**D377**	☐	☑
Survey or research organisations, workers	**D378**	☐	☐
Providers of publicly available information, including public libraries, press and media	**D379**	☐	☐
Providers of privately available information and databanks	**D380**	☐	☑
Traders in personal data	**D381**	☐	☑
Other organisations or individuals *	**D382**		

You should use the space below to give further details if you wish to use one or more of the categories marked with an asterisk (*) above. You should give the code number for each category which you are explaining.

If you wish, you may also write here additional descriptions of Sources and Disclosures:

If you are using the space below, start each description on a new line and indicate whether the item is a Source, a Disclosure, or both.

	A. Source	B. Disclosure
_____	☐	☐
_____	☐	☐
_____	☐	☐
_____	☐	☐
_____	☐	☐

5

Figure 4.3   Application for Registration Form (Page 5)

B.4 Overseas transfers

SPECIMEN

In this section you should name any countries or territories outside the United Kingdom to which you intend to transfer the data.

If none, you should tick this box:

None **T000** ☑

If the nature of your business requires you to transfer the data to any country worldwide, you should tick this box, and indicate your business in the space below:

Worldwide **T999** ☐

Otherwise, tick the appropriate box(es) below:

Algeria	**T001**	☐	Indonesia	**T020**	☐	Norway	**T039**	☐
Argentina	**T002**	☐	Iran	**T021**	☐	Oman	**T040**	☐
Australia	**T003**	☐	Iraq	**T022**	☐	Pakistan	**T041**	☐
Austria	**T004**	☐	Republic of Ireland	**T023**	☐	Philippines	**T042**	☐
Belgium	**T005**	☐	Isle of Man	**T024**	☐	Poland	**T043**	☐
Brazil	**T006**	☐	Israel	**T025**	☐	Portugal	**T044**	☐
Canada	**T007**	☐	Italy	**T026**	☐	Saudi Arabia	**T045**	☐
Cyprus	**T008**	☐	Japan	**T027**	☐	Singapore	**T046**	☐
Denmark	**T009**	☐	Jersey	**T028**	☐	South Africa	**T047**	☐
Dubai	**T010**	☐	Kuwait	**T029**	☐	South Korea	**T048**	☐
Egypt	**T011**	☐	Libya	**T030**	☐	Spain	**T049**	☐
Finland	**T012**	☐	Liechtenstein	**T031**	☐	Sweden	**T050**	☐
France	**T013**	☐	Luxembourg	**T032**	☐	Switzerland	**T051**	☐
West Germany	**T014**	☐	Malaysia	**T033**	☐	Taiwan	**T052**	☐
Greece	**T015**	☐	Malta	**T034**	☐	Turkey	**T053**	☐
Guernsey	**T016**	☐	Mexico	**T035**	☐	USA	**T054**	☐
Hong Kong	**T017**	☐	Netherlands	**T036**	☐	USSR	**T055**	☐
Iceland	**T018**	☐	New Zealand	**T037**	☐	Venezuela	**T056**	☐
India	**T019**	☐	Nigeria	**T038**	☐			

If necessary, you may write additional names or descriptions here; start each on a new line:

6

Figure 4.3   Application for Registration Form (Page 6)

How to apply for Registration

The application form is in two separate parts:

Part A is for information about the applicant and other details covering the whole application.

This part (Part B) is for a description of a Purpose for which personal data are to be held or used, and a description of the data and associated details. You will need to complete one Part B in respect of each Purpose you wish to register.

You should read the accompanying **Notes** booklet before completing the form. The Notes contain rules and conditions which the Registrar will apply, as well as standard descriptions and definitions which you will need to consult. **It is important that you read the Notes carefully.**

In completing form DPR.1, please use a typewriter or, if handwritten, use BLOCK CAPITALS.

Do not use this form to:
Alter or remove an entry already on the Register — use Form DPR.2
Renew an entry already on the Register — in this case you will be sent a renewal reminder.

Further registration packs, and extra copies of Part B, can be obtained from **Crown Post Offices** and from the **Office of the Data Protection Registrar, Springfield House, Water Lane, Wilmslow, Cheshire, SK9 5AX.**

Completed application forms, together with the appropriate fee (see Notes Booklet), should be sent to the Registrar at **P.O.Box 66, Wilmslow, Cheshire, SK9 5AX.** This address must only be used for applications. Other correspondence should be sent to the full address given above — it may be seriously delayed if sent to P.O. Box 66.

How to complete this form

In each section of Part B you may use standard descriptions to provide the detail required. Although you also have the option of writing your own descriptions in free text, **you are strongly encouraged to use the standard description approach.** In most sections this is simply a matter of selecting the appropriate descriptions from the list printed on the form and ticking the corresponding boxes.

The standard descriptions for **Purposes** are not printed on the form but are listed in the separate **Notes** booklet. You will need to read these before filling in the form. You should also refer to the booklet when selecting descriptions for **Data Classes.**

Before completing the rest of the form you should write the application number (copied from the front of Part A) in the box provided on the front of this Part B.

If your application is accepted, the details given in sections B.1 to B.4 will appear on the Register and will be available for public inspection.

If you need more space than is provided for text in any Section, you may continue on page 7.

Form DPR.1 Part B 9/85

Printed in the U.K. for HMSO. Dd 8938928 9/85 W549

7

Figure 4.3 Application for Registration Form (Page 7)

4.12 SUMMARY

Controls are required at all stages of development, from initial system definition (is it a correct use of the organisation's resources?) to system maintenance (is program documentation amended and do the changes affect the data protection registration?). This chapter gives a wide-ranging review of the types of controls required in system development. It has:

- briefly reviewed the areas of risk identified in Wong's onion-skin model;

- presented audit controls to counter these risks within a framework of organisational, application and detailed technical considerations;

- examined the latter three areas of control in greater detail, with particular emphasis on the control of data;

- briefly introduced auditing techniques: test data, audit enquiry packages and the facilities of the Operating System;

- highlighted the difficulties of control in on-line systems and microcomputer applications;

- reviewed the scope of the Data Protection legislation and its implications for the systems designer.

Figure 4.4 gives a summary of the criminal offences created by the Data Protection Act.

4.13 PRACTICAL EXERCISES

The following questions refer to the case study introduced in Chapter 1.

1 Write a short report, based on Wong's model, which systematically identifies the risks to the proposed library system and what controls are required to reduce or eliminate that risk.

2 Develop a proposed coding system for uniquely identifying borrowers.

3 Does the proposed system have to be registered with the Data Protection Registrar?

If it does compile form DPR–1.

If it does not, write a report justifying its exemption to the Data Protection Registrar.

Offence	Liable to prosecution
Holding personal data without being registered or without having applied for registration	Data User
Knowingly or recklessly holding personal data not described in the register entry	Registered Data User
Knowingly or recklessly using, obtaining, disclosing or transferring personal data other than as described in the register entry	Registered Data User. Servants or agents of a registered Data User
Knowingly or recklessly operating as a Computer Bureau in respect of personal data without being registered as such	Computer Bureau
Knowingly or recklessly disclosing personal data without the authority of the person to whom computer bureau services are provided	Computer Bureau. Servants or agents of a Computer Bureau
Failure to comply with an enforcement notice	Data User. Computer Bureau
Failure to comply with a transfer prohibition notice	Data User. Applicant for registration as a Data User
Knowingly or recklessly supplying the Registrar with false or misleading information on an application for registration or for alteration of a register entry	Anyone
Failure to keep the registered address up to date	Registered Data User. Registered Computer Bureau
Intentional obstruction of a person executing a search warrant	Anyone
Failure, without reasonable excuse, to give help reasonably required by a person executing a search warrant.	Anyone

Figure 4.4   Summary of Criminal Offences that the Act Creates

4 Define the data controls that are required in processing the transaction 'Make a reservation'.

The following questions do not refer to the case study.

5 Investigate the current state of the Data Protection Act. Have recent guidelines been issued?; new exemptions created?; case law established?; prosecutions made?; penalties imposed or established?

6 Assess the contribution of the following models to defining controls:

- data flow diagram;

- entity-relationship model;

- data dictionary;

- logical dialogue outline.

7 Investigate the security and audit features of an application software package or an operating system.

5 Designing Data Storage Structures

Designing the contents and structures of data files or databases is a critical activity in the development of information systems. Indeed, the way in which data in an information system is organised, both inside and outside the computer, can affect the speed, cost and feasibility of the desired processing activities. Grosshans (1986) emphasises this importance.

'The objective of any file system is to meet the data management needs and requirements of its users . . . the file system must provide an efficient and effective I/O (input/output) service that provides the functionality and performance required by the users and the pressure of competition' (Grosshans, 1986).

Developing efficient data structures requires the construction of a logical model of the data and the subsequent conversion of this into physical file structures (file or database) which will support the operational transactions, processes and reports of the required system.

Two important analysis techniques form the foundation for this task and these have already been described in detail in the companion text, *Introducing Systems Analysis*. They are logical data modelling, using entity-relationship diagrams and normalisation techniques; and logical process modelling, employing data flow diagrams. The logical data model gives a static view of the system which provides a detailed and reliable foundation for deciding on the contents of both temporary and permanent data structures. Data flow diagrams give a dynamic view of how this data is logically accessed by different processes. The data flow diagram has already been re-introduced in Chapter 2 as a mechanism for the location of the system boundary, separating the human tasks from

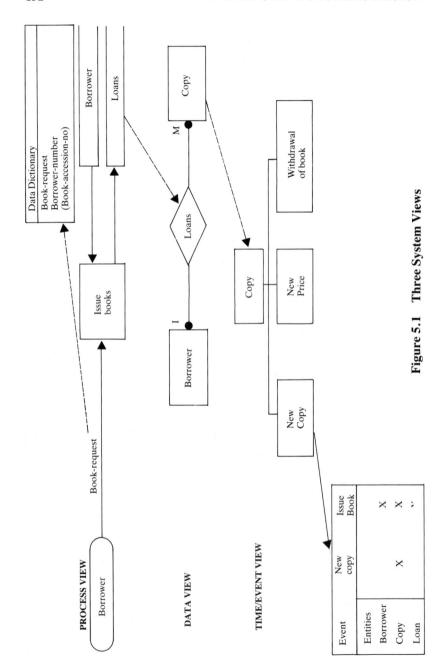

Figure 5.1   Three System Views

the computer-based processes. A third view, the entity life history, highlighting the passage of data through time, is also included in the summary diagram given in Figure 5.1.

The overall aim is to design data structures which are stable yet flexible, so that they can continue to support the organisation's business practices and requirements as they change over time. Such flexibility should make it possible to respond to any system modifications and changes in hardware and software opportunities without requiring a major redesign of the system, or adversely affecting its overall performance.

The discussion in this chapter is divided into two parts reflecting the distinct aspects of data storage design.

a) *Logical Design of Data* to take account of the access requirements of the transactions of the various applications; also referred to as Second Level Design.

b) *Mapping the Logical Design onto a Physical Design* which considers the target hardware and software environment; also referred to as Third Level Design.

A brief discussion of the data storage design issues in the InfoSys Seminar Booking System will conclude the chapter.

5.1   THREE LEVEL DATA DESIGN

Figure 5.2 illustrates the approach to data design. In first level design the initial data model derived from the analysis of requirements usually results in many entity and relationship tables. Direct implementation of these tables into files or databases would lead to a very flexible system fulfilling all the required transactions and capable of easy extension. However, using current hardware and software this implementation is likely to give poor performance both in terms of speed of processing and in response time to queries for some critical activities. This is generally due to the large number of tables (files) that have to be accessed by each process or transaction.

In second level design, the first level data model is thoroughly and systematically checked out to ensure that any subsequent system based on this model will be able to efficiently support all the desired transactions. An initial assessment is made of the functionality and

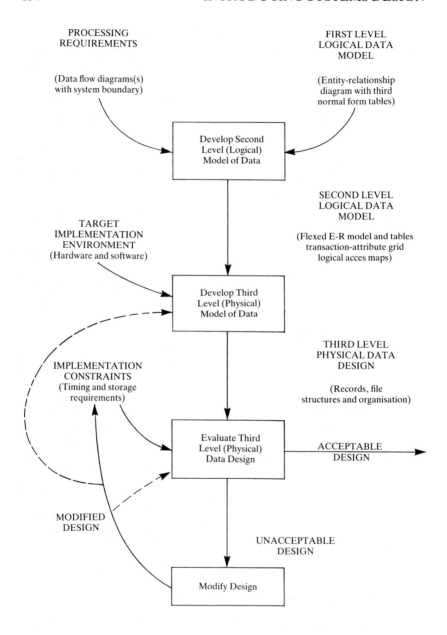

Figure 5.2   Iterative Approach to Data Design

performance of the model in meeting these requirements. This requires an investigation of how each process accesses the data in the various tables. Particularly convoluted access paths, especially for time critical processes, will lead to modifying or 'flexing' the content of the entity and relationship tables to improve the likely performance of the design.

The flexing of the data model may be supported by two useful modelling tools:

1 The Transaction-attribute Grid: used to verify that all data attributes required in each transaction or process are established and maintained during flexing (see Howe, 1986).

2 Logical Access Map: used to diagrammatically show the possible access routes of each transaction (see Martin, 1985).

The culmination of second level design is a further set of entity and relationship tables which still support the required transactions but in a more efficient and effective way. At this stage the data model design is still independent of any hardware or software considerations and is still portable across computing environments – hence it remains a logical model. Limitations of particular computers or programming languages are built into the design at the latest practical point in the design process in order to ensure maximum flexibility and portability of the system in the future.

It is third level design that takes into account the database management system or conventional high level programming language to be used in the actual implementation. The objective of this third level design is the development of a compromise data storage structure that will take into account the requirements and constraints of the environment in which the system is to be implemented. These factors include hardware availability, software facilities and timing requirements of some functions. The objective is to produce an implementation model of the data in which trade-offs between processing times and disk storage have been carefully controlled and not left to chance. Design decisions at this stage are technology and software dependent.

5.2 ITERATIVE DESIGN PHILOSOPHY

Designing the content and structure of data storage has often been considered a specialist systems design activity, on the grounds that many complex factors must be taken into account in arriving at an optimum 'design. In many early computing environments the design of data files demanded considerable skill as both memory and data storage facilities were limited (Bradley, 1982) and these had to be carefully manipulated in the application software. Furthermore, the files often reflected the current hardware capabilities and the physical organisation of data in the manual system as well as established 'rules of thumb' (Waters, 1972). It was not uncommon for many separate files to be developed for individual applications and so the organisation retained a considerable amount of duplicated, and hence redundant, data. Such purpose-built files were normally found to be very restrictive, particularly in the opportunity to share or transfer data between applications.

A number of significant changes have taken place in the last decade:

– The evolution of databases which stress the principles of sharing data.

– The availability of fourth generation languages (4GLs) and revolutionary improvements in the memory and storage facilities of hardware have also lessened the importance of one-off, highly specialised, efficient file or database designs. Current design emphasis is on long term flexibility and accessibility of data to a wide range of applications, some of which will be unknown to the Analyst at the time of design.

– The distinction and separation of the logical and physical aspects of design in a structured approach has the benefit of postponing many potentially restrictive decisions until later in the project. This also has significant advantages in ensuring long term suitability and flexibility. Many applications are unnecessarily restricted because they have been built around the facilities of a particular database management system (DBMS) or 4GL *too early* in the design process.

– Designers have increasingly adopted a prototyping philosophy in system development. An initial system design is put forward and perhaps even implemented in the user environment with the purpose of evaluating its completeness, effectiveness and efficiency in the light of experience (Lantz, 1986). This prototyping approach is inevitably iterative, involving analysis, design, evaluation and modification until the user is satisfied with the results and performance of the system. It does not expect a final detailed design of data structures to be made too early as many future applications will depend on flexibility and easy access to the data. The cost of errors in (or omissions to) the requirements specification can be very high. If an error is discovered and needs to be corrected late in the system life cycle, much extra work is involved. Figure 5.3 is from Boehm (1982).

These trends in system development practices naturally lead to the iterative approach to data storage design which is the central theme of this chapter and was summarised in Figure 5.2. It embodies both a clear separation of logical and physical design of data structures and an iterative approach to arriving at a final database or file design.

5.3   FIRST LEVEL DESIGN

5.3.1   A Logically Simple Redundancy Free Data Model

The first level design of detailed data analysis produces a logically simple redundancy free model. This initial stage has already been described in Chapter 7 of *Introducing Systems Analysis*. It identifies entities and relationships and produces an entity-relationship diagram with a set of supporting tables in at least third normal form. These tables contain no redundant data and thereby eliminate the problems of inconsistent data.

Mills and Skidmore (1987) point out that this initial data model is enterprise-oriented and independent of any factors such as departmental responsibilities, computer hardware and software, and centralisation or decentralisation issues. They suggest that the data model has the following qualities which make it a sound foundation for the design of the system:

– *correct*: precisely documents the enterprise rules;

– *applicable*: supports all current and planned transactions;

– *complete*: includes all necessary entities, attributes and relationships;

– *minimal*: does not include any entities, attributes or relationships which are derivable from other entities, attributes or relationships;

– *independent*: does not depend on any implementation criteria;

– *flexible*: able to evolve with the enterprise.

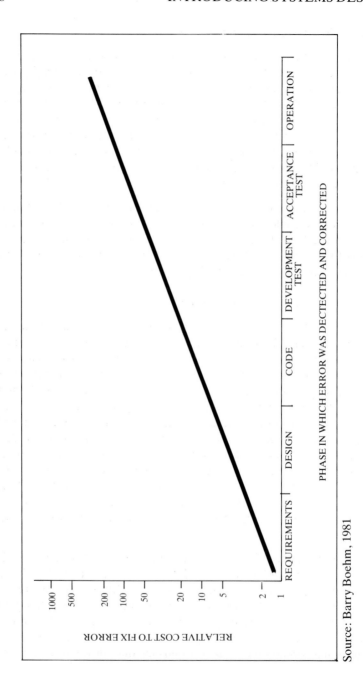

Source: Barry Boehm, 1981

Figure 5.3   Cost of Error Correction Throughout the System Life Cycle

5.3.2   Checking Out the Data Model

First level design is supported by functional analysis which enables the data model to be checked for completeness and accessibility of the attributes. Some difficulties may exist in logically linking one entity occurrence with another in the same model. These are known as connection traps and may prevent some transactions from generating the users' required information. Space in an introductory text such as this does not permit full discussion of this issue and the reader is directed to Howe (1986) for a detailed explanation and discussion of the implications of such problems.

Two tools are suggested here for checking that the first level data model is applicable and complete. These are the *transaction-attribute grid* and the *logical access map*. Other tools such as the process-entity matrix (NCC, 1984) and the entity catalogue (Longworth and Nicholls, 1987) have also been used for this purpose.

5.3.3   The Transaction-attribute Grid

A data model can be checked out by drawing up a transaction-attribute grid which lists all the attributes in each table on one axis and the required transactions on the other. Entries for each transaction are recorded on the grid to represent the storage, retrieval and deletion of data attribute values. In this way the Analyst is able to verify that all stored attributes are used in some way. Every attribute should be stored by a transaction from the data flow diagram, retrieved and modified by other transactions and also have at least one transaction which deletes or archives it. The logical sequence can be further verified by ensuring that an attribute value required by a transaction has been previously stored and not already deleted by any other transaction. Careful examination of a completed transaction-attribute grid will also assist in identifying the most frequently retrieved tables and this will aid physical data design.

The entity-relationship diagram and set of tables in third normal form (Figure 5.4) refer to the example of the Mail Order Book Club (MOBC) order processing system. The reader is referred to Chapter 7 of *Introducing Systems Analysis* for a full explanation of the building of this data model. The posted or preposted identifiers have been printed in bold as in the previous text. A preliminary check against the data flow diagram has already been made to ensure that all the processes of the

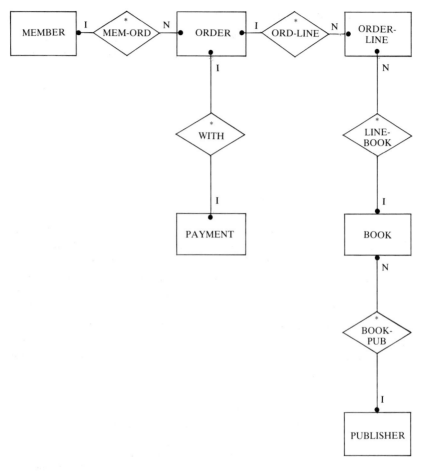

Tables

MEMBER:	(Member-number, member-name, member-address, join-date
ORDER:	(Order-number, order-date, despatch-date, **member-number**
ORDER-LINE:	(**Order-number, ISBN,** quantity-ordered)
BOOK:	(ISBN, title, author, selling-price, cost-price, quantity-in-stock, re-stock-level, **publisher-name**)
PAYMENT:	(Transaction-number, **order-number,** payment-amount, payment-method, clearance-date)
PUBLISHER:	(Publisher-name, publisher-address)

Figure 5.4   Mail Order Book Club: Entity-relationship Diagram and Tables

data flow diagram are supported by the entity-relationship model.

A further check for completeness is performed by the transaction-attribute grid (Figure 5.5). The codes which have been used in completion of the transaction-attribute grid are:

S = store

R = retrieve

M = modify

D = delete

Numbers have been used to indicate the attribute items used as entry points to the tables and indicate the sequence of accesses to the tables. The asterisk indicates that more than one table occurrence is stored, retrieved, updated or deleted. It is clear that this particular transaction-attribute grid is incomplete as some attributes, such as those belonging to the Member entity have no specified transactions which store, update or delete them. Similarly the attributes publisher-address, cost-price and re-stock-level are not used by any of the specified transactions listed. These difficulties must clearly be reconciled by the Analyst before further progress is made. It is at this point that transactions which have been inadvertently omitted or included in the data flow diagram can be identified and corrected.

5.4   SECOND LEVEL DESIGN

5.4.1   Flexing with Performance and Storage in Mind

In second level design the Analyst takes the verified first level data model and undertakes flexing to improve the performance of the model. This is necessary because although the data model will support all specified requirements, it is likely to be slow in processing some transactions. The objective is to flex the logically simple initial model and modify it to ensure its structure is compatible with access requirements and transaction processing times. This separate design process is best undertaken before the Analyst becomes engrossed in the detailed features of a particular hardware or software environment.

Close examination of the way in which tables will be accessed to retrieve relevant data may reveal some lengthy and hence slow routes to fulfil the requirements of a transaction. Transaction processing times

Entity/ relationship	Attribute	Transactions					
		1	**2**	**3**	**4**	**5**	
MEMBER	Member-number	R1		R2	R1		
	Member-name	R		R	R		
	Member-address	R		R	R		
	Join-date	R					
ORDER	Order-number	S2		R1			
	Order-date	S2					
	Despatch-date						
	Member-number	S2		R			
ORDER-LINE	Order-number	S4	R	R			
	ISBN	S4	R2*	R3*			
	Quantity-ordered	S4	R	R			
BOOK	ISBN	R3	R1		R1*		
	Title	R			R		
	Author	R			R		
	Selling-price	R			R		
	Cost-price						
	Quantity-in-stock	R	R				
	Re-stock-level						
	Publisher-name				R		
PAYMENT	Order-number	S5					
	Payment-amount	S5					
	Payment-method	S5					
	Clearance-date	S5					
PUBLISHER	Publisher-name						
	Publisher-address						

Selected MOBC Transaction List (from Data Flow Diagram, Figure 7.29 *Introducing Systems Analysis*)

1 = Verification and clearance of order details
2 = Order consolidation and production of picking details
3 = Generation of member order despatch details
4 = Compilation of offer list
5 = Compilation of a member mailshot and labels

Figure 5.5   Mail Order Book Club: Transaction-Attribute Grid

can be estimated from the average number of accesses to particular table occurrences for a given transaction, and the average access time of the likely storage device.

For example, 'Compilation of the Offer List' (Transaction 4) will have been previously defined in the data dictionary entry for the process. This relatively simple application may only sequentially access the Book table (ie progressing through the row occurrence of the table one by one) if Stock-levels are the only criteria for inclusion of a particular Book on the offer list. However, if this transaction definition is more complex and requires checking the frequency of previous orders for each book during the preceding year, then the transaction would also need to access the Order-Line and Order tables. The two alternative requirements are shown in the section of the transaction-attribute grid shown in Figure 5.6.

5.4.2 The Logical Access Map

The access routes of transactions can be effectively shown by a logical access map. The term 'data navigation diagram' is also appropriate for this model as it graphically depicts the route of a sequence of actions which act upon the entities and relationships of a data design.

A logical access map is superimposed on top of part of the entity-relationship diagram. In this way it provides a useful check that all the attributes required for a particular transaction are present and can be accessed. It also forms a starting point for the Analyst in firming the detailed definition of the processes needed to fulfil the transaction.

The navigation path for each transaction is sketched onto the entity-relationship model to show the sequence of accesses to the entities. These accesses or actions are required to either *create* (ie store), *read* (ie retrieve), *modify* (ie update) or *delete* an occurrence of the entity. In the case of accesses to create or delete entity occurrences the relationships will also have to be made or broken. The sequence of the actions is shown by a number against the entity or relationship symbol. For example, the transaction 4b refers to the process 'Compilation of the Offer List' from the data flow diagram (Figure 5.2). It involves accessing three separate entity tables, Book, Order-Line and Order. This sequence of accesses is shown superimposed on the entity-relationship model in Figure 5.7a. Figure 5.7b shows the same information in vertical format.

Entity/ relationship	Attribute	Transactions		
		4a	**4b**	
MEMBER	Member-number Member-name Member-address Join-date			
ORDER	Order-number Order-date Despatch-date Member-number		R3 R	
ORDER- LINE	Order-number ISBN Quantity-ordered		R2 R2* R	
BOOK	ISBN Title Author Selling-price Cost-price Quantity-in-stock Re-stock-level Publisher-name	R1 R R R R R	R1 R R R R R	

Alternative transactions

4a = Compilation of offer list (based solely on quantity-in-stock)
4b = Compilation of offer list (based on quantity-in-stock and orders
     received during previous year)

Figure 5.6   Partial Transaction-Attribute Grid: 4a and 4b

Retrieval of a single entity occurrence by using one or more attribute values to identify it, is shown by a line with a single arrow head. Access to all or many of the entity occurrences linked via a relationship is shown by a line with a double arrow head. This is illustrated in the access from a particular Book to the Order-Lines for that Book. A single selection occurs in the case of a single Order (identified by the attribute order-number) for each Order-Line. The arrows should not be confused with relationships in the entity-relationship diagram.

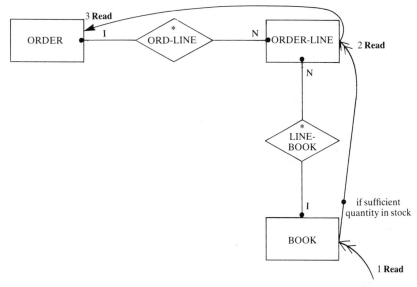

Figure 5.7a   Access Path for Transaction 4b

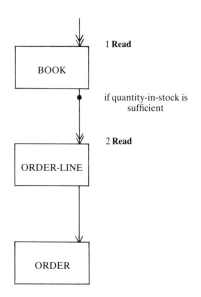

Figure 5.7b   Vertical Format Logical Access Map

Conditional accesses to an entity can be shown by a line broken by a dot with the condition written alongside. Thus the access from Book to Order-Line is broken by a dot since it is dependent upon there being sufficient quantity-in-stock for a particular Book. Mutually exclusive actions can be shown by using a dot on a branched arrow.

A further example is shown in Figure 5.8 and refers to Transaction 1, named 'Verification and clearance of order details'. Errors and exceptional conditions have not been considered in the example for reasons of simplicity. The entities Member, Order, Order-Line, Book and Payment are accessed for the purpose of this process. No attributes from Publisher are required.

In order to establish the access paths of the transaction we need to refer to the data flow diagram and the data dictionary entries which define the processes involved. These show the following sequence of actions.

- The Member record is checked to verify that a valid membership exists.

- If the Member is acceptable then an Order occurrence is made and a link made to the Member entity.

- For each Book on the Order, the Book details are retrieved to check that there is sufficient stock to fill the Order.

- If sufficient stock is available an Order-Line occurrence is created and a link made to the Order entity and the Book entity for that Order-Line.

- When all items are processed, a Payment occurrence is created, an order confirmation is printed and the delivery-date on the Order entry is updated.

The logical access map (LAM) is sometimes annotated with volume and frequency information in preparation for use in the physical file or database design stage. The LAM is useful for checking that all the attributes required are present in the entities and that it is possible to access them. Furthermore, it can also be redrawn vertically (Figure 5.9).

This derives a skeleton high level logical process design, known as a data action diagram and is considered in more detail in the following chapter. Figure 5.10 shows the outline of the definition of the process required to verify and clear the order details.

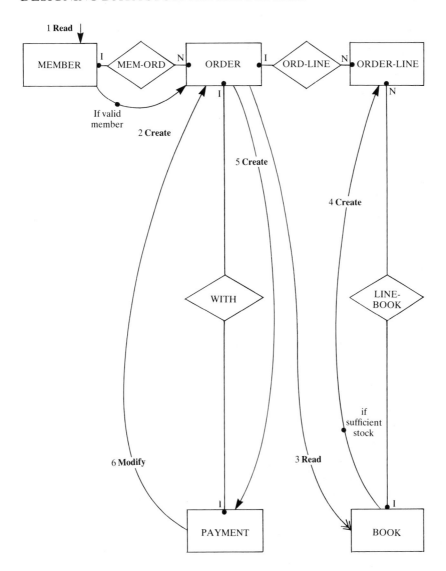

Figure 5.8 Logical Access Map: Transaction 1 – Verification and Clearance of Order Details

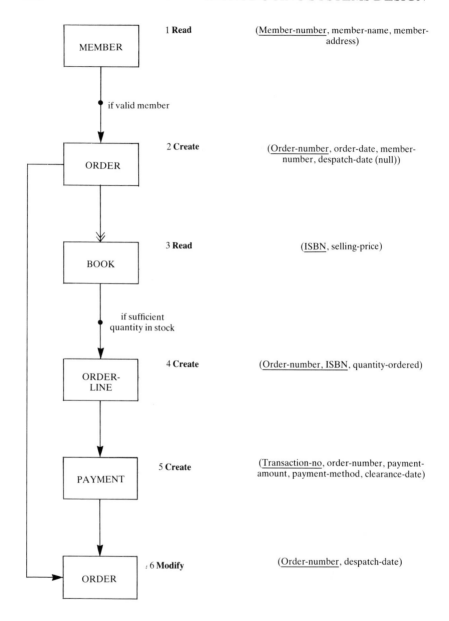

Figure 5.9   Logical Access Map: Transaction 1 – Vertical Format

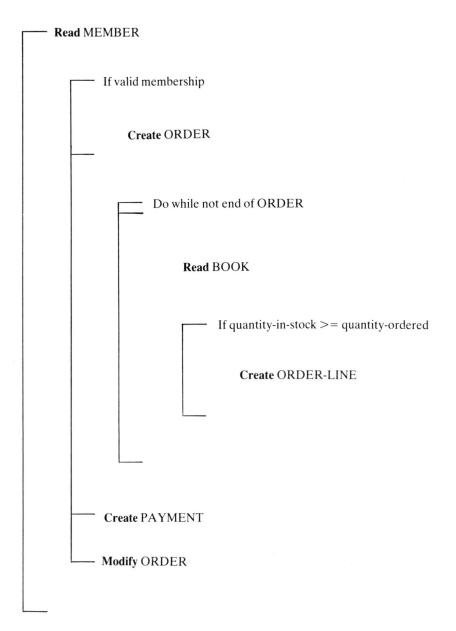

Read MEMBER

If valid membership

Create ORDER

Do while not end of ORDER

Read BOOK

If quantity-in-stock >= quantity-ordered

Create ORDER-LINE

Create PAYMENT

Modify ORDER

Figure 5.10   Data Action Diagram: Transaction 1

5.4.3 Flexing the Data Model

Using these tools (transaction-attribute grid and logical access map) the Analyst may discover the existence of some lengthy access paths which will result in unacceptably slow processing of some transactions. Modifications may be needed to the first level data model to, for example, economise on physical storage or speed up transaction times. This can be achieved in several different ways.

Joining Entity Tables

When the relationship between two entities is one-to-one some storage savings may be made by joining the tables together. In this way the attribute identifier is not duplicated.

Figure 5.11   Data Model with a 1:1 Relationship (subset of Figure 5.2)

For example the entities Order and Payment in Figure 5.11 may be joined together as the relationship between them is obligatory in both directions. It should be noted that this will result in a greater memory requirement for a transaction which needs only to access the attributes relating to an Order. Each table occurrence used by such a transaction (for example, Compilation of the Offer List) will take up more memory space and this may slow down the processing of a batch of such transactions.

First Level Tables

ORDER: (order-number, order-date, despatch-date, **member-number**)

PAYMENT: (transaction-number, **order-number**, payment-amount, payment-method, clearance-date)

The Order and Payment tables become a single Order-With-Payment table after joining. In the second level entity-relationship diagram there is a single Order-With-Payment entity.

ORDER-WITH-PAYMENT: (order-number, order-date, despatch-date, **member-number**, transaction-number, payment-amount, payment-method, clearance-date)

Howe (1986) suggests the creation of a separate table for a non-obligatory 1:many relationship. In the case of the relationship Book-Pub (Figure 5.12) this would require a lengthy access transaction path for a process such as 'Generate the list of all stocked books

Figure 5.12   Data Model with 1: Many Relationships

published by each publisher'. In second level design this can be flexed by treating the many-entity (ie Book) as obligatory and posting the identifier of the one-entity into the many-entity table. In this way publisher-name is posted into Book. When the volumes and frequencies of the relationships are considered it may be discovered that there are a large number of different occurrences of Publisher and since the only other attribute required is publisher-address, these can also be joined together.

BOOK: (<u>ISBN</u>, title, author, selling-price, cost-price, quantity-in-stock, re-stock-level, **publisher-name**)

PUBLISHER: (<u>publisher-name</u>, publisher-address)

The two tables Book and Publisher would become Published-Book after merging.

PUBLISHED-BOOK: (<u>ISBN</u>, title, author, selling-price, cost-price, quantity-in-stock, re-stock-level, **publisher-name**, publisher-address)

The penalty paid for this merging of tables is the storage of a considerable amount of redundant data. In this example the same value of publisher-address may be repeated in many table occurrences of Book. The new table also loses the access to publisher-address by means of publisher-name. Even with the benefit of faster transaction processing time the problems of inserting, deleting and amending this duplicated data would probably, on balance, prevent the merging of these tables.

It would also not be desirable to join the Order and Order-Line entity tables (Figure 5.13) together. Posting all the attributes of Order into

Order-Line results in redundant data since all occurrences of a particular order will have the same order-date and despatch-date. Additionally, it is very likely that some transactions will only require the Order details accessed via order-number. Introducing a limited case of repeating groups by restricting an Order to a specified number of Order-Lines (Orderline1, Orderline2, Orderline3, etc) would also be a possibility, but the result is less flexibility and a constant storage overhead for Orders with less than the agreed number of Order-Lines. If there is no reasonable limit to the repeating group then it is always preferable to leave the entities as separate tables.

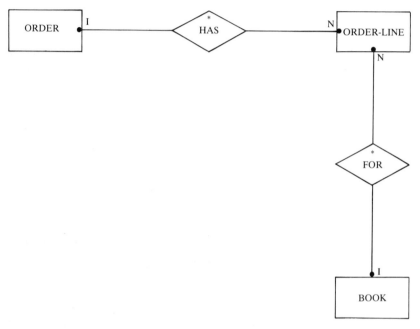

Figure 5.13   Data Model with an Obligatory Many:Many Relationship
(subset of Figure 5.2)

Splitting Tables

If groups of attributes in a table can all be null (ie have no stored value) then there may be a case for splitting one entity table into two or more different entity tables. The aim here is to reduce the data transfer required and/or get more occurrences of the tables into the computer's memory buffer and hence make more data available for immediate access. This will significantly speed up some transaction times.

Figure 5.14   Data Model after Splitting the Member Entity

For example, the first level model may have included a Member entity (Figure 5.14) with attributes to describe the type of membership.

MEMBER: (member-number, member-name, member-address, join-date, business-address, business-tel-number, position, no-of-subordinates)

This may be split into two tables where the Member table becomes Member and Business-Details tables.

MEMBER: (member-number, member-name, member-address, join-date)

BUSINESS-DETAILS: (member-number, business-address, business-tel-number, position, no-of-subordinates)

Two tables will enable some transactions (for example, a mailshot to business users only) to access only the attributes they require.

Creating Derivable Attributes

The values of some attributes can be calculated by accessing several different tables in a particular access route and making appropriate calculations. However, this may be lengthy particularly where responses are required to queries on demand or where calculations are logically complex. The addition of derived attributes will avoid the repetitive recalculation of attribute values and hence shorten the access paths of transactions.

For example, adding the attribute last-order-date to the Member table will eliminate the comparison of all occurrences of the Order table for a particular Member to determine the highest value of the attribute order-date. Similarly, attributes such as quantity-sold-this-month, quantity-sold-this-year, and quantity-sold-to-date will save much processing time, particularly if these data items are frequently required and the Book table has a high volume of occurrences.

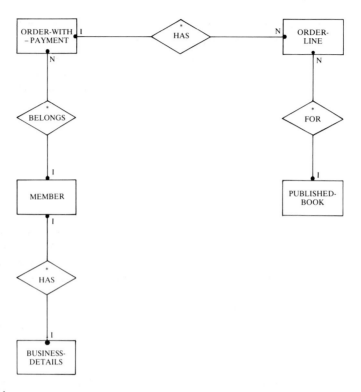

Tables

ORDER-WITH-PAYMENT:	(Order-number, order-date, despatch-date, **member-number**)
MEMBER:	(Member-number, member-name, member-address, join-date)
BUSINESS-DETAILS:	(Member-number, business-address, business-tel-number, position, no-of-sub ordinates)
ORDER-LINE:	(**Order-number, ISBN,** quantity-(ordered)
PUBLISHED BOOK:	(ISBN, title, author, selling-price, cost-price, publisher-name, publisher-address)

Figure 5.15   MOBC: Flexed Data Model with Additional Attributes (Second Level Design)

Flexing the whole of the first level data model in this manner will ensure that the new second level data model will be able to perform at an acceptable level of functionality and efficiency. The transaction-attribute grid and logical access maps will be used to evaluate and document the logical access requirements of the second level data model (Figure 5.15). However, reduced flexibility and maintainability is usually the price paid for the performance gains of the flexed second level design.

5.5   THIRD LEVEL DESIGN

5.5.1   Mapping on to the Implementation Environment

The emphasis so far has been focused on the logical design of data. However, it is the eventual physical implementation that is critical in delivering effective performance to end users. Once the Analyst is satisfied that all the transactions required by the system can be logically supported with acceptable performance, then the design may be developed to take account of the probable hardware and software. This is rarely a completely free choice as most organisations usually already have existing hardware and software and so the Analyst is always constrained in some way by the facilities available and the standards imposed.

Before considering the task of mapping a logical design onto a physical design, some fundamental aspects of the physical environment are discussed.

5.5.2   Fundamentals of the Physical Environment

Information systems always require some data to be permanently stored so that it can be retrieved by processes which need it for updating and generating information. Data attributes are physically stored as *fields* which may be characterised by their size, length and type (integer, packed decimal, ASCII string, etc). *Records* are collections of data fields (normally with a key field for identification purposes) which are required by a process or program. For instance a *student record* system will contain data items such as student-name, home-address, date-of-birth. The key field might be student-name so that given the student-name all the student details could be retrieved from the file. The student record system will contain records of data for each student, each course, each academic year.

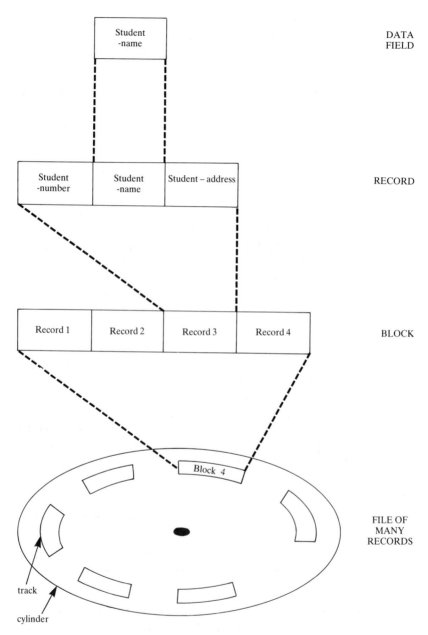

Figure 5.16   Data Field, Record and File Structure

A *file* is a collection of related records organised so that it can be retrieved and physically stored on a storage device. In the case of a magnetic disk, blocks are written on the tracks of a cylinder which form part of the whole disk.

Thus the logical structure is composed of *fields* which represent the attributes of a table, contained in *records* which correspond to row occurrences of a table and *files* corresponding to the table itself. This simple relationship is summarised in Figure 5.16.

Several types of file may also be needed within the information system.

– *Master files* contain essential data which is retained permanently within the system. These are often processed in cycles in a transaction processing system (eg customer master file updated by daily orders). Master files may also be used for reference purposes in information retrieval and may be dynamically updated in on-line systems. In an airline booking system the master files will contain details of available capacity for passengers and freight. Bookings will form the transactions of the system and as these are received the master file information must be updated.

– *Transaction files* accumulate records of events which are cleared off the system at some future time. For instance, the Orders file in an order processing system or Current Loans in a library issue system. The need for historical retrieval determines the frequency of erasure of transaction files. The analysis of all orders received during the past five years may demand that this volume of transactions remain available on the system.

– Other files include *work files* which are needed for the efficiency of system operation, such as sort files. These are generally transient arrangements, transparent to the user and indeed may be copies of other files in the system.

– *Back-up files* are security copies or derivations of master/ transaction files which are needed to allow the reconstruction of the system after corruption.

– *Parameter files* are used in many systems to store singularly occurring items of data (such as the company name and address, the system date, etc) or small tables (such as tax rates or passwords).

Many factors influence the choice of the physical structure of the files, including the characteristics of the devices for data storage. Both Grosshans (1986) and Cunningham (1985) give detailed attention to the physical mechanisms of input/output, using magnetic disk and tape.

In general, file design attempts to meet the following, perhaps conflicting objectives (Waters, 1972).

- *Economical* (ie cost-effective), compared with alternatives.

- *Accurate*, to ensure that all required operational outputs are correct.

- *Timely*, the outputs must be produced on schedule.

- *Flexible*, to cope with unforeseen requirements and change.

- *Robust*, to stand up to variations in the workload.

- *Secure*, to minimise the potential loss of data and service.

- *Efficient*, so as not the waste valuable resources.

- *Maintainable*, for the future.

- *Implementable*, with due regard to available resources, programming skills, and user skills.

- *Compatible*, with existing and planned future systems.

- *Portable*, over a range of hardware/software configurations.

- *Acceptable*, to any organisational design standards.

The following factors must also be considered in arriving at an effective and efficient file design (from NCC, 1984):

- What is the purpose of the file? Is access to its contents to be made 'on demand' or will a time lapse be acceptable between initiating a request for retrieval and the resulting response?

- What access methods are required by the transactions? Will the records be *sequentially accessed*, as in the case of 'calculating the total value of orders not yet despatched', or *directly accessed* to view the attribute values of a particular Order, given the order-number?

- How active is the file? How often is a particular record to be accessed by transactions which enquire or update its contents?

- How volatile are the records comprising the file? How often are records added and deleted from the file? At what rate is the file growing or declining in size during the expected life of the system?

- How large will the file be? The size of the file may be a critical factor when considering the system's overall performance. What response time is required for each process? What security provision is required? Can the file be split for processing/recovery?

- In what sequences is the file required to be accessed for output? The most frequent accesses to a particular file will have a strong influence on how it should be organised. Which process is the most important? Is sorting required or should data be stored in a predetermined sequence?

- What file organisations are possible in the particular hardware environment? Is any further hardware likely to be available? Can greater speeds be obtained by extra storage availability?

5.5.3 Iterative Design Approach

In third level design the Analyst is concerned with mapping the modified tables of the logical second level design to the physical file or database design of a particular language environment. Many of the decisions are more complex than can be illustrated in this chapter. The references for this chapter should be consulted for more detailed coverage of the design process.

The physical design task has been divided into a sequence of design decisions concerning both the individual records and files from both a logical and physical perspective. Figure 5.17 summarises the interrelationship between the logical and physical decisions. The approach is to first consider designing the records and then the files or database. Each step is explained as a sequential process but it is clear that most of the steps are interrelated.

1 Determine the Record Content

Each row occurrence of a logical table is potentially a record. Each attribute in the table is normally a data field in the record description. The row identifier becomes a candidate record key. This mapping may not be the most efficient design but it can be firmly relied upon to support the specified transactions. A Member record (shown in Figure 5.18) is thus required consisting of the following fields: member-

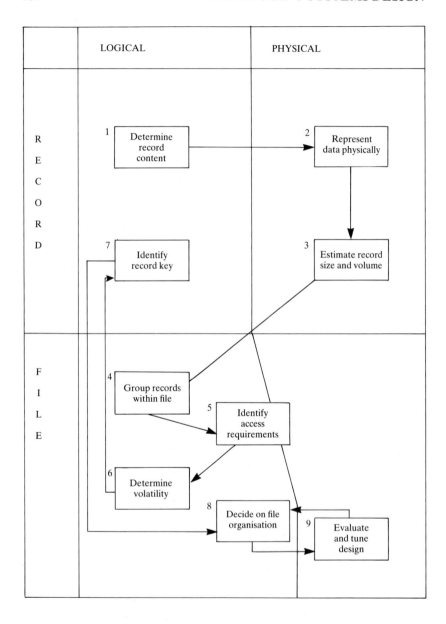

Figure 5.17   Decisions in Record and File Design

number, member-name, member-address and join-date. From the second level model it is clear that the system also requires records for the tables Order, Order-Line and Book.

2 Represent the Fields Physically

The Analyst also needs to recall the physical representation, or format, of each data field from the data dictionary definition. The target software itself will constrain the way in which the data may be held. Records may be restricted to a maximum number of data fields or a

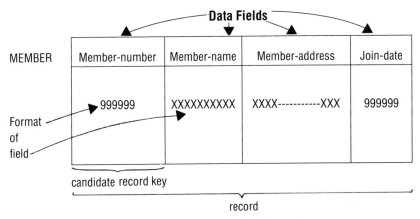

Figure 5.18   A Member Record

maximum number of characters. Further limitations may be imposed on the type of data fields. For example, Ashton-Tate's popular micro-computer database management system dBaseIII allows data fields to be defined as characters or numbers (which may have decimal places) and a data field is limited to 254 characters. However, MicroFocus's Professional COBOL compiler allows the maximum length of a data field to be 8192 bytes if it is alphanumeric but only 18 bytes if numeric.

The variety of data types available in the relational database management system INGRES is shown in Figure 5.19.

The use of codes may be considered where economy of storage is vitally important. Two examples of making storage savings are illustrated in the record specification of a Member record for a system to be written in Professional COBOL (Figure 5.20). The data field member-type has been stored as a code to classify the Member, principally for mailshot purposes. Furthermore, the field last-order-date

Type	Size	Description
Integer	1, 2 or 4 bytes	Displayed as a number
Date	12 bytes	Displayed in a variety of formats
Money	8 bytes	Stored as an actual money value with two decimal places
Text (n)	1-2000 chars	Any string of letters, numbers, punctuation where **n** is the maximum number in the string of text

Figure 5.19   Some Data Types in the INGRES Relational Database Management System

has been defined as a binary field to compress the storage requirements. Variable length records are not supported by this compiler and so it is not possible to make further savings by suppressing the blank spaces in the member-name and member-addresss. Coding of some data fields may also be desirable to achieve an improvement in the speed of processing by reducing the overall size of a record. When the full description is required by processes, a simple look-up table or parameter file can be used.

3 Estimate the Size of Each Record

Early knowledge, even if it is approximate, of the overall size of each record and the maximum number of records, will enable the estimation of the total file storage requirements and the timings of critical transactions. This is achieved by summing the lengths of physical data items to arrive at the actual record length and adding on an allowance for any index overhead. The target hardware and language also place constraints on what is permissible and the record design may have to be modified. There will also be some system overheads which will cause a larger amount of storage to be required than may at first be anticipated.

Designing for the future expansion of the system also requires some allowance to be built into the record definition. Extending a record in

Record Specification NCC

Record description	System	Document	Name	Sheet
Infosys Book Club	ISP	4.4	MEMREC	1

© 1969. The National Computing Centre Limited

Medium: DISK

Record length: Fixed ☑ / Variable ☐
Record format: Fixed ☑ / Variable ☐ — Name
Record size: Words ☐ / Characters ☐ / Bytes ☑
File specification refs: 4.4 / MEMREC
Lay-out chart ref.

Ref.	Position From	To	Level	In system design	In program	Data Type	Size	Align ment	Picture	Occurrence	Value Range
1	01	06		Member-number	MEMNO	C	6		9(6)	1	1-9999
2	07	31		Member-name	MEMNAME	C	25		X(25)		
3	32	121		Member-address	MEMAD))	C	90		X(30)	3 times	Valid date
4	122	124		Join-date	MEMJOIN	B	3		9(6)		P=private. B=business
5	125	125		Member-type	MEMTYPE	C	1		X		
6	126	128		Last-order-date	LASTOR))	B	3		9(6)		Valid date
7	129	140		Future-use	FILLER	C	12		X(12)		

S 44
Author
Issue
Date

Figure 5.20   Member Record Specification

the future may impose the burden of recompilation and possible retesting of all existing programs in the system.

4 Group Records Within Files

This step is confined to the traditional file processing environment and would not be applicable when designing a database. Several logically related records may be physically stored in one file where they will normally be processed together. The second level design may have already covered this by merging tables. In some circumstances different records of the same length may be stored in the same file. COBOL permits different record types to be stored in the same file by use of the 'redefines' clause. This could be used to define a file consisting of an Order record, followed by one or many Order-Line records. The storage of the different logical records in the same physical file is achieved by building a compatible record key (the record key being a concatenation of order-number and a unique line-number) and redefining the record definition. Grouping different record types is not always supported by the target software.

5 Identify Access Requirements

It is necessary to understand the way in which transactions will access the files in order to fulfil their function. These access routes and preferred mode of processing have already been defined by the logical access map and skeleton database action diagram for each transaction. Transactions will need to retrieve and process the records either serially or randomly.

Serial searching is undertaken by examining an entire file, record by record until the required record is found. Binary searches can also be undertaken on a sequentially ordered file in order to find a specific record. Serial processing is the only possibility when accessing records on linear storage devices such as magnetic tapes or punched cards. Figure 5.21 shows a serial file of stock tickets from sales departments of several stores.

Random or Direct Access is where the records are processed by a transaction in neither physical nor logical sequence and hence require a 'direct' route to the desired record. This can be achieved in two main ways, using an algorithm to find the location of the record or via an index.

The access requirements of a selection of the transactions from the order processing system of the Mail Order Book Club may be derived from the transaction-attribute grid in Figure 5.5. Transaction 1 clearly needs to access the Book and Member tables in a direct way. However, serial accesss is required for the Book table in Transaction 4 since the

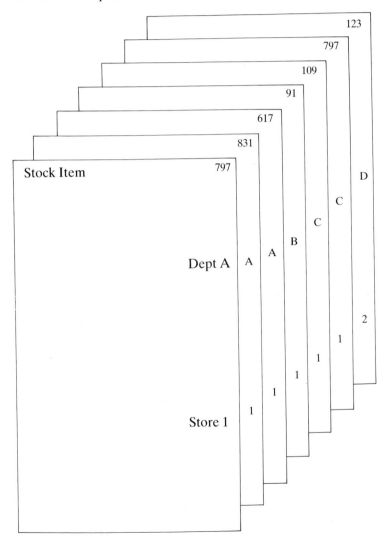

Figure 5.21   A Serial File: Stock Tickets from Sales

whole table needs to be examined record by record for the production of the list. The final choice of file organisation for Book will need to satisfactorily meet both of these requirements.

6 Determine Volatility

The volume of different accesses and the planned growth of the file may affect the way it is organised.

7 Determine the Record Key

Where a file contains a single record type the choice of the primary key is most likely to be the identifier of the original entity table. However, a file may be designed to store several logically related records and then the choice of a suitable primary key is a little more complex. In such a case the primary key will normally contain two logical parts as illustrated in Figure 5.22. The least significant digits in the record key are used to distinguish between the two record types. These will have a zero value in the case of the Order record (header) and positive values up to 99 for the Order-Lines.

Secondary or alternate keys may also be required where access requirements of transactions conflict. Random access may be needed to answer ad hoc queries specifying the value of a given attribute while the rest of the transactions are undertaken through serial processing on a different key. For example, the Order record also requires an alternate key specified as ISB-number for processes demanding direct access. A multiple indexing technique is used extensively on some database management systems but this usually results in increased storage and possible degeneration of system performance, particularly where the file contents frequently change. Reorganisation of the index and possibly the re-construction of the file is required at intervals to maintain acceptable performance.

8 Decide on the File Organisation

The most common file organisations supported by third generation languages, such as COBOL, are briefly described below. Fourth generation languages such as INGRES and ORACLE are built around a relational database structure but may still incorporate the use of several indexes for achieving speedy access to the data. The main considerations in determining the most suitable file organisation are the

```
ENVIRONMENT DIVISION

INPUT-OUTPUT SECTION
     SELECT ORDER
          ASSIGN TO FILE-NAME
          ORGANISATION IS INDEXED
          ACCESS MODE IS DYNAMIC
          RECORD KEY IS ORDER-ID
          ALTERNATE KEY IS ISBN


DATA DIVISION
FILE SECTION


FD ORDER

01     ORDER-HEAD
       02 ORDER-ID
          03  ORDER-NO      PIC  99999
          03  LINE-NO       PIC  99
       02 NOT-USED          PIC  9(8)
       02 ORDER-DATE        PIC  9(6) usage comp
       02 MEMBER-NO         PIC  9(6) usage comp

01     ORDER-LINE REDEFINES ORDER-HEAD
       02 ORDER-ID
          03  ORDER-NO      PIC  99999
          03  LINE-NO       PIC  99
       02 ISBN              PIC  9(8)
       02 ORDER-QTY         PIC  9(4) usage comp
```

Figure 5.22   A MicroFocus COBOL Level II Record Definition

key structure and access requirements of all the processes. There is rarely a perfect solution and the Analyst inevitably decides on a compromise in meeting performance and storage constraints.

Serial and Sequential File Organisations

A *serial* file is a file in which a data record is stored in the next available storage space (Figure 5.23). The records need not be in any particular order and there need not be any relationship between the logical

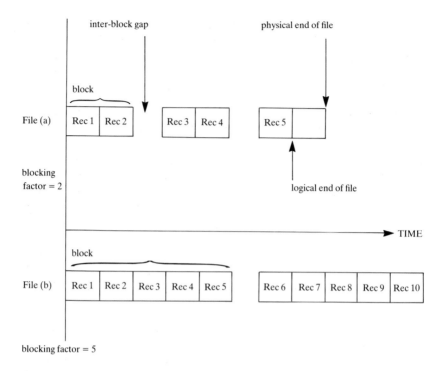

Figure 5.23   A Serial File

position of an item and its physical location on the storage device. The only possible way of accessing the records in a serial file is in the order of physical storage.

Sequential files are ordered on a predetermined primary key and therefore may be retrieved in that sequence. Records are only added at the physical end of serial or sequential files although they may be inserted by rewriting the entire file.

Serial and sequential files are simple and relatively straightforward to maintain. They can be supported by both serial (tape) and direct (disk) access technologies and form a reliable, cheap solution in applications where all the data is always processed in a particular sequence and ad hoc retrievals are rare and not time-critical.

Random File Organisation

A *random* file is one in which records are stored without regard to the primary key sequence. Any available space is used to hold a new record when it is created. The record is accessed by either transforming a key value into a physical disk file address or by means of an index. There are several types of randomly organised files, relative, direct and indexed-sequential. These will be considered very briefly.

A *relative file* is a self-addressing file in which any individual record can be accessed directly. The file may be thought of as a serial string of areas, each capable of holding a logical record. Each one of these areas is denominated by a relative record number. Record storage and retrieval is based on this number. For example, the tenth record is the one addressed by relative record number ten, and is in the tenth record area, whether or not records have been written in any of the preceding areas. Whatever the size of the file, only one disk read or write operation is required to find any record. It is only supported by random access devices such as disks and not by serial tape devices. Each record must have an associated integer key value (ie the relative record number) which will be used to add the record to the file and to retrieve it later.

This type of file organisation has the advantage that records can be quickly and randomly accessed anywhere in the file by simply using the record key as the address. Records can be inserted, updated and deleted at any place in the file, not just at the end. Relative files never need reorganising as the organisation takes place when they are initially created. It is also possible to sequentially access a relative file by taking the record blocks in the order that they are stored. However, the price of this is that each potential record has a space reserved for it and hence the disk may be relatively empty, particularly at times when there are few physical records active.

A *direct file* is one where the key is transformed in some way to find the physical address of the record on the device. Unlike a relative file, it does not require the key to be an integer and the address is a bucket not a record space. In some applications it is not practical to find a key which is ordered sequentially 1 to N. With a direct file organisation the Analyst may specify any type of key, alphanumeric or otherwise, which best suits the application.

Direct files also provide better space utilisation where there are gaps in the chosen record key. The amount of space available to the file is built into a hashing algorithm (or key transformation). Hashing is a technique in which the record key is converted into another value which serves as a storage address. The block found at this address should include the target record, if it exists. All records within a block are physically adjacent to each other as in a serial file. If the target record is not in the block then it may be located in a specified overflow area.

Figure 5.24 shows how a simple hashing algorithm is applied to a selection of records to find their storage location on disk. In this example, the position of the required record is found by dividing the record key by 19 and using the remainder to point to the location address. Each block contains five records.

The overall performance of a direct file is determined by the number of likely collisions which occur (as in the case of record with key 4771

Record key	Block address
1001	13
1291	18
6612	0
2206	2
2472	2
1941	3
1731	2
7712	17
1591	14
4771	2
5431	16
1279	6
6241	9

Hashing algorithm: Division by 19 – block address is the remainder

Block	Key	Data					
0	6612	data					
1							
2	2206	data	2472	data	1731	data	
3	1941	data					
4							
5							
6	1279	data					
7							
8							
9	6241	data					
10							
11							
12							
13	1001	data					
14	1591	data					
15							
16	5431	data					
17	7712	data					
18	1291	data					
19	4771	data					
20							
21							

overflow { 19, 20, 21 }

Figure 5.24   A Direct File: Hashed on the Record Key

which must be stored in the overflow area). In such circumstances the hashing algorithm produces the same address for two records and the record will be stored in or retrieved from an overflow area. The need for additional disk access will result in slower process performance.

The main cost of gaining random access capability via user-defined keys is the loss of being able to sequentially read the records in the file by key. It is possible to start at the first block and access all its records, read the next block and retrieve its records, and so on. However, the records will not be physically stored within a block in key sequence (see Figure 5.24), therefore processes demanding the retrieval of records within a range of dates or account numbers will be extremely slow to execute.

Direct files are most effectively used where fast random access is required to individual records stored on disk. Where the key range does not change significantly, direct files are effective since the hashing algorithm can be tuned to minimise the use of overflow.

Direct access is also possible *via an index*, which is a table giving the physical location of a record in a file corresponding to each record key. The most common indexed organisation is indexed sequential files which maintain the records in sequence by ascending key value. An index structure is thus built on top of the actual data so that the records can be accessed both sequentially and directly by key value.

The structure of an indexed sequential file is illustrated in Figure 5.25. The master index is the highest level index which contains pointers to the next lower level index, the cylinder indexes. Several indexes may be constructed on one set of data records. The data records are then physically maintained within a block in the order in which they were written. If the index is ordered in the same key sequence as the data, it is called the primary index, and the data is accessed by the primary key. All other indexes ordered in different sequence from the data records are called alternate or secondary indexes.

Locating a particular record is achieved by following the index tree from the master index or root to the target data block. The block containing the target record is then read in order to locate the record with a matching key. If this search is unsuccessful then the record will be found in the associated overflow area and hence this will require the reading of at least one further block of data (as in the case of Badley in

1000 records are stored sequentially in blocks of 8.
Each index block contains 100 entries.

Master Index

Record key	Block address
Dixon	950
Mason	951
Wroe	952

Cylinder Index

Record key   Block address

950	Aylesbury	1000	Barrett	1001	Dixon	1002	
951	King	1021	Lindon	1022	Mason	1024	
952	Tyson	1036	Wroe	1041			

Data records (keys shown for illustration purposes only)

1000	Abbey	Anderson	Anderton	Ashton	Aylesbury			
1001	Baard	Babbage	Bait	Bamford	Barnacle	Barnes	Barnett	Barrett
1002	Chiswick	Cristal	Dixon					
1003								
1027	Badley							

Figure 5.25   Indexed Sequential Organisation

Figure 5.25). Some blocks in Figure 5.25 are not full, as an allowance for expansion was made when the file was created.

Insertion of a new record must be undertaken in the correct location, in the correct sequence. If the appropriate block is full then one or more records with higher key values must be pushed out of the primary data block and into the overflow area.

Indexed sequential files are generally slower than direct files since the time taken to traverse the index tree is greater than that needed to hash a record key to find its address. There is also a disk space overhead associated with the maintenance of the various indexes. However, it is a very flexible method of file organisation because it has the facility for both sequential and direct access.

In highly volatile indexed sequential files the use of overflow blocks to store insertions gradually increases. The file therefore becomes less efficient with operation and the retrieval of a particular record is only achieved by several block retrievals. This leads to a periodic necessity to reorganise the file and its associated indexes.

Indexed sequential is a very popular file organisation as both random and sequential access to the data records is supported. However, whilst this is a common file structure on large mainframes where disk space is plentiful, it is less acceptable in microcomputer applications and frequent file reorganisation will normally be needed to ensure efficient performance.

Inverted File Organisation

An inverted file may be considered where there is a need for flexible and efficient data retrieval. Inverted files are organised so that records may be retrieved by giving values of any data item in the record structure. The data forming a logical record is grouped and stored by data item value rather than as a contiguous record for each entity. An index is kept for each data item value, or data item range, and holds an entry for each record possessing that value or range.

This structure enables quick response to queries on non-key fields such as 'Which Books have a selling-price over £10?' An inverted file will access only those records meeting this criterion and acts as an alternative to searching every record in the file and retaining the matching records. Figure 5.26 shows an inverted file structure for the Book file. It has been partially inverted on the attributes selling-price, author and publisher-name. It is therefore easy to answer queries such as:

– Which books are in the range £10–20 selling-price?

– Which books are stocked for author 'L Payne'?

– Which stocked books are by the publisher 'NCC'?

Selling price directory	
Key	Pointer
0–5	
6–10	1,2,3
11–20	4,5
21–30	6
>30	

Author directory	
Key	Pointer
A Parkin	1,
S Jones	2,
L Payne	4,5,12

Publisher directory	
Key	Pointer
NCC	1,2,4
Arnold	3,5
Wiley	6,45

Block	Book key	File data title	cost-price
1	21	Systems Analysis	9.50
2	22	Systems Design	9.40
3	24	Data Analysis	7.50
4	25	Data Security	12.00
5	26	Security	12.50
6	29	Artificial Intelligence	25.00
7			
8			
9			
10			
11			
12	45	Networks	12.50

Figure 5.26   A Partially Inverted File

5.5.4   Relational Databases

The choice of a particular file organisation obviously constrains the future use of that data by new applications. These may suggest that a different file organisation is more suitable. The result, in many cases, is the creation of duplicated copies of data in files designed for specific purposes. When this data needs updating several physical records in different files must be accessed which produces problems in control and maintenance of the integrity of data. Consequently, file processing systems are often rigid and inflexible and so do not easily allow the integration of new applications.

Database management systems (DBMS) organise the data in order to ensure data independence. Clear separation of logical and physical design of data structures is the basis of a relational database. A relational database is perceived by its users as a collection of simple two-dimensional tables. Unknown to the user, these tables may be physically stored by the DBMS in a number of possible ways. The tables containing third normal form data structures can be manipulated by selection, projection and/or joining, to meet different information needs. Chapter 7 of *Introducing Systems Analysis* includes detailed discussion on the derivation of tables in third normal form.

A significant benefit associated with a relational database is that in many cases the first level data design can be implemented without flexing. The following approach to the design of relational databases is based on the logical data model discussed earlier.

1. Construct third normal form tables corresponding to each entity and specify the identifiers for each table. Each attribute will be represented as a field in a table.

2. Many-to-many and many-to-many-to-many relationships also need to be represented by tables. The primary key for these tables is likely to be a combination of the primary keys of the entities participating in the relationship.

3. Posted and preposted identifiers (sometimes known as foreign keys) are then specified to represent one-to-one and one-to-many relationships in the logical model. Alternate index fields for the file may be used for this purpose. Any required restrictions should also be specified at this point. For example, a foreign key field may not be allowed to be null because the relationship was previously defined as obligatory (by the use of a dot inside the entity in the logical model). This is the case with the foreign key member-no in the Order table, since the logical model stated that an Order could not exist without being related to a Member.

4. Some on-line update operations should be prohibited to ensure that the integrity of the whole database is maintained. For instance it is desirable that a Book is not deleted whilst Order-Lines exist, since

data such as price and title would then become unobtainable. Similarly, the foreign key member-no is not permitted to be updated in the Order table since it again has a mandatory relationship and its update would mean that the Order would now belong to a different Member!

5 Tuning the physical table structure may be necessary if the operation of the system is unacceptably slow. Performance benefits may result from creating an index where there are frequent requirements for Join operations over the foreign key and its matching primary key. For instance, the operation of processes which join the Order and Member tables on member-no could be improved by creating an index on the Order table with composite keys, Order-No, Member-No.

The above design procedure should be iterated until a satisfactory performance for the most critical transactions is achieved.

The documentation for the database design can then be expressed in pseudo data definition language statements. The first level design tables from the Mail Order Book Club have been used in Figure 5.27 as illustration.

Weighing up the Parameters

The primary considerations in deciding upon file or database organisation are the access requirements of processes and the nature of the record key. These can be used as an overall indicator to the type of file organisation, before the Analyst weighs up the performance, disk utilisation, maintainability, and ease of use of the selected file organisation in a cost and benefit exercise for the whole application. Decisions on the type of file organisation are becoming less critical as hardware technology improves in performance and storage facilities. The emphasis is moving towards file designs which offer flexibility and maintainability and hence offer opportunities for future expansion without massive overheads of reorganisation and rewriting.

Evaluate and Tune Design

The Analyst will now consider whether the initial physical data design (often referred to as 'a first cut design') will produce an acceptable level of performance. Some adjustments will be necessary and the overall performance of the system is inevitably a compromise. This will be

```
CREATE TABLE MEMBER
        PRIMARY KEY (MEMBER-NO)
        FIELDS (MEMBER-NO, MEMBER-ADD, JOINDATE);

CREATE TABLE ORDER
        PRIMARY KEY (ORDER-NO)
        FOREIGN KEY  (MEMBER-NO IDENTIFIES MEMBER
                NULLS NOT ALLOWED
                DELETE OF MEMBER RESTRICTED)
        FIELDS (ORDER-NO, ORDER-DATE, DESPATCH-
                DATE, MEMBER-NO);

CREATE TABLE ORDER-LINE
        PRIMARY KEY (ORDER-NO, LINE-NO)
        FOREIGN KEY  (ISBN IDENTIFIES BOOK
                NULLS NOT ALLOWED
                DELETE OF BOOK RESTRICTED)
        FIELDS (ORDER-NO, LINE-NO, ISBN, QUANTITY-
                ORDERED);

CREATE TABLE BOOK
        PRIMARY KEY (ISBN)
        FOREIGN KEY  (PUBLISHER-NAME IDENTIFIES
                PUBLISHER)
        FIELDS          (ISBN, TITLE, AUTHOR, SELLING-
                PRICE, COST-PRICE, QUANTITY-IN-
                STOCK, RE-STOCK-LEVEL,
                PUBLISHER-NAME);

CREATE TABLE PAYMENT
        PRIMARY KEY (TRANSACTION-NO)
        FOREIGN KEY  (ORDER-NO IDENTIFIES ORDER
                NULLS NOT ALLOWED
                DELETE OF ORDER RESTRICTED)
        FIELDS          (TRANSACTION-NO, ORDER-NO,
                PAYMENT-AMOUNT, PAYMENT-
                METHOD, CLEARANCE-DATE);

CREATE TABLE PUBLISHER
        PRIMARY KEY (PUBLISHER-NAME)
        FIELDS          (PUBLISHER-NAME, PUBLISHER-
                ADDRESS);
```

Figure 5.27   Data Definition Language Statements for the Creation of MOBC Tables

considered further in the next chapter, with process design decisions affecting the way that the files are organised and accessed.

5.6   INFOSYS: DATA STORAGE DESIGN

5.6.1   First Level Design: Seminar Bookings

The data analysis of the seminar bookings system at InfoSys has been described in Chapter 7 of *Introducing Systems Analysis*. This analysis resulted in the entity-relationship diagram and third normal form tables shown in Figure 5.28. Logical process modelling by means of data flow diagram also further revealed that the seminar bookings system must, as a minimum, be able to support the transactions also listed in Figure 5.28.

5.6.2   Second Level Design: Seminar Bookings

We must first establish that the process view of the data flow diagram and the static view of the first level data model are consistent with each other, complete and able to support the events identified on the entity life histories. The first level data model (Figure 5.28) can be verified for completeness by using a transaction-attribute grid shown in Figure 5.29. The entries in this grid indicate that many of the on-line transactions require access to the majority of the tables in order to fulfil their functions. This must raise the issue of whether the response time for processing such transactions would be satisfactory. The first level model may be flexed by considering the combination of some of the tables to reduce the delaying effect of multiple table accesses.

The principle of flexing can be illustrated by examining Transaction 5 – the 'Generation of a Booking Confirmation' – resulting in an output like that shown in the sample layout form of Figure 5.30. It is likely that a booking confirmation would cover several seminars. However, in order to keep the design example as simple as possible, it has been assumed here that a separate Seminar Booking Confirmation will be sent to each delegate for each booked seminar.

It is also necessary to add a few other details to this case study to allow the example to continue.

– The model will need to store some additional attributes such as a seminar-charge (including the accommodation charge if applicable) in order to be able to retain a booking for later confirmation. The

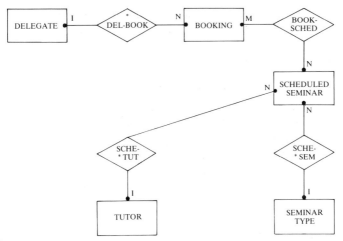

Tables

SEMINAR TYPE:	(seminar-number, title seminar-charge, no-of-days)
SCHEDULED SEMINAR:	(**seminar-number, date**, venue, **tutor-name**)
BOOKING:	(booking-number, amount-due, amount-paid, booking-date, **delegate-number**)
DELEGATE:	(delegate-number, delegate-name, delegate-address)
TUTOR:	(tutor-name, tutor-grade)
BOOK-SCHED:	(**booking-number, seminar-number, date,** no-nights-accommodation)

- Acceptance of seminar bookings
- Generation of a delegate list for a given seminar
- Generation of a schedule of future seminars
- Generate a list of delegates requiring accommodation for a given seminar
- Production of a confirmation of booking to be sent to each delegate

Queries:

- How many delegates have been booked on a particular seminar?
- What alternative dates can be offered for a fully booked seminar?

Figure 5.28   InfoSys Seminar Bookings Data Model

Entity/ relationship	Attribute	Transactions						
		1	2	3	4	5	6	7
SEMINAR-TYPE	Seminar-number	R_2		R_2		R_5		
	Title	R		R		R		
	Seminar-charge	R		R		R		
	No-of-days	R		R		R		
SCHEDULED SEMINAR	Seminar-number	R_1	R_1	R_1	R_1	R_4		R_1*
	Date	R_1	R_1	R_1	R_1	R		R
	Venue	R	R	R		R		
	Tutor-name		R	R				
BOOKING	Booking-number	S_4	R_3		R_3	R_1		
	Amount-due	S_4				R		
	Amount-paid	S_4				R		
	Booking-date	S_4				R		
	Date-confirmation-sent					S		
	Delegate-number	S_4	R		R	R		
DELEGATE	Delegate-number	S_3	R_4		R_4	R_2		
	Delegate-name	S_3	R		R	R		
	Delegate-address	S_3	R			R		
BOOK-SCHED	Booking-number	S_5	R		R	R_3*	R	
	Seminar-number	S_5	R_2		R_2	R	R_1*	
	Date	S_5	R_2*		R_2*	R	R_1	
	No-nights-accommodation	S_5			R	R		
TUTOR	Tutor-name							
	Tutor-grade							

Selected Transaction List (from data flow diagram)

1 Acceptance of seminar bookings
2 Generation of a delegate list for a given seminar
3 Generation of a schedule of future seminars
4 Generate a list of delegates requiring accommodation for a given seminar
5 Production of a confirmation of booking to be sent to each delegate
6 How many delegates have been booked on a particular seminar?
7 What alternative dates can be offered for a fully booked seminar?

Figure 5.29   Seminar Booking System: Transaction-Attribute Grid (Based on First Level Model)

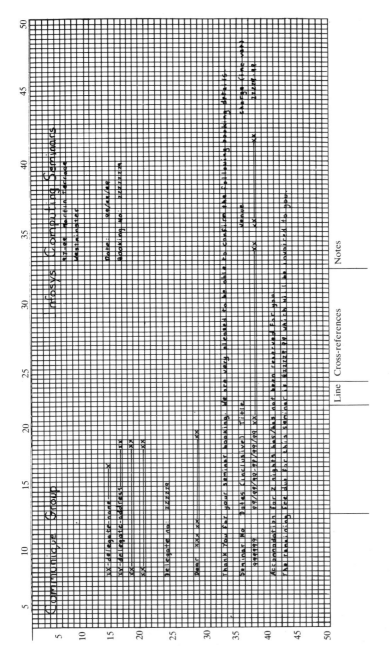

Figure 5.30 InfoSys Seminar Bookings: Booking Confirmation Layout

first level data model introduced in the companion text has been further developed and refined to contain all the necessary attributes for the production of this system output.

- It is an operational requirement that printing the booking confirmations be run as a batch process at the end of each day. This will enable full use of the printer for other processes required throughout the day.

- A control requirement must also be incorporated into the system design to record that a booking has been confirmed to a delegate. A further attribute date-confirmation-sent has been added to the Booking table for this purpose. This field must be updated when the confirmation process is run, but is presently omitted for simplicity.

A judgement must now be made on whether the access paths for the transactions are likely to be too lengthy and hence not give the required performance. The access path for Transaction 5 has been identified on the logical access map shown in Figure 5.31. Some volume data has been added to assist in the flexing decision. However, the lengthy navigation path seems to suggest that some modifications to the table structures will be necessary.

The access path can be shortened by combining the Seminar-Type and Scheduled-Seminar tables and the Booking and Delegate tables respectively. The consequences of such flexing must be considered in detail.

- Seminar-Type and Scheduled-Seminar. A merged table would be unable to include a new seminar until it has been scheduled for presentation. Removal of scheduled seminars, which have already been presented, causes the loss of data about the type of seminar and its charge. Table merger will also require some procedural controls to be built-in to ensure that the scheduled-seminars are not deleted before any processes requiring the seminar-charge information have been completed. However, it will enable InfoSys to keep a different charge for seminars of the same type (ie seminar-number) held on different dates and provide 'customised' titles according to the anticipated audience.

- Booking and Delegate. Merger of these two entities is likely to cause some significant problems. Bookings deleted from the table

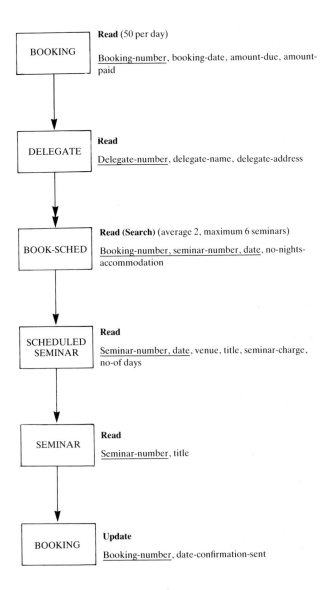

**Figure 5.31 Logical Access Map: Generation of the Booking
Confirmation Slip**

will lead to the loss of delegate information and so these people cannot be included in mailshots for future seminars. This is contrary to one of the major strategic objectives of the company.

The main benefit of the merger of entities is the reduction in the

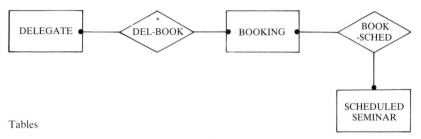

Tables

SCHEDULED SEMINAR: (**seminar-number**, date, title, seminar-charge,
                       no-of-days, venue, tutor-name, tutor-grade)
BOOKING: (**booking-number**, amount-due, amount-paid,
                       booking-date, **delegate-number**)
DELEGATE: (**delegate-number**, delegate-name, delegate-address)
BOOK-SCHED: (**booking-number, seminar-number, date,**
                       no-nights-accommodation

Figure 5.32   InfoSys Seminar Bookings: Second Level Data Model and Tables

processing time of Transaction 5. However, the penalty for this is the flexibility of the model and additional storage requirements, caused by additional attributes and necessary attribute duplication.

Compromises made during the flexing of the model should be considered very carefully. Initial modifications may not lead to overall improvements when all the transactions of the system are considered. However, in other circumstances an alteration designed to improve one transaction can have additional benefits in other parts of the system. For example, the addition of an attribute 'number-of-delegates-booked' adds some redundancy into the model but the query specified in Transaction 6 will now be fulfilled with a single table access, rather than a serial search through the entire Book-Sched table to aggregate the number of bookings made.

Many other flexing exercises are possible but cannot be described in detail here. Figure 5.32 gives the details of the data model after second level flexing has been undertaken. A further transaction-attribute grid should be constructed on the new tables of the second level data model (shown in Figure 5.33).

Entity/ relationship	Attribute	Transactions						
		1	2	3	4	5	6	7
SCHEDULED SEMINAR	Seminar-number	R₁	R₁	R₁	R₁	R₅		R₁*
	Date	R₁	R₁	R₁	R₁	R₅		R
	Venue	R	R	R		R		
	Tutor-name		R	R				
	Tutor-grade			R				
	Title	R		R		R		
	Seminar-charge	R		R		R		
	No-of-days	R		R	R	R		
BOOKING	Booking-number	S₂	R₃		R₃	R₁		
	Amount-due	S₂				R		
	Amount-paid	S₂				R		
	Booking-date	S₂				R		
	Date-confirmation-sent					S		
	Delegate-number	S₂	R		R	R		
DELEGATE	Delegate-number	R₃ (S₄)	R₄		R₄	R₃		
	Delegate-name	R (S₄)	R		R	R		
	Delegate-address	R (S₄)	R			R		
BOOK-SCHED	Booking-number	S₅	R		R	R₄*	R	
	Seminar-number	S₅	R₂*		R₂*	R	R₁*	
	Date	S₅	R₂*		R₂*	R	R₁*	
	No-nights-accommodation	S₅			R	R		

Selected Transaction List

1 Acceptance of seminar bookings
2 Generation of a delegate list for a given seminar
3 Generation of a schedule of future seminars
4 Generate a list of delegates requiring accommodation for a given seminar
5 Production of a confirmation of booking to be sent to each delegate
6 How many delegates have been booked on a particular seminar?
7 What alternative dates can be offered for a fully booked seminar?

Figure 5.33   Transaction-Attribute Grid (After Second Level Design)

Record Specification
NCC

Record description	System	Document	Name	Sheet
Booking Record.	ISP	4.7	BKGREC	1

Medium: Disk. | Record length: Fixed ☑ Variable ☐ | Record format: Fixed ☑ Variable ☐ | Record size: 30 | Words ☐ Characters ☐ Bytes ☑ | File specification refs.: 4.4 / BOOKFILE | Lay-out chart ref.:

	Ref.	Position From	Position To	Level	Name: In system design	Name: In program	Data Type	Size	Alignment	Picture	Occurrence	Value Range
Key	1	01	06	02	BOOKING-NUMBER	BKGNO	C	6		9(6)	1	
	2	07	09	02	BOOKING-DATE	BKGDATE	P	3		9(6) usage comp	1	Valid date
	3	10	13	02	AMOUNT-DUE	BKGAMT	P	4		9(5)v99	1	
	4	14	16	02	AMOUNT-PAID.	BKGPAID	P	4		9(5)v99	1	
	5	17	19	02	DATE-CONFIRMATION-SENT	BKGCON	P	3		9(6) usage comp	1	Valid date
Alt Key	6	20	22	02	DELEGATE-NUMBER	BELNO	P	3		9(6) usage comp	1	
	7	23	30	02	FUTURE-USE	FILLER	C	8		X(8)	1	

S 44
Author | Issue | Date

Figure 5.34 Booking Record Specification

5.6.3 Third Level Design: Seminar Bookings

Third level design is illustrated by two separate target software environments. A conventional programming language (MicroFocus's COBOL Level II) and a relational database management system (Relational Technology's INGRES).

File Design in a PC-based COBOL Environment

The contents of the physical records are derived from the tables included in the second level data model (Figure 5.32). One possibility would be to implement four record types, Delegate, Booking, Seminar and Book-Sched, corresponding to the second level entity and relationship tables. The design of the Booking file will be considered in some depth and the other files a little more briefly as much of the argument is similar in nature.

- Record Definition. The size and format of each data item in the Booking record is derived from the data dictionary entries for the entity and from the input/output requirements for each field (see Chapters 2 and 3). The primary key is chosen as the table identifier (booking-number) and delegate-number is assigned as an alternate key to enable the direct access of the Booking file records by this field.

- Record and File Sizing. Maximum lengths of all data fields for the record are summed to give the total record length. COBOL is a conventional programming language and so all programs must be re-compiled when a record is extended in size. Consequently, it is advisable to add spare space which may be used up during the maintenance and evolution of the system. The record specification is documented in Figure 5.34.

- Data Storage Estimation. The estimation of the file sizes indicates the minimum storage capacity required on the selected hardware. Depending on implementation circumstances a further allowance would normally be made. An increase of 1.25 to 1.5 times the calculated storage requirement is typical. This calculation has been undertaken for all four files in Figure 5.35.

- Total Storage Estimation. A further addition to the data storage requirement must be made for programs and spooled output files. In specifying hardware requirements the Analyst must also

File	Record Size (bytes)	Average No of Records	Maximum No of Records (5 times)	Average File Size (bytes)	Maximum File Size (bytes)
SEMINAR	120	500	2,500	60,000	300,000
BOOKING	30	5,000	25,000	150,000	750,000
DELEGATE	150	4,000	20,000	600,000	3,000,000
BOOK-SCHED	21	10,000	25,000	210,000	525,000
				1,020,000	4,575,000

Figure 5.35   Estimation of File Storage Requirement

consider how and where security copies of the data files are to be made.

- Storage Medium. The storage of the Booking file appears to be the most critical as it is too large to fit on most floppy disks. A large capacity tape back-up or removable hard disk is required to ensure that the system can be recovered easily and speedily.

- Access Requirements and Devices. The overall requirements of the four files for direct and sequential access are shown in Figure 5.36. Examination of this table confirms that the Booking file needs to be on-line for many of the queries. A disk storage device would therefore be the most likely choice as the primary requirement is for direct access. The exception to this is Transaction 5 which produces the booking confirmation slips. The latter is a sequential processing transaction which needs to access every record from a selected date.

- File Organisation. The most probable file organisation for the Booking file is either:

  • Indexed-sequential using the Booking-number as the record key;

  • Relative file using Booking-number as the record key;

  • Direct file using a hashing algorithm on the sequential Booking-number.

The first two suggested file organisation methods are supported by the

File Key	DELEGATE (Delegate-no)	BOOKING (Booking-no)	SEMINAR (Seminar-no Date)	BOOK- SCHED (Booking-no Seminar-no Date)
Transaction 1 Acceptance of seminar bookings	D		D	
2 Generation of a delegate list for a given seminar	D	D	D	S (= seminar- no, + date)
3 Generation of a schedule of future seminars			S	
4 A list of delegates requiring accommoda- tion for a given seminar	D	D	D	S (= seminar- no, + date)
5 Production of a confirmation of booking to be sent to each delegate	D	S	D	S (= booking- no)
6 How many delegates have been booked on a particular seminar?	D		D	S (= seminar- no, + date)
7 What alternative dates can be offered for a fully booked seminar?			D	S (= seminar-no)

Key
D = direct access required on primary key
S = sequential access required
( ) brackets contain the data fields searched on in serial access search

Figure 5.36   InfoSys Seminar Bookings: File Access Matrix

MicroFocus COBOL Level II language but the direct file method would require the programmer to write special file processing routines. The last option has therefore been discounted and the choice for the

Booking file constrained to either an indexed-sequential file or a relative file.

On some hardware, the indexed-sequential organisation may be slower than the relative file and would incur the space and performance overhead associated with the maintenance of an index. The Booking file is likely to be fairly volatile as the file is continually being added to (for new bookings) and it will be diminished in size by the removal of records (for bookings which have ceased to be useful after the presentation of the seminar). The Booking records for current and forthcoming seminars are also required to be on-line. It is likely that the use of large-memory computers with fast disk devices will result in a satisfactory performance with an indexed-sequential file for the volume of Bookings data currently envisaged. However, some reorganisation of an indexed-sequential file will be needed periodically to avoid fragmentation of the file and the consequent decline in its performance.

Using a relative file organisation requires the full potential of the growth of the Booking file to be known initially in order to assign the space for the whole key range. On balance, a relative file may be slower than the indexed-sequential in performing processes like the production of booking confirmations which demand sequential processing. The bookings will be received and stored in random order of seminar presentation. If a large number of these bookings have been deleted from the file when the seminar is past or the booking cancelled, then sequential processing will be slow. Consequently, this data storage structure has been rejected.

The design of the other files will now be briefly considered.

- The Scheduled-Seminar file is a master file which requires referencing by many transactions. We may consider creating a new unique sequential key field (eg scheduled-seminar-no) rather than the concatenated fields seminar-no and date, particularly if there is a need to select seminars by date or title. Indexed-sequential is the most versatile file organisation for this type of file.

- The Book-Sched file acts as a multiple index to link the records in the Bookings file to the records in Scheduled-Seminars. It also has to be directly accessed on either the booking-number or the combination of seminar-number and date, and then sequentially processed to retrieve all the records with these values. The file organisation best suited to this type of file is again indexed-sequential, since it can employ a sequential search using the 'read-next' function.

An alternative design would be to define the Book-Sched record as a Booking Line record for each Scheduled-Seminar booked. This would be stored in the same file as the Booking header record using the redefinition facility in COBOL. This is similar to the Order and Order-Line example discussed earlier in the chaper.

– The Delegate records are also likely to be stored as an indexed sequential file. Both direct and sequential access is required to this high-volume file.

The constraints of the hardware and software environments will have a significant influence on the physical implementation of the files and records. It is important that these physical design decisions be fully documented to agreed organisation standards for the benefit of construction and maintenance of the system. Many system documentation standards (for example NCC, SSADM and LSDM) have been designed to document both the logical and physical features of a system design and some organisations have developed their own hybrid sets of documentation standards. The computer record specification for the COBOL environment example illustrated in Figure 5.34 was produced to the NCC documentation standards (1978).

File Design in a PC-based INGRES Environment

In a relational DBMS such as INGRES the first cut data design is much simpler to implement. The tables of the first level data model can be supported without amendment, merging or further splitting. Flexing of the design may be needed if the performance of the system is not acceptable to the user, particularly with complex queries or large table handling. No flexing of the first level model has been undertaken for this example. The storage of the Booking table will be considered in detail.

Tables can be stored physically in a number of data structures in INGRES.

– A *heap* stores the rows (records) in the table randomly and unordered. New rows are added at the bottom of the table regardless of what the rows contain. In order to retrieve a particular record the system will scan the entire table. The table may also be converted into a *heapsort* for processing a particular transaction, but new records will still be stored at the end of the table, until it is converted again. This is likely to be relatively slow for the retrieval of a particular booking record.

- *Hashed* tables store each row at an address determined by the value of a column of a row (ie the booking-number in this case). The hashing technique is undertaken by INGRES and does not need to be worried about, only the key field or combination of key fields must be specified. This option would speed up the queries or processes which require exact matching of data in the key column (eg booking-number).

- *ISAM* (indexed sequential access method) is a structure which facilitates both retrieval of exact matching and matching ranges of values. A directory of sequentially stored keys is initially searched and the table itself does not need to be completely scanned to locate a particular row.

- *B-Tree* is a fast access method achieved by efficient indexing of the actual data in the table. This is particularly efficient when there is a large number of rows.

Relational Technology (1985) suggest that:

- if the table is small and/or a fast response time (less than 5 or 10 seconds) is required use a heap storage structure;

- if the table is large and if most queries require an exact match on the same column, then use a hash structure on that column;

- if the table is large and if the queries require both exact and range matches on one or more columns, use an ISAM structure on these columns.

Using the above guidelines the suggested data structures for the seminar booking tables are:

Booking	ISAM	(high volume and range match on booking-date needed)
Delegate	HASH	(high volume and exact match on delegate-number needed)
Scheduled-Seminar	HEAP	(low volume can be sorted and searched when required)

Book-Sched   B-TREE   (very high volumes and efficient retrieval of the rows are required using some parts of the concatenated key)

In this environment tables can be extended to include new fields as required. Consequently there is no need to include a filler data field as in the previous COBOL example.

5.7 SUMMARY

Designing the files of an information system is a critical activity. The defined structures may affect the required performance, cost and hence overall feasibility of the overall software solution. This chapter has presented an iterative approach to the design of data storage structures. It has:

- Suggested that design must be undertaken in two stages. The first stage requires the construction of a logical data model. This is subsequently converted into physical file or database structures which support the necessary transactions, processes and reports.

- Shown that design is based upon two major *analysis* models – data flow diagrams and entity-relationship diagrams.

- Established first level design as the definition of a redundancy-free data model. The tables in this model are in at least third normal form and support a model that is independent of all enterprise issues.

- Flexed the first level model into a second level design which consists of data tables that support the transactions more effectively. The price to be paid for this better performance is reduced flexibility in the design. Two techniques help the flexing process – the transaction-attribute grid and the data action diagram. The flexing itself usually consists of joining or splitting entity tables or creating derived attributes.

- Defined third level design as a physical implementation for an agreed hardware and software environment. These usually impose constraints on the designer and hence the data tables are no longer implementation independent.

- Suggested an iterative design approach to third level design and illustrated this with a case study using COBOL and INGRES as the target software.

Iteration has been a particular theme of this chapter. Moving from first to third level design demands changes in diagrams, table structures and transaction-attribute grids. These changes are very time-consuming to do manually. The automation and verification of this iteration is essential for the successful adoption of this approach. Furthermore, certain elements of the iteration have demanded estimates and guesswork. Hence if the results of the iteration can be *simulated* then the performance of a design becomes more predictable. Automatic iteration and simulation permits different flexes to be tried out in different hardware and software environments. The implications of this are discussed in the final chapter.

5.8 EXERCISES

The following questions refer to the library case study introduced in Chapter 1.

Using the data model given in Chapter 1 as the first level design:

1 Construct a transaction-attribute grid for the ten transactions specified in the case study.

2 Construct logical access maps for three selected transactions.

3 Flex the first level design into an appropriate second level model. This flexing should take into account that Transactions 3, 4, 7, 8 and 10 are particularly critical.

4 Produce a revised transaction-attribute grid for the second level model and logical access maps for Transactions 3, 4, 7, 8 and 10.

5 Flex the second level model into a third level model for a:

- third generation language with which you are familiar (COBOL, BASIC, PL/1, etc);

- fourth generation language with which you are familiar (INGRES, ORACLE, PROGRESS, etc).

The following questions do not refer to the case study.

6 Investigate a particular implementation of a language and report on which file organisations it supports and its advice (if any) on when these should be used.

7 Investigate other methods which support the flexing of a data model through the stages of design.

6 Process Design

6.1 INTRODUCTION

This chapter examines the design of processes. The logical foundation of these processes is summarised in the data flow diagrams, with the detailed logic stated in appropriate decision trees, decision tables and Structured English statements, supported by the data dictionary. The tools for modelling processes introduced in the companion text (Chapter 4, *Introducing Systems Analysis*) still remain appropriate for the declaration of the processes of the new design. However, they do not provide a way of creating the overall structure and partitioning of that design or provide sufficient detail for programming. This chapter introduces the *structure chart* and gives rules for its presentation and construction. The potential use of such a chart in prototyping is also discussed.

The suggestion is also made that structure charts are insufficient in themselves for providing a basis for detailed design specifications. Consequently, *action diagrams* are introduced as a comprehensive method of summarising the detailed logic of the modules of the structure chart. Examples of these diagrams are presented in the latter part of the chapter.

In many respects structure charts and action diagrams have a similar relationship to the data flow diagram as second and third level data modelling. The data flow diagram produces a transformation-driven definition of processes which may have certain undesirable features – such as redundancy and inefficiency in store structures. These are rectified in the design stage by flexing through further versions of the model (see Chapter 5).

In the same way, programs written from the process definitions of the data flow diagram are likely to exhibit undesirable software design features such as low maintainability, poor robustness and reliability, and coding duplication and inefficiency. Consequently, we need to build on the logic of the data flow diagram in a way that fulfils the functional requirements but with surer and sounder foundations.

6.2   FUNCTIONAL DECOMPOSITION

Functional decomposition is the term applied to the process that successively breaks down the general functional views of what is to be achieved into many small sub-functions, which can be implemented in program code. In performing functional decomposition, the designer will move from general process descriptions, such as Forecast-Demand, to specific definitions that handle detailed circumstances, exceptions and procedures. This progression in design will use the information gathered in the logical system definition, primarily from the levelled data flow diagrams, as well as prompting the gathering of further information.

This decomposition is a reflection of our general problem-solving approach. We normally deal with complexity by dividing it into manageable 'chunks'. Functional decomposition enforces hierarchical ordering. The successive division of functions leads to a tree-like structure with more detail given at the lower levels of the hierarchy.

This arrangement is enhanced if it defines a set of relatively independent modules which can be removed and amended with predictability. Module independence is an important objective of system design. It makes systems simpler to understand, more maintainable and easier to extend and enhance.

Structure charts are a form of functional decomposition. An example of a structure chart is given in Figure 6.1.

6.3   STRUCTURE CHARTS

Figure 6.1 illustrates the three main features of a structure chart.

– The modules are shown in rectangular boxes.

– Arrowed lines represent the control relationships between modules.

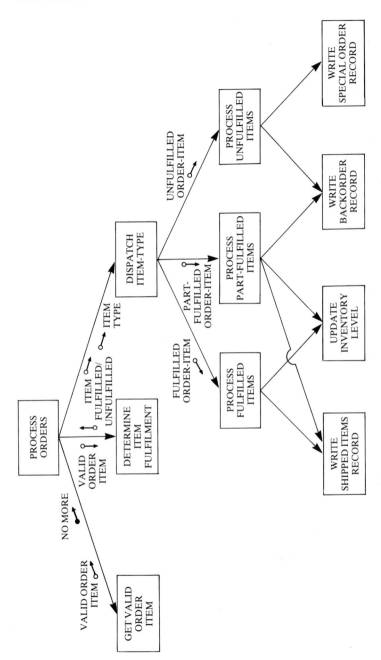

Figure 6.1   An Example Structure Chart

This example Structure Chart (taken from Gane and Sasson, 1980) is still incomplete. It is unbalanced (only the right hand output side has been detailed) and the communications between modules are sketchy. However, it does illustrate the general layout and notation of a Structure Chart.

– The communication between modules is shown by small arrows with a circle at the tail of the arrow shaft.

These represent three elementary constructs of a structure chart and are used in the vast majority of notations, and extensions to the notation are also given in many texts. However, our decision to produce supporting action diagrams makes such developments less important, because instances of (for example) iteration, optionality and termination, will be dealt with in the detailed notation of the action diagram. We feel that further notation confuses and clutters the structure chart.

Each of the basic concepts can now be examined in greater detail:

Module: A module is a collection of program statements with five basic attributes:

– An input: What it receives from the module that invokes it.

– An output: What it returns to the module that invoked it.

– A function: What it does to its input to produce its output.

– A mechanism: The code or logic which allows it to undertake its function.

– Internal data: Data to which it alone refers.

At present we are only concerned with the first three of these attributes, concentrating on what a module does rather than how it does it.

On the structure chart, the module is shown as a rectangular box with an explanatory name inside it. These names should follow similar principles to those outlined for naming processes in data flow diagrams – an active verb followed by an object or object clause (see Chapter 6 of *Introducing Systems Analysis*).

```
┌─────────────────────────┐
│                         │
│        VERIFY           │
│      ACCOUNT-NO         │
│                         │
└─────────────────────────┘
```

Pre-defined modules are shown by the addition of lines parallel to the vertical lines of the box. This is a module that already exists within a library of modules maintained by the organisation and consequently will not have to be written afresh for this particular application.

```
┌─────────────────────────┐
│ │                     │ │
│ │     COMPUTE         │ │
│ │     UNION-          │ │
│ │     DEDUCTION       │ │
│ │                     │ │
└─────────────────────────┘
```

Control relationships between modules: The structure chart shows the interrelationships of modules by arranging them at different levels and connecting modules in those levels by arrows. An arrow between two modules means that program control is passed from one module to the other at execution time. The first module is said to call or invoke the lower level module. Three rules control the relationship between modules:

– There is only one module at the top of the structure. This is usually called the root or boss module.

– The root passes control down the structure chart to the lower level modules. However, control is always returned to the invoking module and so a finished module should always terminate at the root.

– There can be no more than one control relationship between any two modules on the structure chart. Thus, if module A invokes module B, then module B cannot invoke module A.

Communication between modules: Two types of information are passed between modules:

– Data: this is shown by an arrow with an open circle at its tail. In the example shown below, the module GET CUSTOMER DETAILS invokes the module FIND CUSTOMER NAME by passing the Customer Account Number. The name of the data item is written alongside this *data couple*.

– Control: control items are used to direct program control and show error or end of file conditions. In the example shown below, the *flag* Account Number OK is sent to the calling module to confirm that the requested account number does have a valid account name. This *control couple* is shown by a filled-in circle on the tail of the arrow.

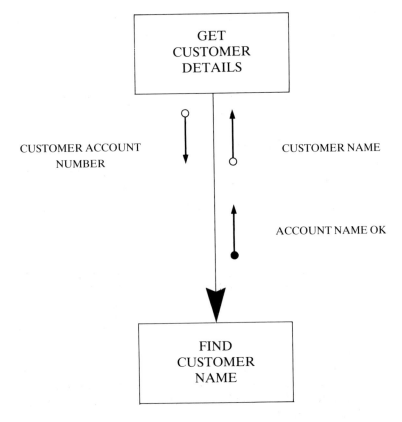

In many practical instances it is physically impossible to show all the control couplings on the structure chart. Consequently, it may be advisable to adopt the principle that such couples are shown only when *there is no other coupling* between modules, ie no data coupling takes place.

6.4   MODULE DESIGN REQUIREMENTS

The previous section has introduced the notion of the structure chart. Such a hierarchical structure should present many advantages in management, development, testing and maintenance. However, such advantages will only accrue if the module design reflects two particular qualities:

– Independence.

It is vital that modules are as independent as possible so that any change in one module has limited effect on any other modules. This is the issue of *coupling*.

– Strength.

Secondly, each module carries out a single problem-related function. This is the issue of *cohesion*.

6.4.1   Module Design: Coupling

One of the objectives of good design is to minimise coupling. The modules should be as independent as possible. This will ensure that:

– There is less chance of an error being 'rippled' through the system.

– The effect of a change in one module has limited effect on other modules.

– Maintenance and re-coding of one module does not require detailed knowledge of the coding of other modules. A module can be withdrawn and replaced without affecting other modules.

– The action of adding new modules to the system is simple and predictable in its effects.

Such independence is a goal of many complex systems – not just computer-based information systems. The failure of many car manufacturers to follow principles of modular design is often brought painfully home in car maintenance!

Independence may be achieved by: eliminating unnecessary relationships, and minimising the number of necessary relationships.

Five types of coupling between modules may be identified:

– *Data Coupling*. The exchange of data items between modules. This is necessary for module control and communication, and so is quite harmless as long as the data items are kept to a minimum.

– *Stamp Coupling*. This occurs when a whole data structure is passed to a module and in that structure there are data items which are irrelevant to the calling module. Any change in this data structure will affect all modules that use it even if those modules do not refer to the item or items which have been changed. Consequently, stamp coupling introduces dependencies between modules that should be unrelated.

This is not to say that data structures should never be passed. The useful shorthand of structures has already been recognised (Chapter 6 of *Introducing Systems Analysis*), but the problems of introducing superfluous data must be recognised.

– *Control Coupling*. This happens when the calling module passes a flag intended to control the logic of the called module. This has the effect of closely linking the logic of the two modules. The calling module must know how the called module is organised if it is to send the correct control information. Control flags which tell a module what to do are not permissible. However, descriptive flags (Account Number OK) are acceptable, because they give information not orders. Control in the hierarchy should be passed through data couples not flag couples.

– *Common Coupling*. Two modules are common coupled if they refer to the same common data area. These common data areas are defined within the context of the target programming language. In Fortran COMMON can be used to declare common areas across SUBROUTINEs and FUNCTIONs. In COBOL, a DATA DIVISION is accessible to any paragraph in the PROCEDURE DIVISION. Common coupling can lead to problems in error rippling, maintenance and inflexibility.

In such instances the value and meaning of the variables in the data area depend upon the state of the system. In one application known to the authors, the meaning of seven flag data fields depends totally on the programs that are accessing them.

– *Content Coupling*. Two modules have content coupling if one module refers to the internal workings of the other. Any changes made to either module will lead to the failure of the other.

Content coupling is the worst type of coupling as it produces systems which are virtually unmaintainable. At the other end of the spectrum, data coupling is essential, but it must be controlled. Examples of data, stamp, control and common coupling are given in Figure 6.2.

6.4.2 Module Design: Cohesion

This is concerned with examining the internal activities of a single module. In general, one module should perform only one task. Modules which try to perform many tasks – validate input, process data, output

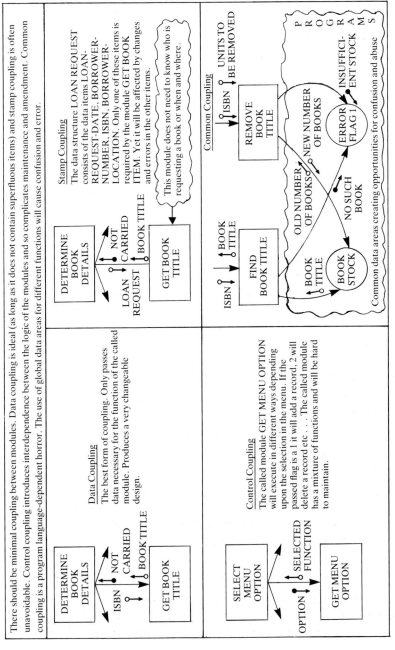

There should be minimal coupling between modules. Data coupling is ideal (as long as it does not contain superfluous items) and stamp coupling is often unavoidable. Control coupling introduces interdependence between the logic of the modules and so complicates maintenance and amendment. Common coupling is a program language-dependent horror. The use of global data areas for different functions will cause confusion and error.

Data Coupling

The best form of coupling. Only passes data necessary for the function of the called module. Produces a very changeable design.

Control Coupling

The called module GET MENU OPTION will execute in different ways depending upon the selection in the menu. If the passed flag is a 1 it will add a record, 2 will delete a record etc . . . The called module has a mixture of functions and will be hard to maintain.

Stamp Coupling

The data structure LOAN REQUEST consists of the data items LOAN-REQUEST-DATE, BORROWER-NUMBER, ISBN, BORROWER-LOCATION. Only one of these items is required by the module GET BOOK ITEM. Yet it will be affected by changes and errors in the other items.

This module does not need to know who is requesting a book or when and where.

Common Coupling

Common data areas creating opportunities for confusion and abuse

Figure 6.2   Diagrammatic Summary of Coupling

results – are difficult to define and maintain. By their very nature their complexity will lead to coupling problems. Hence good coupling should help enforce good cohesion. There are seven forms of cohesion.

- *Functional Cohesion.* A module is said to be functionally cohesive when it consists of data items that all contribute to the execution of one task. Such modules are overwhelmingly single-minded. They GET AN EMPLOYEE NAME not print or validate it.

- *Sequential Cohesion.* In this instance the activities within the module are related to each other in such a way that the output of one activity becomes the input to the next. Thus the module consists of a sequence of actions.

- *Communicational Cohesion.* This is a module that performs a number of activities on the same input or output data. For example, the input data Customer Account Number may be used within one module to find Customer Name, Customer Address, Customer Balance, Customer Sex, etc.

In general functional, sequential and communicational cohesion are all desirable or acceptable. The latter may create some coupling problems (another module may wish to use Customer Balance) so a certain amount of vigilance is necessary.

- *Procedural Cohesion.* A procedurally cohesive module is one whose internal activities seem to bear little relationship to each other. The activities in the module may be organised in a sequence but it is *control* rather than *data* that is passed between them. A procedurally cohesive module is usually a bits and pieces module mopping up the activities that have not been catered for elsewhere.

- *Temporal Cohesion.* These modules are similar to procedurally cohesive modules in that they tend to consist of activities that occur at the same *time*. Their activities are actually more closely related to those in other modules and consequently they often exhibit very 'tight' coupling.

- *Logical Cohesiveness.* A logically cohesive module is one where the selection of activities within the module is dictated from outside. The module contains activities of a general kind, only one of which is selected through the common interface. This creates content coupling problems as well as complicating maintenance.

– *Coincidental Cohesiveness*. This occurs in modules with activities which have no logical connection with each other. It is an extreme case of logical cohesiveness. At least the activities of the latter were of the same type. In a coincidentally cohesive module the activities have no temporal, procedural or logical connection. The modules have probably been created by the 'machete method', cutting up longer programs into a 'modularised' design. Consequently, the modules are just there! Their homelessness should give us strong clues about the rest of the design!

Examples of cohesion are given in Figure 6.3. In general, procedural, temporal, logical and coincidental cohesion must be avoided.

6.4.3 Module Design: Other Considerations

Although cohesion and coupling are important criteria for module design other design issues must be taken into account.

1 *Factoring*. Modules should not be too large. In the context of commercial programming Page-Jones has suggested that a module might be a:

PROGRAM (or less ideally a SECTION or PARAGRAPH): COBOL

SUBROUTINE or FUNCTION: Fortran

FUNCTION : C, APL, PL/1 or Algol

PROCEDURE, FUNCTION: Ada or Pascal (Page-Jones, 1988.)

A number of maximum sizes of modules have been suggested (Weinberg, 1978). 'Certainly, all the code of a module should be visible on one page of listing or on two facing pages' (Page-Jones, 1981). This normally sets an upper limit of 120 lines. Myers has suggested that 'experience has shown that a well-structured program has an average module size of 40–50 high level executable statements (ie excluding declarative and comment statements)' (Myers, 1978).

It is important to recognise that there are no absolute standards, which may lead to arbitrary divisions based on program length rather than considerations of cohesion and coupling. However, it

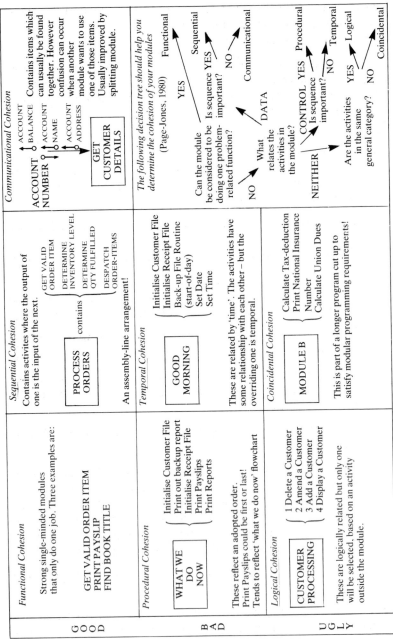

Figure 6.3   Diagrammatic Summary of Cohesion

must be acknowledged that many modules (particularly in 4GLs) are much too long for comfort. Functionally limited modules are much easier to program, control and maintain.

Factoring will, by its very nature, encourage functional cohesion. This is likely to create general modules which can be used a number of times in the system as well as being added to the company library for future system development.

2 *Decision-splitting.* A decision has two phases. The first is the recognition of that decision (Account Name is valid) and the second is the action that results (send Valid Transaction Flag). Decision-splitting should be avoided as the recognition and the action should be in the same module.

3 *System Shape.* There are essentially four types of modules on a structure chart.

   – *Co-ordinating Modules.* These control the activities of subordinates.

   – *Data Collection Modules.* These are responsible for the collection and validation of data coming into the system.

   – *Data Output Modules.* Such modules arrange the format and distribution of output data.

   – *Transformation Modules.* These receive data from the collection modules and transform it into a form suitable for the output modules.

The general location of these modules on the structure chart is illustrated in Figure 6.4.

The aim is to produce a balanced structure chart that can be read top to bottom and left to right. The higher modules contain broad, logical statements and the lower ones have restricted physical ones. The left hand side sees the data coming into the system and the right hand side describes the distribution of that data once it has passed through the transformation modules in the centre.

4 *Error Reporting.* The module that recognises and detects the error should report it.

5 *Editing.* Perform simple validation first. Thus errors of syntax are checked before those of semantics. For example, in the data item

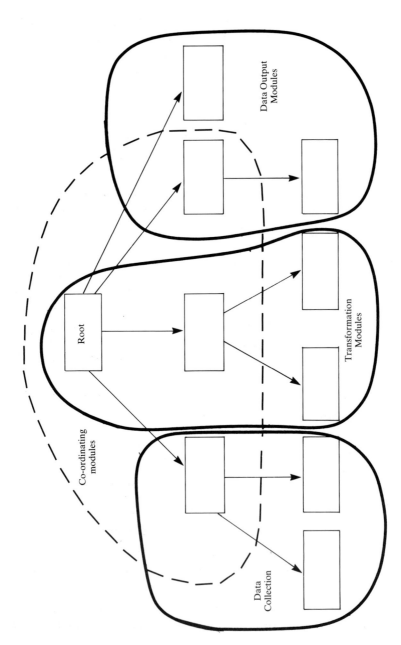

Figure 6.4   Types and Positions of Modules in a Structure Chart

entries Sex=Mile and Discharge-Reason=Maternity the entries are checked independently (leading to the correction of Mile to Male) before the entries fail on the cross-validation. Thus a syntax validation module would be at a lower level than the semantic check.

6 *State Memory.* Avoid modules which use items whose value has to be taken over from one call to the next. A module should be constructed so that it acts each time like the first occasion on which it was called. It should require no state memory – a figure dependent upon a past existence.

7 *Initialisation and Termination.* Generalised initialisation and termination routines are difficult to maintain because of their poor cohesiveness and high coupling. The rule is to initialise as late as possible and to terminate as soon as possible.

8 *Restrictivity/Generality.* Restrictive modules can normally be identified by their hard-coding. The module can only deal with specific values and not with any parameter passed to it by the calling module. In contrast, modules are too general when they provide for excessive breadth in the passed parameters. This restrictiveness/generality is applicable to function as well as data. Some software packages provide functions which, in all probability, will never be used by the overwhelming majority of its customers.

9 *Fan-in/Fan-out.* Fan-out refers to the number of immediate subordinates of a module. It is suggested that there should be no more than seven such subordinates.

Fan-in is the number of immediate superiors of a module. This should be kept high but within the boundaries dictated by good cohesion. In general, a high fan-in should indicate a good design because it illustrates how the designer has been able to use the module in different contexts and applications. Alternatively, and less acceptably, is that it might hide disastrous levels of coupling.

These nine design guidelines are dealt with in more detail elsewhere (for example Page-Jones, 1981; Myers, 1978; Gilbert, 1983; Page-Jones, 1988).

We now have an idea of the structure chart and design guidelines for constructing the modules. The next question must be, where do we get the content from?

6.5 CONTENT OF THE STRUCTURE CHART: FROM DATA FLOW DIAGRAM TO STRUCTURE CHART

There are two main strategies for converting the data flow diagram of analysis into the structure chart of design. These are:

– transform analysis;

– transaction analysis.

The word *strategy* is important. Both give a set of guidelines and suggestions – not a cookbook transformation. However, 'if you follow the steps of the strategy you will get in sight of a good result, but you will rarely attain perfection' (Page-Jones, 1981).

6.5.1 Transform Analysis

Transform analysis passes through five main steps:

Step 1: Draw a Data Flow Diagram

The development of data flow digrams is covered in Chapter 6 of the companion text, *Introducing Systems Analysis*. A simple example for a payroll system is shown in Figure 6.4 and this will serve to demonstrate the transform as well as providing a reminder of the basic features of a data flow diagram.

Step 2: Identify the Central Transform

The central transform is the essential function of the data flow diagram. Candidates for this role may be identified by pruning off the so-called afferent and efferent flows of the diagram.

The *afferent* data flows are concerned with the entry of data and the validation of this input. These may be pruned away because they are simply concerned with filtering erroneous data out of the system. They *prepare* the data for the central transform. In a perfect world they would not be needed because the input data would never contain errors.

The *efferent* data flows are those flows which distribute data from the prime function to the identified recipients. These flows are normally concerned with formatting and presenting the data in a certain way. Again, in a perfect world, these would not matter as the user would not be concerned with appearance and format.

Thus the central transform is what is left when the data arrives and

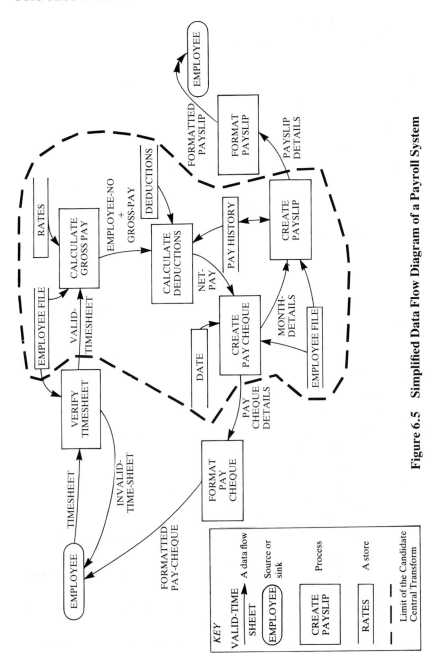

Figure 6.5   Simplified Data Flow Diagram of a Payroll System

leaves in a raw, but logically complete and correct form. Figure 6.5 shows a candidate central transform for the payroll system.

The location of the boundary of the transform will clearly have elements of subjectivity. However, it is better to proceed with the design to see what happens rather than to spend too much time arguing whether a process should or should not be regarded as part of the central transform.

Step 3: Produce a First-cut Structure Chart

The data flow diagram has no hierarchy and so this now has to be identified or imposed. Transform analysis suggests two ways of establishing the root or boss module. *Either* using a process in the central transform which seems to be the most important, *or* creating a new boss for all the processes to hang off.

The candidate processes in the central transform of the payroll model are:

- Calculate Gross Pay

- Calculate Deductions

- Create Pay Cheque

- Create Payslip

None of these appear to be a possible root, nor do they appear to provide sequential cohesion for any newly elected boss module. The reason for this lies in the balance of the activities. There are no afferent flows to provide the right type of system shape as well as providing cohesion within any root module. This can be remedied by including the flow from the verified timesheet in the module definition, hence:

- Get Valid Timesheet

- Calculate Gross Pay

- Calculate Deductions

- Create Pay Cheque

- Create Payslip

presents a sequentially cohesive Produce Payroll module. Figure 6.6a shows the structure chart for this new boss module.

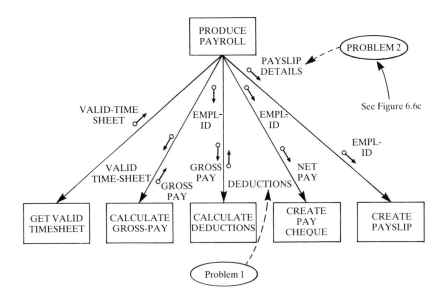

The calculation of a deduction
requires a **selection** amongst
alternative rates. Empl-ID would
have to include some selection
parameter. This causes logical
cohesiveness.

Figure 6.6a   Structure Chart for Produce Payroll Module

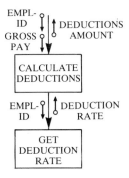

Figure 6.6b   Deductions Store Module for Produce Payroll Module

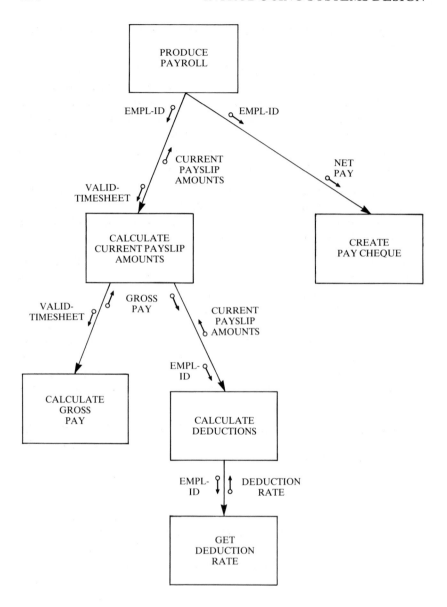

**Figure 6.6c   Produce Payroll Module Incorporating Calculate Net Pay
Module**

The production of this structure chart immediately highlights two problems.

Calculate Deductions is logically cohesive. The deduction rate is selected from outside the module and consequently it currently holds a series of deductions any one of which might be used at a given time. This may be solved by splitting the module into two. A higher level module can now calculate the deductions based upon a rate supplied by a lower module. This lower module accords with the deductions store shown on the data flow diagram. This is shown in Figure 6.6b.

Problem two is encountered when trying to write the details of what is sent to the pay cheque. The amount on the cheque is determined by gross pay minus deductions. However, there is no module to create this result. This is remedied in Figure 6.6c.

The transformation of Figure 6.6c can now be checked with the central transform of the data flow diagram. The module Calculate Gross Pay only receives a valid time report at present. This would be acceptable if all employees were paid at the same rate. However, this is unlikely to be true (hence the Rates store in the data flow diagram) and so the chart again needs extending. A similar store access is made by the process Calculate Deductions which needs to know the Pay History of the employee because some deductions are dependent upon cumulative Year-to-Date pay. The role of these stores must be recognised in the structure chart.

Figure 6.6d represents the structure chart of the first part of the central transform and illustrates how it has been completed by cross-checking with the data flow diagram.

Step 4: Revise and Enhance the Structure Chart

The other second level modules can now be expanded by referencing the data flow diagram. Check that read and write modules have been created for accessing sources, sinks and stores. Figure 6.7 presents an annotated structure chart for the simplified payroll system.

Step 5: Check the Structure Chart

Check out the structure chart by a formal 'walkthrough' of the chart and the data flow diagram. This is a formal version of what was required in the development Steps 3 and 4.

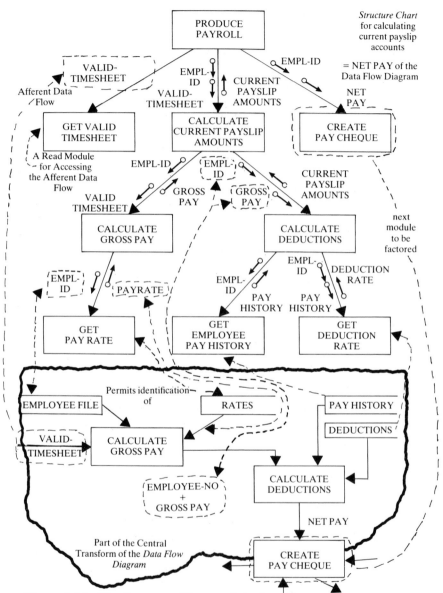

Structure Chart for calculating current payslip accounts

= NET PAY of the Data Flow Diagram

Figure 6.6d   The Structure Chart and the Data Flow Diagram for Part of a Simplified Payroll System. (Selected Connections shown by dotted lines)

6.5.2   Transaction Analysis

Transaction analysis is essentially a supportive technique to guard against control coupling and logical cohesion. It is a recognition of the fact that a large number of systems are transaction-based and that many of these transactions (add a customer, delete a customer, modify customer details, etc) are superficially quite similar. Furthermore, it also recognises that many developers have tried to exploit this similarity by sharing code between transactions, usually with extravagant use of conditional jumps, flags and switches. This leads to tangled code that incurs high maintenance overheads.

Transaction analysis suggests that, however similar transactions appear to be, they should always be dealt with by different modules. These transaction modules (typically; create, add, delete, modify, list) are co-ordinated by a *transaction centre* module that determines the required action and passes it to the appropriate module.

In most respects a transaction centre is essentially a particular type of process on the data flow diagram – a control switching centre. It typically reflects the situation where four or five alternative flows emanate from a process that has received one input (see Figure 6.8). In practice, transform analysis tends to be the major strategy for producing the structure chart, supported by transaction analysis where appropriate.

6.6   COMMENTS ON THE STRUCTURE CHART

Structure charts are time-consuming to draw and edit. Physical limitations do not allow the comprehensive annotation of data couples or the complete specification of control couples. The omission of the latter may help clarity but at the cost of the completeness of the model.

Automated tools are a particular boon to structure charts. The graphical editing facilities permit the re-positioning and re-definition of modules. The high resolution of advanced workstations allows the definition of complete – and readable – coupling annotation. Furthermore, as Sharp (1988) has commented, the manual translation of data flow diagrams into structure charts can be 'tedious and time consuming' for anything but small systems. A complete or partial automation of transform analysis is obviously very desirable. Sharp describes a tool (Transform Analyser) to do this; a further step in design automation.

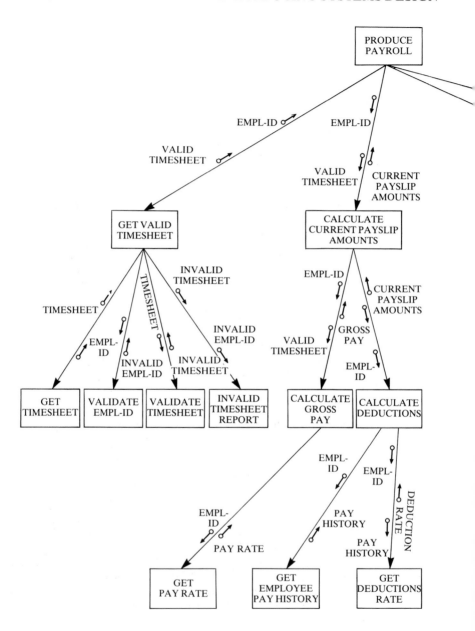

Figure 6.6   Structure Chart for the Simplified Payroll System

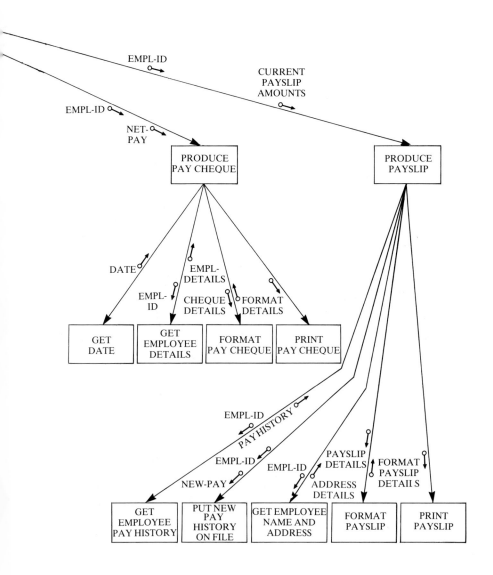

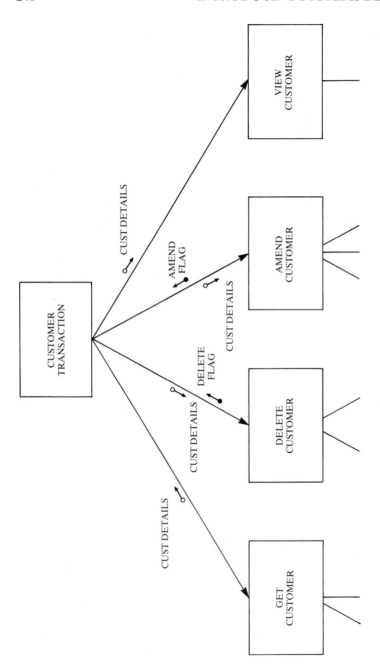

Figure 6.8   A Transaction Centre

In our view transform analysis provides a very useful technique for moving from a logical to a physical design. Structure charts are shown in many texts, but there is often very little indication of where such charts *have come from* and the design guidelines behind them. These charts are often used as the start of some process (particularly program design) rather than the result of some previous activity. In contrast, transform analysis has the birthright of the data flow diagram. The structure chart has a parent – it is conceived and not ordained.

However, whilst such charts give a basis for developing the physical system they are cluttered by data and control information. This information is insufficient for detailed design, but too much for the clarity of the structure chart itself. Consequently structure charts can look very complex and intricate but still not contain sufficient control structure details for programming. Hence, we prefer to see the structure chart as an important step in the transition from logical to physical design, but to leave the description of module details to a more appropriate technique – action diagrams – introduced later in this chapter.

6.7 STRUCTURE CHARTS: OTHER USES

6.7.1 Functional Allocation

Each module has to be allocated to a mechanism that can undertake that module. Three broad options are available from a spectrum of possibilities.

- The process is carried out by a human being. This is usually reserved for decisions which require important subjective judgements, or are sufficiently 'one-off' that they do not justify data collection and interpretation.

- The process is carried out by some combination of human being and computer. For example, the process Allocate-Priority may describe the allocation of priorities to customers by a Customer Service Manager. He may undertake this task by supplementing his subjective observations of the firm with buying pattern data provided by a computer system. In reality, many processes fall into this category.

- The process is carried out completely by computer. This is possible when it is feasible to completely predict the states and actions of the system. The computer is a *rule-following* machine. Therefore, it may only be used in circumstances where those rules can be identified and completely defined. Grindley and Humble (1973) identified four main areas where the computer appeared to contribute to success. Briefly, these were:

- *Improved performance in repetitive tasks.* If a task can be found that is essentially predictable and repetitive then it can almost certainly be carried out more successfully by using a computer. This is because of the rule-following nature of the machine that will cause it to consistently and tirelessly carry out the specified tasks. In contrast, few human beings are rule-following, preferring to wilfully choose different paths and alternatives to keep control over the activities of the work system. In addition, the human being may become tired, forgetful, inaccurate and inconsistent.

- *Increased volume of repetitive tasks.* Even if clerks are cajoled into performing repetitive tasks the inherent lack of job satisfaction leads to the need to seek compensation in the form of raised salaries. The result is that firms with large processing requirements cannot afford to maintain an 'army of clerks' and so turn to the computer to perform the required volume of processes.

- *Humans released for discretionary tasks.* Relieving humans of routine rule-following work leaves them extra time to perform the more discretionary tasks of management. This is essentially what has happened to accounting in the last two decades, losing the overhead of bookkeeping to the computer, and giving more time for budget management, corporate strategy and financial planning.

- *Improved control method.* This is concerned with cases where a decision, once solely made by human judgement, may be improved by the contribution of some rule-following data processing. This often covers circumstances where the rules have been too complicated or the volume of data too great to make it practicable for human beings to do.

Thus the designer is concerned with *allocating* the module to a suitable medium – human, human/computer, computer and then specifying the module in some way. In certain instances this will be a

Clerical Procedures Document, in others it will be a specification for a computer program. This allocation is a design decision.

6.7.2 Prototyping

Top-down incremental implementation is the term given to the strategy of implementing the top module of the structure chart first and then progressing downwards through the hierarchy of the chart. Modules which await full implementation are represented by *stubs* which permit the rest of the system to work properly. These stubs are written in such a way that they pass data realistically around the system even though many modules are not yet complete. Module stubs are usually simple data passing programs that output values instead of computed parameters. Efferent modules which are concerned with output and display may simply be represented by stubs which proclaim:

'Option 5: Print Leavers Report is not yet available'.

Program stubs are replaced by programs as development progresses.

The order in which modules should be developed greatly depends upon the nature of the system under consideration. However, a level-by-level implementation will seldom be desirable. Users will be more concerned with the afferent and efferent modules as it is these upon which they will judge the accuracy, friendliness and usefulness of the system. Prototyping the input and output may also be used to help define the requirements of the system in the first place.

Thus input, output and interface design (see Chapters 2 and 3) will be a priority in the development of the afferent and efferent modules. This will enable the demonstration of a running system with a simulated central transformation that can be used to determine the correct content and format of input and output as well as agreeing the nature of the interfaces.

In contrast, prototyping the central transformation is likely to be of significance only to the designer. Candidate modules for prototyping include:

- those which have to produce output within an agreed or determined response time;

- those which have to process a large amount of input data;

- those with complicated algorithms.

In general, the demands of each system and the environment in which that system is being developed will determine the order of the incremental implementation. A possible prototype plan for the simplified payroll system is given in Figure 6.9.

1 Develop outline timesheet, payslip and pay cheque. These draft inputs and outputs will be used to test the processes developed in the system.
2 Write Calculate Gross Pay and Calculate Deductions modules using unverified input data. Check that correct net pay is produced.
3 Write Create Pay Cheque and Create Payslip modules. Check that details produced are correct and sufficient.
4 Review output document with user. Agree format. Write Format Pay Cheque module.
5 Discuss input errors with user and write Verify Timesheet module.
6 Complete testing.

Figure 6.9   Prototype Development Plan for a Simplified Payroll System

The structure chart can also be used as a basis for software package selection. Some (or all) of the modules identified in the chart may be provided by a commercially available software package. This will permit competing packages to be evaluated against requirements rather than against checklists. Furthermore, if no package is available, then the design may be confidently partitioned between bespoke and packaged solutions. A hypothetical division of the payroll system is given on the data flow diagram of Figure 6.10.

6.8   ACTION DIAGRAMS

Although the importance of structure charts has been recognised, their limitations have also been acknowledged. Consequently, we wish to introduce action diagrams as a supporting tool, one which is well suited to the presentation of the detailed logic of a module.

Action diagrams have five important characteristics:

– They are relatively easy to learn and teach.

– They are suitable for automation. An action diagram editor is

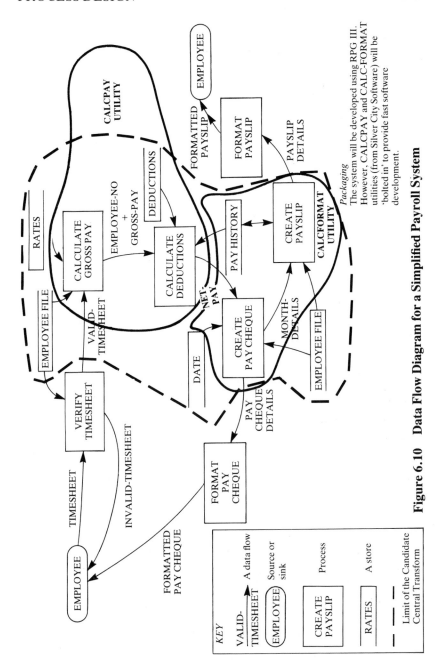

Figure 6.10 Data Flow Diagram for a Simplified Payroll System

Packaging
The system will be developed using RPG III. However, CALCPAY and CALC-FORMAT utilities (from Silver City Software) will be 'bolted in' to provide fast software development.

KEY

VALID-TIMESHEET → A data flow

EMPLOYEE — Source or sink

CREATE PAYSLIP — Process

RATES — A store

- - - Limit of the Candidate Central Transform

available for the IBM PC from Database Design Inc.

- They are particularly suitable for using with 4GLs. The action diagram technique can easily be customised to reflect the syntax of different languages.

- They use a tree-like structure. Figure 6.11 shows the action diagram for the module hierarchy of the payroll example. The economy of the representation should be self-evident.

- The same tools can be used at different levels. A single technique extends from a general overview down to program coding level.

```
PRODUCE PAYROLL
      GET VALID TIMESHEET
      GET TIMESHEET
      VALIDATE EMPL-ID
      VALIDATE TIMESHEET
      INVALID TIMESHEET REPORT


      CALCULATE CURRENT PAYSLIP AMOUNTS
      CALCULATE GROSS PAY
        GET PAY RATE
      CALCULATE DEDUCTIONS
        GET EMPLOYEE PAY HISTORY
        GET DEDUCTIONS RATE


      PRODUCE PAY CHEQUE
      GET DATE
      GET EMPLOYEE DETAILS
      FORMAT PAY CHEQUE
      PRINT PAY CHEQUE


      PRODUCE PAYSLIP
      GET EMPLOYEE PAY HISTORY
      PUT NEW PAY HISTORY ON FILE
      GET EMPLOYEE NAME AND ADDRESS
      FORMAT PAYSLIP
      PRINT PAYSLIP
END PAYROLL
```

Figure 6.11   Action Diagram for the Simplified Payroll System

6.8.1   Action Diagrams: Diagramming Conventions

Brackets

The brackets enclose a series of actions. These actions might range from a high level process definition to specific lines of program code. For example, the high level process, Fulfil An Order placed by an established customer, might look like this:

┌─Fulfil an Established Customer Order

│   Check Credit Limit

│   Check Goods Availability

│   Pick Order

│   Despatch Order

│   Raise Invoice

└──── Check Remittance against Invoice

The program code for totalling the salaries of each department in the organisation can also be represented in a similar top to bottom sequence.

Total Salaries by Department

┌────USE PEOPLE

│   INDEX ON DEPARTMENT TO TEMPER

│   USE PEOPLE INDEX TEMPER

│   TOTAL TO SUMMARY ON DEPARTMENT FIELDS SALARY

│   USE SUMMARY

└──── LIST DEPARTMENT, SALARY

The action list may be conditional:

┌────IF CUSTNO=INVALID

│   SET FLAGREP TO ZERO

│   PRINT 'Invalid Customer Number'

│   PRINT 'Please re-enter Customer Code'

│   SET ENTERTRY to ENTERTRY+1

└────ENDIF

In all instances the action list is entered at the top and performed sequentially before exiting at the bottom.

Conditions

Some actions are only executed if a certain condition holds. For example, the process Check Trade References only applies to new customers. The Condition statement in the action diagram below has a split bracket to show what actions should take place if the condition is true and what actions if it is false. Both sets of actions end at a common exit point (the end of the bracket) and resume a top to bottom sequence.

Fulfil a Customer Order

IF the Customer is a New Customer

Request Bank References

Request Trade References

Place Order on Hold

Establish Credit Limit

ELSE

Pick Goods

Despatch Order

Raise Invoice

Check Remittance Against Invoice

ENDIF

Case Structure

The ELSE structure represents two mutually exclusive conditions, the order is either placed by a New or Established Customer. In some circumstances there are many such mutually exclusive conditions and these form a case structure where only one of several conditions is true at any one time. For example:

```
┌──── CASE
│
├──── WHEN OPTION = C
│     Create New Customer
├──── WHEN OPTION = A
│     Amend Customer Details
├──── WHEN OPTION = D
│     Delete Customer Details
├──── WHEN OPTION = L
│     List Customer Details
├──── WHEN OPTION = E
│     Exit to Operating System
├──── WHEN OPTION NOTEQUAL TO CADLE
│     Display 'Entry invalid'
│     Display 'Please re-enter option required'
└──── ENDCASE
```

This type of structure was introduced in the companion text (*Introducing Systems Analysis*) and it is particularly appropriate in the definition of menu options – typically defined in a transaction centre module.

Repetition

It is often necessary to repeat a set of actions for a series of transactions. In such circumstances the repetition is shown by a double bar at the top and a thicker vertical line in the bracket.

```
┌═══ FOR ALL Valid Orders
┃
┃    Pick Goods
┃
┃    Despatch Order
┃
┃    Raise Invoice
┃
┃    Check Remittance Against Invoice
┃
└──── ENDFOR
```

The repetition structure may be controlled by a condition. This may state that the actions within the bracket are only executed *while* a certain condition is true (DO WHILE). In the example shown below the variable AGAIN is tested at the *beginning* of every iteration of the loop and the actions will be executed until the user inputs a N(o), whereupon control returns to the main menu. In this example the user may fail to pass the authorisation procedure or may have chosen the wrong option in error. In such circumstances the variable AGAIN is not set to Y and so the DO WHILE loop is not executed.

```
┌── DO Add Customer Option

    Display 'Please Wait'

    Display 'Add Customer Records Option'

    Perform authorisation checks

    ┌── DO WHILE AGAIN=Y

        Enter Customer Code

        Retrieve Customer Record

        Display 'Any More Customers?'

        Accept input of AGAIN

    └── END DO WHILE

    Display number of records added

    Return to Main Menu

└── ENDDO
```

In some circumstances the actions in a process are executed *until* a certain condition is reached (DO UNTIL). In this instance the actions are first executed and then the UNTIL condition is tested. If this condition is false then the actions in the bracket are executed again. The iteration of the loop continues until the UNTIL condition becomes true.

This testing of the loop is subtly different to that of the DO WHILE construct. In the previous example, the actions within the loop may never have been executed because the user failed either the authorisation procedure or to recognise that the wrong menu option had been selected. In contrast, the DO UNTIL construct executes the loop instructions *at least once* because the condition is not tested until the loop is executed. The distinction between DO WHILE and DO UNTIL is made explicit in action diagrams by drawing the test statement at the part of the bracket where the test is made.

```
┌── DO WHILE AGAIN=Y
└── END DO WHILE

┌── DO UNTIL
└── UNTIL AGAIN=Y
```

For example:

```
┌── DO Add Customer Option
│    ┌── DO UNTIL
│    │    Enter Customer Code
│    │    Retrieve Customer Record
│    │    Display 'Any More Customers?'
│    │    Accept input of AGAIN
│    └── UNTIL AGAIN=Y
│    Display number of records added
│    Return to Main Menu
└── ENDDO
```

Escape

Certain conditions will demand that particular actions are skipped. For example, in one of the action diagrams used above, there is a need for an Authorisation Procedure. As the definition currently stands, the failure of this procedure will lead to the user being returned to the Main Menu. This is unlikely to be acceptable as we would wish to trip and track such attempted incursions. Consequently a termination arrow can be used to cut through successive brackets with the escape condition written to the right of the escape arrow. The arrow may pass through any number of brackets and program execution resumes at the level indicated at the point of the arrow.

For example:

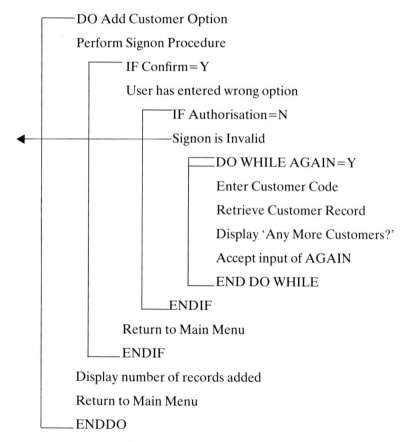

```
┌────DO Add Customer Option
│    Perform Signon Procedure
│         ┌──IF Confirm=Y
│         │  User has entered wrong option
│         │       ┌──IF Authorisation=N
◄─────────┼───────┤──Signon is Invalid
│         │       │    ┌──DO WHILE AGAIN=Y
│         │       │    │  Enter Customer Code
│         │       │    │  Retrieve Customer Record
│         │       │    │  Display 'Any More Customers?'
│         │       │    │  Accept input of AGAIN
│         │       │    └──END DO WHILE
│         │       └──ENDIF
│         │  Return to Main Menu
│         └──ENDIF
│    Display number of records added
│    Return to Main Menu
└────ENDDO
```

Further Structures

NEXT Iteration

A NEXT structure is an arrow in a repetition bracket which does not break through that bracket. If the condition to the right of the arrow is fulfilled then control transfers to the next iteration of the loop. This is useful when the loop has to be broken for some reason but then resumed.

Procedures

Subroutines and subprocedures can be drawn on an action diagram. These are drawn as round-cornered boxes with the subprocedure name inside the box. The details of these procedure boxes are given on a separate action diagram. The procedure notation can be expanded to include procedures which have yet to be designed and those which are called more than once in an action diagram.

```
┌─────────────────────────────┐
│                             │
│           FIND              │
│         MISMATCH            │
│                             │
└─────────────────────────────┘
```

```
┌─┬───────────────────────────┐
│ │                           │
│ │        COMPUTE            │
│ │        DEDUCT             │
│ │                           │
└─┴───────────────────────────┘
```

The bracket wordings of the action diagram can be altered to fit the target fourth generation language. Many of the constructs given above are similar to the Structured English conventions introduced in the companion text, *Introducing Systems Analysis*. In fact, action diagrams can be seen as a 'visual' Structured English, with diagramming conventions highlighting and simplifying the structure of the content.

6.9   PROCESS DESIGN AT INFOSYS

Figure 6.12 is the Level 1 data flow diagram repeated from *Introducing Systems Analysis*. A tentative central transform has been drawn encompassing the following processes:

– Retrieve Customer Details

– Create a New Customer

– Determine Stock Position

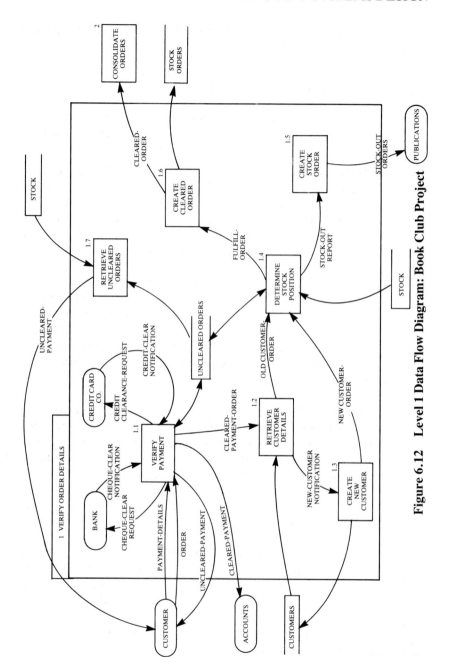

Figure 6.12   Level 1 Data Flow Diagram: Book Club Project

The incoming data flow is Cleared Order Payment, while the outgoing flows are Fulfil Order and Stock Out Report.

A suggested structure chart for this central transform is given in Figure 6.13. A number of points are worth making about this chart:

- Customers supply certain details (Cust Name) on their order form. The customer identifier is not requested (this reflects a management decision) and so it is retrieved in the system itself.

- Cust Names that do not give an identifier (Cust-ID) are passed to the Create New Customer module which records other details (Cust Details) and allocates a new ID. It soon became clear in the development of this chart that Create New Customer is subordinate to Retrieve Customer Details – although both appear in the candidate central transform of the data flow diagram.

- The Determine Stock Position module identifies the order items, order item quantity fulfilled, order item quantity unfulfilled and the new inventory level for each order item on the order. The latter value is passed to a module that updates the inventory. If the new inventory level (NIL) is below the reorder level for that item, then a reorder quantity is raised and passed to the module Create Stock Order.

  In an earlier draft of this chart the module Update Inventory was drawn as subordinate to Determine Stock Position. However, this led to the passing of the reorder quantity between Determine Stock Position and Process Orders. In most instances this would be unwanted and so cause unnecessary stamp coupling.

- Store-date has been added to the system to record the creation date of the uncleared order.

Importantly, the development of the structure chart now permits a re-drafting of the data flow diagram, so again stressing the complementary nature of most of the techniques used in systems analysis and design. The redrawn diagram is given in Figure 6.14.

The modules on the structure chart can now be presented in detail in action diagrams. For example:

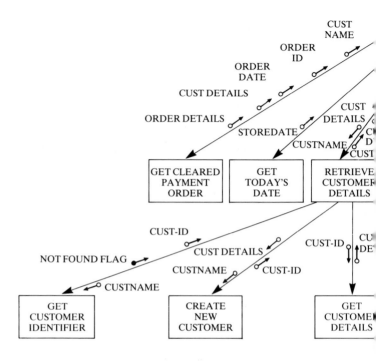

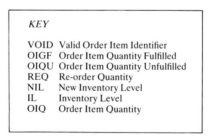

KEY

VOID Valid Order Item Identifier
OIGF Order Item Quantity Fulfilled
OIQU Order Item Quantity Unfulfilled
REQ   Re-order Quantity
NIL   New Inventory Level
IL   Inventory Level
OIQ   Order Item Quantity

Figure 6.13   Par

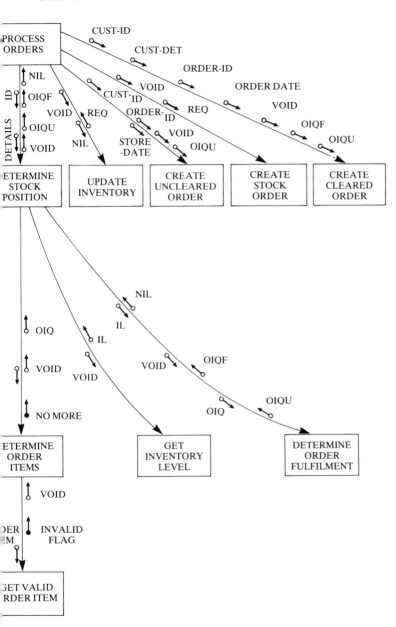

Structure Chart: InfoSys

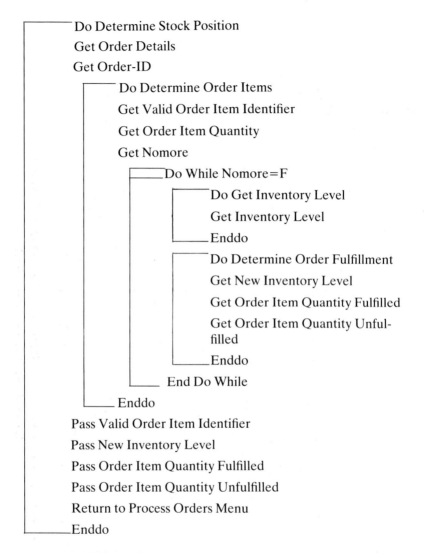

Do Determine Stock Position
Get Order Details
Get Order-ID
    Do Determine Order Items
    Get Valid Order Item Identifier
    Get Order Item Quantity
    Get Nomore
        Do While Nomore=F
            Do Get Inventory Level
            Get Inventory Level
            Enddo
            Do Determine Order Fulfillment
            Get New Inventory Level
            Get Order Item Quantity Fulfilled
            Get Order Item Quantity Unful-
            filled
            Enddo
        End Do While
    Enddo
Pass Valid Order Item Identifier
Pass New Inventory Level
Pass Order Item Quantity Fulfilled
Pass Order Item Quantity Unfulfilled
Return to Process Orders Menu
Enddo

6.10   PROCESS SUMMARY

This chapter has introduced two powerful and complementary techniques for process definition. The first, the structure chart, was presented as an important step in the transition from the logical design to the physical one. It displays the data flow diagram in more detail, and in a hierarchical format suitable for software implementation. The structure

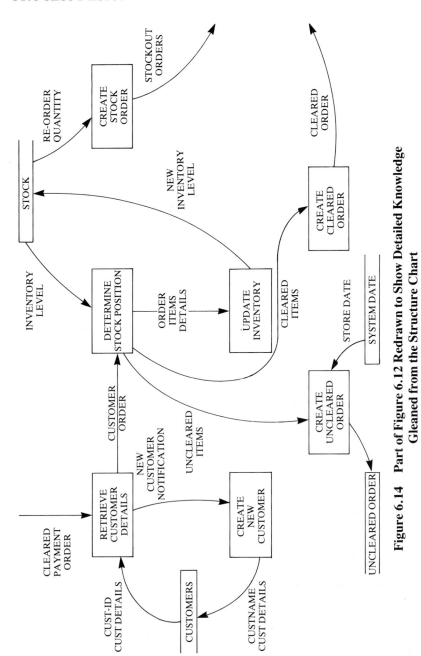

Figure 6.14 Part of Figure 6.12 Redrawn to Show Detailed Knowledge Gleaned from the Structure Chart

chart also provides a powerful aid to functional allocation and prototyping through top-down incremental implementation.

Action diagrams document the detail of the modules. Structure charts do have a mechanism for showing control but it tends to produce messy and cluttered diagrams. Furthermore, the control information shown is insufficient for program development, particularly if automatic code generation is required.

6.11   REVIEW OF THE DESIGN TASK

This and the previous four chapters have considered five design aspects of the system:

- Input and output design based upon the data flows of the data flow diagram and their supporting data dictionary entries (Chapter 2).

- Interface design underpinned by understanding the requirements and skill levels of users and operators explored within the context of the data flow diagram (Chapter 3).

- Control design from the detail of the data dictionary (Chapter 4).

- File and database design based upon the entity-relationship model and supported by the entity life history and the data dictionary (Chapter 5).

- Process and program design based upon the data flow diagram and supported by the data dictionary (Chapter 6).

Each chapter has introduced design models which ease the transition from the logical to the physical design.

However, it must be recognised that all of these design tasks (particularly file and process design) are inter-dependent. For example, the definition of detailed procedures in an action diagram will require knowledge of file or database structures and may, in turn, affect those structures by demanding a change in the second or third level data model. The order in which the design tasks have been tackled in this book reflects preoccupation rather than rigid sequence. Input and output design will be a *preoccupation* of the earlier stages of design, while detailed program development will be a major factor in the later stages. The iteration and interaction between all the aspects of design must be recognised and appreciated.

Packaging

The physical design must now be coded. Programs will be written to produce the agreed input and output screens and reports. These will reflect the defined interfaces and controls as well as accessing the correct files and databases. The programs will then be tested on the target hardware and tuned and amended where necessary (see Chapter 7).

The amount of actual code-cutting will vary with the development tool. The general goal must be to reduce time-consuming coding and so screen and dialogue designers and program and system generators may be employed to undertake part or all of the task.

However, even quicker development is possible if all or part of the system is implemented using an application software package and the principle of this has already been introduced in this chapter (see Figure 6.8). This begs an important question:

Is it necessary to undertake all the design tasks if the target software is likely to be a software package?

The answer to this question must be NO. In such circumstances there is little point in spending much time on file, database and program design because there is very little control over these factors in a 'closed' application package with no direct access to code and files. It is the recognition of this that has guided the order of the last four chapters. We suggest that a minimum set of information for software selection should be:

- Input and Output requirements (Chapter 2)

- Interface requirements (Chapter 3)

- Controls required (Chapter 4)

These are still needed in the detail required for a bespoke solution. The package must produce the outputs required and manipulate inputs with the necessary precision and control. Interface issues are particularly important as it is often *differences* in the interface that distinguish a package from its competitor. These may be supplemented by first and second level data models designed to support an understanding of the problem area as well as appreciating the effect of the required inputs and outputs.

A simple structure chart (with minimal annotation) will help explore the interface and provide clues about the modularity of the application package (what happens when I delete a customer?). This sub-set of the design tasks provides criteria for the selection of a package. It ensures that competing products are evaluated *against requirements*, rather than against a checklist. This issue is re-visited in Chapter 8.

6.12 SUMMARY

This chapter has introduced the design of processes through two major techniques – structure charts and action diagrams. It has:

- introduced the notation and construction of structure charts;

- provided guidelines for module construction and content, reflecting principles of cohesion and coupling;

- given two major strategies – transform and transaction analysis – for converting a data flow diagram into a structure chart;

- explored how the structure chart can be used as a basis for functional allocation, prototyping and software package selection;

- introduced the notation and construction of action diagrams and recognised how they can be used to supplement the structure chart;

- applied structure charts and action diagrams to the InfoSys case study;

- paused to review the design task, particularly in the light of the target software solution being an application package.

6.13 EXERCISES

The following questions refer to the case study given in Chapter 1.

1 Develop a structure chart for the library application.

2 Support each module with an action diagram defining the detailed logic of the process.

3 Provide appropriate 'packaging' for the implementation.

7 System Implementation

7.1 INTRODUCTION

This book has considered several important areas of design. Input, output, interface and control considerations (Chapters 2 to 4) which will shape the database, file and process specifications examined in Chapters 5 and 6. The physical design of the files and processes, and the way that development takes place, will vary with circumstances. For example, a set of formal specifications – consisting of file layouts (from third level design), program specifications (structure charts supported by action diagrams), inputs, outputs, interfaces and controls may be handed over to programmers for coding. This handover can be relatively formal, with documents recording the passing of control from the analysis to the programming team and, ultimately, back again. In other circumstances there may be no particular cut-off point between the design models and their physical implementation. The power and accessibility of 4GLs and the ability of Computer Aided Software Engineering (CASE) tools to produce code in such languages is making this more common. Artificial boundaries between analysis, design and development, once enshrined in data processing department hierarchies, are becoming increasingly irrelevant.

However, whatever software is used or organisational arrangements adopted, the newly developed system must now be delivered and implemented. This chapter examines two aspects of this implementation. The first looks at the practical tasks that must be completed – testing, conversion, documentation and training. The second is a consideration of the different implementation strategies that can be adopted – pilot implementation, parallel running and direct changeover.

263

7.2 PRACTICAL TASKS

Testing

During the programming stage each programmer or programming team will perform their own program testing to the specifications laid down by the designer. The completed programs are then passed to the designer for further testing. He will be anxious not only to examine the delivered programs but also to prove their interfaces with the rest of the system. Testing will be performed by both *desk checking* – comparing the program flowcharts with the original specifications – and by *running* the programs using *test data*.

Test data should be manually compiled and the results produced by the system compared with the appropriate clerical figures or the current computer system. So, for example, in a system designed to produce and print examination certificates, a sample of students' data should be taken and entered into the new computer system. The generated certificates can then be compared with their clerically produced counterparts and discrepancies investigated.

It is also important that the system correctly identifies errors and omissions and testing for these is especially critical. Common error tests include the input of:

– oversize and undersize data items;

– incorrect formats;

– out of range items;

– no data at all;

– invalid combinations;

– negative numbers.

Outputs also have to be validated, particularly those which are a little unusual, such as the nil Statement and the multi-page Invoice. Testing is a vital but time-consuming activity. It is inevitable that errors will be found. These may be due to incorrect programming, misunderstanding of specifications or simply omissions in the original design. The amendments required must be coded by the programmer, and the programs and system retested. This retesting is very important because the requested amendments may have caused unwanted side effects and so new errors and problems may appear. One of the most common sources of faults in programs is the fixing of other faults!

The best method of preventing errors is not to introduce them in the first place. The models introduced in this book and its companion text have aimed at reducing the chance of error in specification. Research has consistently demonstrated that it is cheaper to fix errors in the early stages of development rather than in the later ones. Both books in this series have tried to lay the foundations of good design. The modular structures derived through functional decomposition (see structure charts in Chapter 6) should reinforce these foundations by isolating errors and reducing their effect on the rest of the system. Time spent on proving the specification is time well spent, particularly if the specification can be automatically turned into a program.

It is also at the system testing stage that the *timing* aspects of the system become clearer. Required response times (a maximum of ten seconds for retrieval of patient data), processing times (all employee records updated in two hours) and output schedules (all examination certificates produced in one week) must all be checked. Problems that are due to inefficient programming or misspecified files may be tackled by the designer. This may mean a return to the third level model for file re-structuring, or the use of faster programming languages in certain modules. Problems due to hardware not achieving its claimed specification must be taken up with the supplier. Modules which have particular timing constraints are candidates for early development and testing in the incremental approach advocated in Chapter 6.

A modular approach also permits progressive testing. The following steps are recommended (adapted from Keen, 1981):

- *Module Testing.* Validating the internal code of a module:

  - Desk Check: a manual 'walkthrough' of the program prior to compilation, checking code against specification statements.

  - Compile: a clean compilation is required.

  - Test data: once the module is known to work then it must be checked to see if it works as specified.

  - Linking: testing the interfaces between tested modules.

- *Suite Testing.* Validating the operations of a suite of interconnected modules. This seeks to test that a logical sub-system is working correctly and that data is passed properly between the modules in this sub-system. Candidate sub-systems should be derived from the structure chart. The afferent and efferent modules are two obvious candidates for suite testing.

- *System Testing*. This is designed to ensure that the sub-systems work properly together. Such testing should pass through the following phases:

  • Single run: testing the system over a single pass of test data.

  • Cyclic Tests: testing the system over several cycles of processing. This is to ensure that it correctly deals with end-of-day, end-of-month and end-of-year routines.

  • Volume Tests: up to this point the minimum set of test data has been used. This must now be extended to examine how the system copes with agreed volumes and possible overloads.

  • Clerical Tests: testing all aspects of the interface between the user and the system.

System testing is a time-consuming activity. Keen has suggested that it could 'well consume one half of the project's total expenditure' (Keen, 1981). The use of automated aids to assist the production of test data (eg from a data dictionary) and for detecting program errors is obviously very helpful. If automation extends to program development then a rigorous method of constructing specifications should ensure bug-free programs. However, current hand-crafted experience dictates otherwise. Errors often seem to come from surprising areas, particularly when the development software is being pushed to its limits. One of the authors of this book has been part of a team developing a software product that has been held up by errors in the proprietary 4GL and in the proprietary operating system!

Whatever the circumstances, however, it must be recognised that testing represents the last opportunity for preparing the system modules before their exposure to users and the harshness of the real world. From now on any errors or idiosyncracies will become public knowledge.

File Conversion

Most systems require an established set of files if they are to be immediately operational. Thus an Order Entry system will need such files as customer data, outstanding orders, products, etc. This may demand a large file conversion task (when moving from one computer system to another) or a large, one-off data entry when systems are being computerised for the first time. This conversion leads to both programming and management tasks.

If the files are currently held on a computer system then it should be possible to move the data from the present implementation to the target hardware and software. There are many companies that offer this service although both cost and compatibility should be thoroughly investigated. It may also be necessary to write certain routines, such as stripping off control characters, to modify the data format after conversion.

Data entry programs will also have to be written for data that is to be collected for the first time. The designer may be able to use the data input routines of the proposed system for entering current information into the computer. However, it is more likely that a certain amount of historical data will also be required and this facility will not be available in the normal input routine. A simple example will illustrate this. A system for maintaining Mail Order customers required the recording of the Date of Last Order. This was not entered on the input screen as it could be picked up automatically from the Operating System. Consequently, the proposed input screen could not be used for entering established customers as their Date of Last Order could have been any time within the last decade. A special file creation program had to be written to capture Date of Last Order together with other historical data required by the system.

In general, the designer will have to develop a suite of file creation programs. These will have to be specified, written and tested with the same care as those produced for the proposed operational system. It is likely that a certain amount of re-routeing of input data will also be required. For example, the user may be asked for customer details which are then used to create two or three complete or partial files. Validation and verification are vital in file creation programs. It is the stage when the users begin to lose their established filing methods for something that is less tangible. Errors are pounced upon and confidence may quickly ebb away.

The task of *organising* the creation of files must also be approached with meticulous detail. Entering 50,000 customer records is a daunting, not to say boring, task. The clerical resources of the department may not be sufficient or willing to undertake such activities on top of their daily work. The employment of temporary staff or the use of computer bureau facilities must be considered. It may be possible to phase the file creation by entering established records over a period of time, in parallel with the running of the operational system. This requires a certain discipline to ensure that the completion of data entry does not stretch too far into the future and, in addition, it has the disadvantage of the system operating for some considerable time with incomplete files.

In summary, file conversion creates important technical and operational requirements which have to be planned for by the designer. Poor planning may lead to delayed or erroneous file creation.

Preparation of Documentation

Documentation is a constant task in system development. The analysis and design methods introduced in this book and its companion text have produced documentation which has been useful in both understanding and communicating the problem area. In this way the documentation provides *prompts* for action not just a *record* of actions (see Chapter 4 of *Introducing Systems Analysis*).

The methods introduced so far have permitted the documentation of three views of the system under consideration:

- The current physical system: typically modelled with system flowcharts, decision tables, etc. (See Chapters 4 and 5 of *Introducing Systems Analysis*.)

- The logical system: modelled with data flow diagrams and entity-relationship models. Checked out with entity life histories. (See Chapters 6, 7 and 8 of *Introducing Systems Analysis*.)

- The planned logical and physical system: this has been the major concern of this book. Where necessary the logical models have been supplemented with detailed techniques such as structure charts and action diagrams.

All of these views of the system are underpinned by a data dictionary (see Chapter 8 of *Introducing Systems Analysis*). Furthermore, the business justification of the development of the system is well documented in the Strategic Plan and the resultant Feasibility Study (see Chapters 2 and 3 of *Introducing Systems Analysis*).

The latter stages of a project give the opportunity to tidy up this system documentation and to ensure that it actually does reflect the proposed physical system.

Implementation Documentation

Three further types of documentation are associated with the implementation itself.

Training Documentation. Training documentation is likely to be concerned with two principal tasks:

i) Easing the transition from the current system to its successor. Many of the users of the proposed system can better understand its function when it is explained in the *context* of current procedures. This before and after approach provides a commonly understood reference point which should help the confidence of apprehensive users.

ii) Providing detailed tuition in the operations of the proposed system. There is a tendency to believe that the functions of the system can be learnt from large technical User Manuals. This is very unlikely. Most of these manuals are too long, present all information at the same level of detail, and *describe* operations rather than *explain* them. It is very unlikely that the user will have either the time or the motivation to work systematically through such a manual. Even if they did, it is uncertain whether they could successfully place the information in the context of their own application and hence separate the important from the trivial. These large manuals fail to recognise the distinction between *learning* and *reference*.

Documentation for learning will typically set objectives, explain concepts and commands relevant to those objectives and then test the mastery of those commands to examine whether the objectives have been achieved. Such documentation may use conventional media and methods – handouts, lectures, tests – in the traditional setting of a training course. Alternatively, Computer Based Tuition (CBT) may be considered, particularly where the users are spread geographically and cannot be spared from their everyday tasks. Certainly CBT has particular relevance in computer training as the medium of training is also the objective of that training. The Barclaycard training initiative (Dean and Whitlock, 1983) demonstrates a 'piggybacking' approach where trainees use identical terminals to those they will use in their daily work, while a simulation using dummy data permits them to practise precisely the operations that they will carry out when using the real system.

User Documentation. The point has already been made that user manuals should be reference rather than learning documents. Such manuals will need to reflect the expertise and vocabulary of the variety of users involved in the system, and it is preferable to write a series of documents aimed at different *types* of user rather than to produce one all-encompassing manual whose weight ensures that it will never be used. Manuals should concentrate on the issues that concern users the most – *functions* (how to do something, eg create a customer, delete a product type) and *errors*. It is particularly important to include some basic information on how to get started. Some problems are caused by being unable to start the machine or enter the software.

These manuals will be the user's main point of reference when the system is operational and so possible problems should be anticipated and documented. This can save unwanted time-consuming phone calls after the system has been implemented. Procedures for calling support (who should I phone in your department?) and requesting system amendments and enhancements should also be documented.

Operations Documentation. The operations section of the Data Processing department will be responsible for the day-to-day running of the system. They will need to know the normal operating procedures and how to respond to errors. Much of this information will be derived from the detailed design and program documentation. The typical contents of Operations Documentation is listed below:

Identity of programs and their execution sequence for each program:

Input required and format

Files required

Processing logic

Output produced

Error conditions, messages and response

Machine components used

Set up requirements

Distribution and processing of output

Maintenance programmer responsible for the system

User responsible for input

Normal cut-off date for input

Normal run cycle

(Adapted from Lucas, 1981)

These operational details are obviously very important. The system may produce the payslips successfully, but someone must have responsibility for loading the paper at a certain time, readying the printer and collating and distributing the output in accordance with a defined timetable. Operators need documentation and training.

Training

Elements of the training task have been considered in the previous section. Training will cover the retraining of current staff and the recruitment of new personnel. The latter will involve job specifications, advertising, salary advice and interviewing. Retraining will require planning and co-ordination.

For training to be effective, it must be clear *what it is trying to achieve*. This may be clarified through the setting of objectives. Parkin (1988) distinguishes between three levels of objective. The first type demands the recall of facts – thus objectives are defined in terms of specific facts that have to be recalled.

'given any department name, the trainee should be able to recall the department code, and vice versa.'

Comprehension is a different type of objective. In this instance the trainee should be able to 'both recall the facts and describe or illustrate them using words, actions or examples which are different from those the instructor used.' Parkin provides an example of this. The objective should not be to 'understand the Highway Code' but a series of objectives which might include:

'To be able to give his or her own examples of where a driver should not overtake.'

Finally, objectives might be defined in terms of application, where the trainee has to use his or her knowledge in different situations of the same general type. Such an objective should not be to 'appreciate the company's rules for giving credit' but rather:

'Given the customer's time and cash credit limit, and aged account balances, to decide whether or not to satisfy a request for a stated further amount of credit.'

(All examples – Parkin 1988)

In practice, the objectives of the training course are likely to be a mixture of recall, comprehension and application.

The setting of objectives for training will suggest ways of delivering that training, eg lectures, tutorials, case studies, simulations, practice, reading and computer-based material are all candidate methods. The objectives might suggest a combination of media, an approach well demonstrated by the Open University who combine video, audio, tutorial texts, conventional books, case studies, practicals and lectures in the delivery of its courses. Indeed, an appreciation of the different types of objective will suggest a mixed-media approach as conventional text is unlikely to satisfy all the application objectives. The agreed methods of delivery determine the training documentation that is required. In some circumstances it will be a handout, in other instances an on-line tutorial.

Once the material has been delivered, then the attainment of the trainee and the effectiveness of the training methods used must be assessed. The evaluation of the trainee might be through an end of course test, a subjective assessment, a statistical report from the authoring language used to produce the CBT material, or some combination of all three. Similarly, the effectiveness of the trainer and the training materials should be assessed (perhaps through end of course questionnaires) and appropriate action taken.

Unfortunately too much training is poorly planned and presented at the wrong level, failing to take the expertise and expectations of staff into consideration. To compound this, management are often reluctant to give training sessions the time or resources they require. This often manifests itself in under-funding training or not releasing staff for sufficient time from their daily duties. As a result, many systems are implemented with users and operators who do not fully understand their tasks and roles. This greatly reduces the chance of a successful implementation.

It should be clear that the tasks of implementation – system testing, file conversion, documentation and training – all require careful planning and co-ordination. Certain tasks must not be left too late (rushed user manuals are usually unimpressive), done too early (operator training months before the system will go live) or in the wrong sequence. Implementation is a *project* in its own right and will benefit from controls that are applicable to any project (see Keen, 1981). There is sometimes a tendency to relax during implementation believing that all the hard work is done. This is false confidence; lack of control and planning in implementation can undo months of good system and programming work.

7.3 IMPLEMENTATION STRATEGIES

The changeover from the old to the new system can be arranged once the computer system is tested and approved. Three possible strategies are available.

Parallel Running

In this method, the old and new systems are run simultaneously for an agreed period of time and results from the two systems are compared. Once the user has complete confidence in the system the old system is abandoned and transactions are only passed through the new one. Parallel running places a large administrative overhead on the user department because every transaction has effectively to be done twice – once through the established procedures and then again through the new computer system. Results have to be cross-checked and the source of errors located. This will lead to system modifications if problems are discovered in the computer system.

This method does have the advantage of having a 'fail-safe' system to fall back on should the new system crash for some reason. System problems can then be sorted out and the parallel run resumed. However, the duplication of effort can be something of a mixed blessing. Many operators and users still tend to rely on the established system and so some problems never appear until this has been abandoned. In addition, it may be difficult to justify a parallel run for the whole cycle of processing. Problems may only appear at, say, the end of the financial year, months after the 'fail-safe' manual system has been phased out.

In summary, it could be claimed that parallel running is perhaps the safest, costliest and most time-consuming way of implementing a system.

Pilot Implementation

Two different possibilities exist. The first may be seen as a sort of retrospective parallel running. This takes historical data, say the last three months' invoices, and the output produced is compared with the known results. This is, in effect, a large set of test data, and although this is not a bad thing in itself it does not really give the users and operators the experience and urgency of live processing.

The second type of pilot implementation does use live operations. Instead of *all* the transactions being passed through the new system, as in parallel running, only a limited number are entered into the computer system. This may be on a sample basis (say one in every ten) if this still facilitates cross-checking or, perhaps more realistically, by entering only certain sections, departments or accounts. This gives practice in live processing and reduces the overheads of duplicated entry. It is less rigorous in its testing than parallel running because only a limited set of transactions are used. However, experience suggests that the type of transaction which causes the system to crash is to be found in one of the other nine or in another department; a fact that is only found out when the existing system is abandoned and full live running commences.

Direct Changeover

The final strategy is to implement the new system completely and withdraw the old without any sort of parallel running at all. Thus processing of the current system may end on a Friday night and all transactions pass through the new computer system from Monday morning onwards. There is no 'fail-safe' system at all. Direct change-over has none of the cost and time overheads of the previous two methods. Neither does it permit the old loyalty to the replaced system to be reflected in the relative performance of the two systems. It clearly demands very thorough testing and well-planned file creation and training strategies. All operations of the system must be understood at the moment of going live because the opportunity for gradual training and further testing does not exist. Thus direct changeover is the quickest and most complete of the three implementation strategies but it is probably the riskiest.

In certain instances there is no real alternative to this method. These tend to be:

- where there is little similarity between the old and the replacement system so that cross-checking is not possible;

- where the cost of parallel running is so prohibitive that it is cheaper to pay for the mistakes of a direct changeover.

Where possible, direct changeovers should occur in slack periods and take advantage of natural breaks in the operations of the organisation, such as industrial holidays.

7.4 POST-IMPLEMENTATION REVIEW

The final delivery of a system provides the opportunity to review the whole conduct of the project. Achievements, failures, surprises and assessments all provide experience which can be used to improve the development of future projects. Thus the review is not only concerned with user satisfaction (and tuning the system to improve that satisfaction), but also with the way that the whole project was conducted.

The criteria for the success of the project were established in the Strategic Plan (see *Introducing Systems Analysis* – Chapter 2) and the performance of the system must now be regularly monitored against these criteria. It was the business objectives set out in that document which provided the justification for the technical activity that has been the focus of the two texts. We must ensure that our technical achievements are successfully contributing to those objectives. If they are not, then our technical expertise is devalued, if not wasted.

7.5 SUMMARY

This chapter has considered the final stages of systems development. It has:

- recognised the significance of testing and the need to approach it in a rigorous manner, progressing from module to system testing;

- reinforced the point that rigorous specification techniques are required to reduce errors;

- identified the problem of converting files from the current to the proposed system, particularly where there is a large amount of 'one-off' data input;

- restated the role of documentation in the project and the need to carefully plan the content and bulk of user documentation;

- recognised the need for carefully executed training which is properly established and evaluated;

- introduced three strategies for implementing the new system.

Above all, implementation needs care and attention to detail. Sloppiness and cutting corners at this stage can devalue months of hard work.

7.6 EXERCISES

The following questions refer to the case study introduced in Chapter 1.

1 Develop a plan for the testing of the proposed library system.

2 List the documentation that will be provided with the proposed system.

3 Draw up a training schedule and budget for the employees that will use the new system.

4 What implementation strategy will be used and why?

The following question does not refer to the case study.

5 Assess the documentation provided by an application software package or operating system with which you are familiar. How would you wish to change it and why?

8 Reflections

Contemporary systems analysis and design is being radically affected by four important trends:

i) The increased formalism of system development methods introduced by the structured systems revolution and discernable in most proprietary methodologies (such as SSADM, YOURDON, STRADIS, MODUS, etc). This formalism is based on the introduction of logical modelling into the development life cycle. Typical models include data flow diagrams, entity models, entity life histories, and structure charts. This has been recognised in the texts by the explicit and detailed introduction of a selection of these tools and techniques.

ii) A counter-reaction to this formalism from the proponents of prototyping, who advocate an incremental approach to information system development. The principles of prototyping were introduced in the first chapter of *Introducing Systems Analysis* and examples have been given, where relevant, for each task in the development cycle. A formal mechanism for controlling prototyping, the structure chart, was introduced in Chapter 6 of this book.

iii) The emergence of powerful system development languages that threaten to replace conventional programming languages such as COBOL and PL/1. These fourth generation products vary considerably in their power, price and functionality.

iv) The development of powerful CASE (Computer Aided Software Engineering) tools that look likely to change the working patterns and norms of systems developers. Candidates for automation have been identified in the system development tasks as the texts have progressed.

In many respects these four trends are interrelated and it is useful to provide a more detailed review of the progress of formalism, automation and prototyping.

8.1 PROTOTYPING

The principle of prototyping was introduced in the first chapter of *Introducing Systems Analysis*. Prototyping stresses the early delivery of a working system that can be used to refine user requirements and system characteristics.

> 'Prototyping addresses the inability of many users to specify their information needs, and the difficulty of systems analysts to understand the user's environment, by providing the user with a tentative system for experimental purposes at the earliest possible time. The user's experiences with this experimental system indicate modifications to incorporate into the prototype, leading to a new series of user experimentation.' (Janson and Smith, 1985.)

Hence, the prototype is successively refined in a series of iterations until it eventually becomes an acceptable reflection of the user's requirements.

The possible role of prototypes has been threaded throughout the two texts with relevant examples given in the context of the task under consideration.

Prototyping – Advantages

Alavi (1984) suggested the following advantages:

1 The prototype is real. It provides the user with a tangible means of comprehending and evaluating the real system and giving useful and meaningful feedback.

2 It gives a common base line or point of reference for both users and designers. It is an effective way of sharing a 'model' of the system.

3 Users are enthusiastic. They perceive that something is being done and that their comments influence the final design.

4 Prototyping helps the correct definition of requirements. It should ensure that the nucleus of the system is correct before committing development resources to the whole system.

5 Prototypes establish better working relationships between designers and users.

Prototyping – Disadvantages

1 Prototypes can be oversold; the limited functionality and rough interfaces of the prototype can be disappointing to some users. There is almost a culture of 'trying to crash the system' by inserting spurious dates, names and operations. The likelihood of crashing is much greater in a prototype built to display functionality rather than robustness.

2 Prototypes are difficult to manage and control. Traditional life cycle methodologies have specific milestones and deliverables which are absent from an approach which stresses an evolving system.

One of the undoubted attractions of prototyping to the developer is that it gives the feeling of 'getting on with the job', rather than creating abstract models on paper. Many are impatient to begin the 'real task' of 'code cutting'. Consequently, there is a danger that prototyping will become a euphemism for maverick development and under-preparation. A poor fit between software and application can too easily be shrugged off as 'it's only a prototype', when in fact it is a reflection of poor analysis and design.

If prototyping is to be successful it needs to be controlled. The use of the structure chart to plan the content and progression of the prototype (see Chapter 6) is recommended. In this way the designer can allocate sensible priorities to successive module development, whilst at the same time retaining a perspective of the whole task. Similarly, the client or user can share this perceived scope of the prototype and hence is aware of the functionality of the successive deliveries of the software.

3 It is difficult to prototype large information systems.

'It is not clear how a large system should be divided for the purpose of prototyping or how aspects of the system to be prototyped are identified and boundaries set.' (Alavi, 1984.)

4 It is often difficult to maintain user enthusiasm. Prototypes may satisfy user requirements but not those of the information system developers. The prototype may have temporary file structures, simulated program modules and poor coupling and cohesion. Objectives of good design must dictate that developers resist pressure to move onto new projects before cleaning up the old ones.

If prototyping is to be successful then it is essential that the prototype is created quickly.

'Common to most prototypes is the requirement that they should be constructed quickly to give timely feedback into the development life cycle'. (Alexander and Potter, 1987.)

Four general 'types' of prototype tools were suggested:

- Application packages

- Program generators

- Re-usable code

- Fourth Generation Languages (4GLs)

However, it is becoming increasingly clear that not all 4GLs adequately support prototyping. The product philosophy of some packages is concentrated upon the overall definition of the system and is therefore at pains to capture the detail of this development. This is usually reflected in completeness checks of the application (so important in detailed system development) that cannot be overruled (file not found, variable not yet defined, exceptions not specified, variable type mismatches). This effectively prevents a partial definition of the system. The strength of such software – ensuring comprehensive specification – is at the same time its weakness. It cannot distinguish between omissions which are designed to support a prototype and unplanned errors caused by an incomplete specification.

It is also clear that many 4GLs have performance problems (see for example, Prizzant, 1986).

'Unfortunately, 4GLs and prototyping packages have been over-sold. Even worse, they were sometimes presented as tools that rendered structured analysis obsolete.' (Yourdon, 1986.)

Thus if a 4GL is being selected for prototyping applications then it is important that such features are evaluated in the selection of the product. It should not be assumed that all 4GLs are suitable for prototyping or are applicable in all circumstances.

Fourth generation products also influence two other major trends identified in the introduction to this chapter. The increased formalism of analysis and design has meant that the first stages of the life cycle are likely to be lengthened and hence increase the overall time for the delivery of systems. However, this can be reduced if the development part of the cycle can be shortened by using a 4GL product. Consequently, the overall project time may be maintained (or indeed reduced), but the emphasis of the cycle will have altered. More effort will be placed in the definition stages where research shows mistakes to be at their costliest.

Secondly, the desire of software vendors to produce an all-encompassing product has meant that many are now supplying 'front-end' CASE facilities to their software. So, for example, logical definition tools – such as data flow diagrams and entity models – are provided in the package to guide the definition of program and database structures. This should reinforce the completeness of the definition but possibly at the cost of being able to construct incomplete prototypes that are not supported by the data dictionary definition.

Prototyping – Summary

The emergence of 4GLs has provided opportunities for the incremental development of systems using a prototype approach. However, not all 4GLs are good prototyping tools as some aim for completeness of system development in a way that precludes the generation of partly-specified systems. Furthermore, controversy about machine performance (an issue we do not wish to discuss here) and a lack of skills and standardisation has held back their acceptance by the data processing community.

The process of incremental development must be controlled if it is to be successful. Vague definitions of a 'prototype system' invariably lead to misunderstandings and disappointment. Clients and designers both need to be aware of the order of module development and the scope of successive prototypes. The structure chart is an excellent medium for defining and communicating the progressive implementation of the system.

8.2   AUTOMATED SYSTEMS DEVELOPMENT

This book and its companion text, *Introducing Systems Analysis*, have stressed the need for logical information systems models which are independent of organisational arrangements and hardware and software implementation. However, the adoption of such logical models extends the development life cycle. This increase in the number of activities has meant that the automation of some of these tasks is essential, otherwise the long development times associated with the conventional life cycle become even greater. Ed Yourdon has identified this perception of increased duration as one of the reasons for not adopting structured techniques (Yourdon, 1986).

There are clear candidates for automation. Nick Jones (1988) in his account of the development of the LBMS tool Automate+ identifies the following areas:

i)   Logical data modelling. Data flow diagrams, entity relationship models and entity life histories are the three major models used to present a logical view of the information systems of the enterprise. These three models are pictorial, and interrelated through the details maintained in a common data dictionary.

ii) Relational data analysis. Data analysis derives a set of Third Normal Form tables that satisfy certain automatable criteria.

iii) Physical design. This technique takes logical models produced by (i) or (ii) and generates a physical database design which is typically represented as a text file for input to a DBMS schema compiler. It may also be feasible to simulate the performance of the database design and hence try different data designs and perhaps even different products in the search for adequate response and processing times.

Current automated tools are primarily concerned with:

i)   The diagramming of common models – data flow diagrams, entity-relationship models, entity life histories. The interactive development and editing of such models can save a considerable amount of time.

ii) The verification of these models against the contents of the data dictionary. For example, a certain data item may be contained in an output from a process and did not enter this process either from an incoming data flow or from a store, nor was it produced by the activity of the process itself.

iii) The validation of models against each other, so highlighting inconsistencies between different views of the data. For example, is a create activity shown on an entity life history – but not on the relevant data flow diagram?

Automated tools (like the term 4GL) seems to cover a wide range of software facilities – from diagram editors to fully integrated support environments (IPSE). Part of this width of definition is confused by the parentage of the product. IPSE tends to be the term used by software engineers, searching for a program support facility – while CASE tools is the preferred term of many information systems professionals – looking for a project support environment. Furthermore, CASE appears to be a term preferred by American commentators while IPSE is favoured by UK and European practitioners. A useful division has been suggested by Slusky (1987) who distinguishes between three levels of CASE or IPSE.

CASE 1 tools are orientated towards logical modelling. They primarily provide graphical facilities for model manipulation together with the validation of these models using a shared data dictionary. 'The methodological foundation for these products was constructed in numerous theoretical works on structured systems analysis and design and on models implementing this foundation, such as data flow diagrams, structured analysis models, logical data models, entity-relationship models, structure charts, etc.' Slusky identifies Excelerator and Stradis/Draw as two typical CASE 1 tools.

CASE 2 tools are primarily aimed at prototyping. These produce executable code from the specified logical models. They may be more restricted in the supported set of logical models than the CASE 1 products, preferring to adopt one modelling method to drive database and program definition. ORACLE, MicroFOCUS and MANTIS are given by Slusky as typical CASE 2 tools.

CASE 3 products encompass CASE 1 and CASE 2 tools but also introduce project management facilities for planning, control and execution of the project. Most of these products are only just coming to the marketplace. Examples might include the Information Engineering Facility (IEF), Maestro and Teamwork.

In some respects the IPSE/CASE division is a temporary one and reflects divisions in backgrounds and perceptions. CASE tools are coming from an information systems perspective and are often produced in terms of particular information systems methodologies. In contrast, IPSEs have their background in software engineering problems and are largely orientated to that. Consequently they tend to be less product or methodology specific.

The next generation of IPSE (CASE 3 tools) is likely to support both software and information engineering problems and so integrate all the activities of information systems development.

Figure 8.1 taken from Slusky summarises the facilities that might be expected from CASE/IPSE tools.

The Effect of Automation

What will be the likely effect of the trend of automation on the development life cycle and the activities of analysts and designers? John Windsor (1986) has suggested the following changes in information systems development because of the CASE/IPSE revolution.

i) CASE will provide the structure of the task. The input requirements of the software will demand the required level of problem definition and functional analysis. If the definition is incomplete, then development cannot continue.

   Documentation standards play a similar role in manual development but are often foiled by the sheer complexity and diversity of the task. 'Flexible' humans permit incomplete definition on the grounds of project deadlines.

ii) CASE will permit the proper consideration of alternative designs. Currently, an Analyst only has time to pursue one basic design. Most other possibilities are discounted at an early stage because time and cost does not allow their proper evaluation. CASE tools permit the exploration of different boundaries, technologies and requirements by stimulating the effect of these parameters.

   'Through the use of the ability to quickly and easily investigate alternatives the analyst becomes capable of generating a 'best' system, a system that will most closely meet the needs of the client.' (Windsor, 1986.)

CASE facilities	CASE categories		
	Development		Integrated
	Modelling	Prototyping	control
	CASE I	CASE II	CASE III
Primary facilities			
Graphics	Yes		Yes
Data dictionary			
Environment entities	Yes	Yes	Yes
Application entities	Yes	Yes	Yes
Documentation			
Document graph	Yes		Yes
Word processing	Yes		Yes
Analysis			
Graphics analysis	Yes		Yes
Entities analysis	Yes	Yes	Yes
User input/output prototype			
Screen design	Yes	Yes	Yes
Data entry execution		Yes	Yes
Report design	Yes	Yes	Yes
Report execution		Yes	Yes
Data manipulation prototype			
Program generation		Yes	Yes
Program execution		Yes	Yes
Syntax conversion		Yes	Yes
Database prototype			
Database generation		Yes	Yes
Database query/update		Yes	Yes
System project management			
Project planning			Yes
Project execution			Yes
Project control			Yes
Auxiliary facilities			
Migration (export/import)			
Dictionary migration	Yes	Yes	Yes
Program migration		Yes	Yes
Database migration		Yes	Yes
Help maintenance	Yes	Yes	Yes
Custom modifications customisation for new methods and standards	Yes		Yes
Housekeeping			
Backup/restore		Yes	Yes
CASE set-up/monitoring		Yes	Yes

Source: Slusky, 1988

Figure 8.1   Summary of CASE/IPSE Tools Facilities

iii) Error handling, audit and security – usually addressed at the end of the development cycle – can be tackled much earlier in the project. Consequently, such factors become much more an integral part of design rather than being tacked onto the end of a project.

iv) Delivered systems should be much more comprehensive and accurate. They should have a longer survival time because of the rigour of the development process.

v) The use of code generators should significantly speed up the coding part of the development life cycle.

vi) The CASE software imposes and maintains documentation standards. This should considerably ease the maintenance burden.

However, Windsor also feels that the major advantages of automated development tools are also potential weaknesses. For example:

i) Standards may become too inflexible. The standard is driven by the tool rather than the needs of the organisation.

ii) There are no rules to tell you when to stop investigating alternative systems.

iii) Code generators may produce verbose programs which are slow to run and difficult to interface with other parts of the system.

Automation – Summary

Thus CASE/IPSE tools are likely to have profound effects on the future delivery of information systems. In the first instance they will make the structured techniques, and their associated logical models, much more accessible. One of the factors that has undoubtedly held back the spread of these methods has been the time taken to use them manually.

Secondly, the use of the definition tools to automatically produce code will change the balance of the development life cycle as well as improving the reliability and functional correctness of the source programs. Time spent 'hand crafting' programs and systems will be reduced. At this point the CASE tool meets the 4GL – either as an integrated 'front-end' or as a complementary tool that can pass the required information in an acceptable format.

However, there is a tendency to be seduced by automation. The business context of computerisation must not be forgotten in the construction of increasingly elaborate models that are internally consistent but of little significance to the enterprise. Furthermore, the Analyst must avoid retreating into an abstract world that ignores the 'messy' nature of reality and the idiosyncracies of users, operators and managers. The interpersonal skills of analysis and design will still be required. Any attempt to turn information systems development into a set of interrelated technical activities misses essential points and is doomed to failure. A detail which we take up in the next section.

8.3   RESTATEMENT OF PHILOSOPHY

The two texts have shared a common philosophy in their refusal to embrace any proprietary methodology and in their pursuit of a 'top-down' approach to systems development (see *Foreword*). It now seems appropriate to revisit, extend and further justify this stance.

Methodology

Peter Checkland's need to attach an appropriate designation to his 'soft systems' work (Checkland, 1981) causes him to reflect upon the meaning of such terms as methodology, technique and philosophy. He identifies three current conceptions of methodology (from Kotarbinski, 1965), of which the praxiological 'the science of ... ways of expert procedures' is the one most appropriate to the methodologies offered in the commercial systems development marketplace. These methodologies are essentially offering an expert way of doing things.

We decided not to adopt a proprietary methodology for four main reasons:

1 None of the methodologies are demonstrably applicable in all development circumstances. They tend to be more relevant to large organisations with significant computer resources undertaking complex projects. Research has shown that smaller organisations face significant system development problems which need tackling in a systematic way (Wroe, 1987).

2 Most methodologies tend to over-technicalise analysis by presenting it as a series of increasingly complex models, where the skill of manipulating the model can quickly dwarf the 'real-life' application. There can be a tendency, in education, to flex the case study

or application to suit the model, rather than the other way around. This is dangerous – the proof of the pudding should be in the eating.

Kimmerly (1984) accuses many Analysts of having restricted vision. He recognises the:

'failure of both practising systems analysts and computer science academicians to stress adequately the importance of aesthetics, imagery and other precursors of creativity in the methodology of the discipline.'

'Due in part to the legacy of various 'structured revolutions', creativity has not only been comprehensively de-emphasised, but has come to be regarded as something to be avoided altogether.'

3 Most methodologies do not appear to significantly recognise the 'organisational context' of the application, or indeed the personal skills of the individual Analyst. This issue is examined in greater detail below.

4 The absence of acceptable metrics and a seeming reluctance to undertake empirical research means that there is little quantitative evidence to support efficiency claims. Journals carry many articles describing different analysis and design techniques – but are less blessed with papers about their quantifiable, or even subjective, success.

Consequently, we feel that the wholesale adoption of a proprietary methodology is not appropriate for general introductory analysis and design training. Proprietary courses are essentially a 'second step' after the developer has mastered basic skills and techniques and is in a better position to appreciate and evaluate the presented methodology.

Hence, our preferred approach has been to select techniques from certain proprietary methodologies where they suit the purpose at hand. A technique (again borrowing from Checkland) is a specific programme of action that can be practised and learnt, and repeatedly executed with a fair chance of success. Some of the techniques we have introduced (such as decision tables) are more precise (in a learning context) than others (such as structure charts), but we should expect this. Some techniques (such as serving a fast swerving tennis ball) defy repeated success, while others always guarantee the correct result.

The technique approach can be used as:

i) A grounding in techniques before examining their detailed use in the context of a proprietary methodology.

ii) A basis for a 'toolkit' approach to analysis and design that gives the practitioner a set of tools which can be selected to suit different circumstances. This is not dissimilar to the craftsman choosing appropriate tools to undertake different tasks and circumstances.

The toolkit approach seeks to recognise the variety and richness of all real-world applications. This variety manifests itself along three related axes (see Figure 8.2):

– *Technical*. This concerns itself with the technical skills of the developer and with his or her technological knowledge. The mastery of techniques lies along this axis. So do other learning and training skills (network management, COBOL programming, hardware maintenance).

– *Organisational*. The technical solution will be affected (at least) by the size and structure of the organisation, its products, services and geographical distribution, the personalities and skills of the managers concerned and the organisational norms of status, control and reward. Deciding the *appropriate* technology is not an easy matter. There are plenty of examples where information systems failure has been caused by the selection of a too complex solution, and still others where lack of ambition has led to the under-use of technology. The analyst must be sensitive to the organisational context of his work, understanding that different skills and solutions will be required in what may, at first technical sight, appear to be familiar territory. The great variety of organisational contexts makes us nervous about recommending a 'one best way' approach.

– *Human*. People model reality in a number of ways. It seems clear to us that individuals find certain techniques more appealing and comfortable to use. They come to perfectly acceptable solutions by concentrating upon a particular perspective. This is probably most marked in the distinction between the static (entity relationship model) and dynamic (data flow model) of the organisation. Some practitioners are more at home with the former and use it to drive their analysis work, while others prefer to concentrate upon the

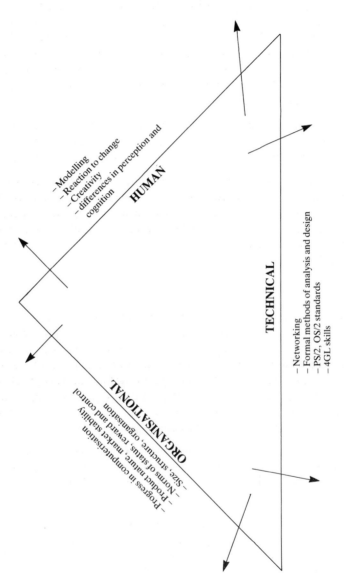

Figure 8.2   Axes of Variety

latter. What we must avoid is dogma, typified in a recent prescription by a practitioner that 'entity modelling must come first'. The answer to this is that it *depends*, both upon the modelling perception of the analyst and on the organisational application. We are not saying that analysts should exclude techniques from their toolkit (after all, they never know when they will need them), but that they should recognise and exploit their own modelling preferences and abilities.

The toolkit approach stresses sensitivity to the organisational and human issues that confront an analyst. It recognises that a heavy methodological hammer is not needed to crack every project nut.

'Of course, systems have been built using single strategies or even no formal one ... However, there are several arguments that strongly suggest that the quality of applications and the application development process is highest when methods representing several strategies are used together in a balanced way.' (Zimmerman, 1983.)

Top-down Approach

In general, a 'top-down' approach to system development is preferred. This is a reflection of the belief that systems should be developed in the context of the business requirements and that this can best be achieved by building systems downwards from an understanding of the enterprise's strategic requirements. Information systems must support critical business areas. The practice of computerising 'obvious' applications, such as payroll and accounting ledgers has often led to a fragmented computer strategy that does not use resourses effectively.

The point is put succinctly by Ian Macdonald (1988) when he suggests that the key concept of the future is non-procedurality, concentrating on *what* you want to have done, rather than the *detail* of how this is to be achieved.

'This is a vitally important feature because it places all of the stress in systems development on being able to describe what the business is about. Methodologies must therefore focus on business modelling.'

The strategic role of information systems is gaining increasing popularity and this has been reflected in *Introducing Systems Analysis*.

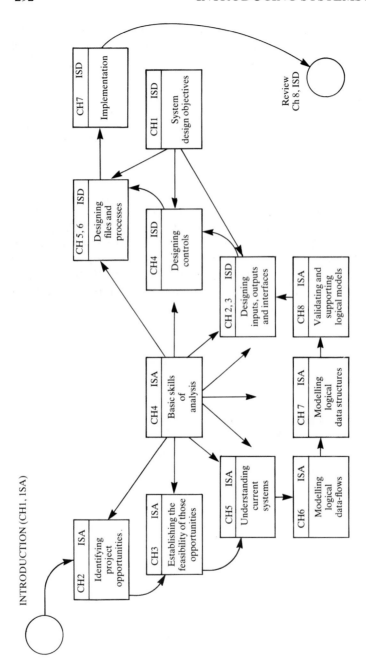

Figure 8.3   A Simple Model of the Progression of Analysis and Design Through the Two Texts

Furthermore, in a recent survey (Brancheau and Wetherbe, 1987) strategic planning was identified as the most critical issue facing information systems professionals over the next three to five years. They comment that:

'Strategic planning has long been a difficult and important issue . . . It has perennially ranked first in studies of this kind.'

In fact, it was also found to be the most important issue in their previous survey commissioned in 1983.

Finally . . .

Systems development has now been considered from strategic planning (Chapter 2 of *Introducing Systems Analysis*) to implementation (Chapter 7 of *Introducing Systems Design*). This progression is summarised in Figure 8.3. The delivery of appropriate information systems remains a complex, challenging but ultimately rewarding task. We hope that we have provided a detailed and interesting introduction to this world, and the issues that are important in it.

Bibliography and References

CHAPTER 1

Adie C, *SAA and the Common User Access*, EXE, July 1988, pp 10–15

Aktas AZ, *Structured Analysis and Design of Information Systems*, Prentice-Hall, 1987

Gane C, Sarson T, *Structured Systems Analysis: Tools and Techniques*, McDonnell Douglas, 1985

Martin J, *Fourth Generation Languages*, vols 1 and 2, Savant Research Institute, 1984

Parkin A, *Systems Analysis*, 2nd edition, Edward Arnold, 1988

Schott F, Olson M, Designing usability in systems: driving for normalcy, *Datamation*, 15 May 1988, pp 68–76

Shackel B, Ergonomics in the design for usability, *Proceedings of the Second Conference of the British Computer Society Human Computer Interaction Specialist Group*, 23–26 September 1986, pp 44–64

Skidmore S, Wroe B, *Introducing Systems Analysis*, NCC Publications, 1988

CHAPTER 2

Abbott J, *Presentation of Computer I/O for People*, NCC Publications, 1983

Eason KD, Managing technological change. The process of introducing information technology, *Organisations, Cases, Issues, Concepts*, Paton R, et al, eds, Harper and Row, 1984

Parkin A, *Systems Analysis*, 2nd edition, Edward Arnold, 1988

Skidmore S, *Business Computing*, Edward Arnold, 1987

Wroe B, *Successful Computing in a Small Business*, NCC Publications, 1987

CHAPTER 3

Adie C, *SAA and the Common User Access*, EXE, July 1988, pp10–15

Cakir A, Hart D, Stewart H, *Visual Display Terminals: A Manual Covering Ergonomics, Workplace Design, Health and Safety, Task Organisation*, John Wiley, 1980

Coats RB, Vlaeminke I, *Man–Computer Interfaces, A Guide for Software Design and Implementation*, Blackwell, 1988

Downs E, Clare P, Coe P, *Structured Systems Analysis and Design Methodology*, Prentice-Hall, 1987

Gaines BR, Shaw MLG, *The Art of Computer Conversation*, Prentice-Hall, 1984

Gwei GM, Foxley E, A flexible synonym interface with application examples in CAL and help environments, *Computer Journal*, vol 30, no 6, 1987

Hebditch D, in: Shackel B, ed, *Man–Computer Communication*, vol 2, Infotech, 1979

Martin J, *Design of Man–Computer Dialogues*, Prentice-Hall, 1973

Mehlmann M, *When People Use Computers – An Approach to Developing an Interface*, Prentice-Hall, 1981

Schott F, Olson M, Designing usability in systems: driving for normalcy, *Datamation*, 15 May 1988, vol 34 (10)

Shackel B, Ergonomics in design for usability. Designing for usability, *Proceedings of the British Computer Society Second Annual Conference of the Human–Computer Interaction Group*, 23–26 September, 1986

SSADM Reference Manual Part 2, Version 3.1, March 1986, Central Computer and Telecommunications Agency

CHAPTER 4

Bourne C, Benyon J, *Data Protection: Perspectives on Information Privacy*, Leicester University, 1983

Chambers A, *Computer Auditing*, Pitman, 1986

Data Protection Registrar, *The Data Protection Act – 1984*, HMSO

Data Protection Registrar, *The Data Protection Act – Guidelines*, 1985 onwards

Douglas I, ed, *Audit and Control of Systems Software*, NCC Publications, 1984

Elbra RA, *Guide to the Data Protection Act*, NCC Publications, 1984

Martin J, *Security, Accuracy and Privacy in Computer Systems*, Prentice-Hall, 1973

Norman ARD, *Computer Insecurity*, Chapman and Hall, 1983

Peat, Marwick, *The Data Protection Act Handbook*, 1984

Thomas A, Douglas I, *Audit of Computer Systems*, NCC Publications, 1981

Warner M, Stone M, *The Data Bank Society*, Allen and Unwin, 1970

Wong KK, *Computer Security: Risk Analysis and Control*, NCC Publications, 1977

CHAPTER 5

Bradley J, *File and Data Base Techniques*, Holt-Saunders, 1982

Boehm B, *Software Engineering Economics* Prentice-Hall, 1982

Cunningham M, *File Structure and Design*, Chartwell-Bratt, 1985

Date CJ, *A Guide to DB2*, Addison Wesley, 1984

Date CJ, *An Introduction to Database Systems*, Addison Wesley, 1987

Grosshans D, *File Systems Design and Implementation*, Prentice-Hall, 1986

Hanson O, *Design of Computer Files*, Pitman, 1982

Howe DR, *Data Analysis For Data Base Design*, Edward Arnold, 1986

Lantz KE, *The Prototyping Methodology*, Prentice-Hall, 1986

Longworth, G, Nicholls D, *SSADM Manual*, NCC Publications, 1987

Martin J, *Diagramming Techniques for Analysts and Programmers*, Prentice-Hall, 1985

Mills GM, Skidmore S, Data modelling and data design, *CARIS Working Paper No 21*, School of Mathematics, Computing and Statistics, Leicester Polytechnic, 1987

NCC, Systems Training Library, Book 7: *Systems Design Techniques*, 1984

Relational Technology Ltd, *A Guide to INGRES*, 1985

Waters S, File design fallacies, *Computer Journal*, 1972, vol 15, no 1, pp 1–4

CHAPTER 6

Coleman M, Pratt S, *Software Engineering*, Chartwell-Bratt, 1986

Gilbert P, *Software Design and Development*, SRA, 1983

Grindley K, Humble J, *The Effective Computer*, McGraw-Hill, 1973

Myers G, *Composite–Structured Design*, Van Nostrand, 1978

Page-Jones M, *Practical Guide to Structured Systems Design*, 1st edition, Prentice-Hall, 1981

Page-Jones M, *Practical Guide to Structured Systems Design*, 2nd edition, Prentice-Hall, 1988

Sharp H, Accelerating the analysis–design transition with the transform analyser. Benyon D, Skidmore S, *Automating Systems Development*, Plenum Press, 1988

Weinberg V, *Structured Analysis*, Prentice-Hall, 1978

CHAPTER 7

Dean C, Whitlock D, *Computer Based Training*, 1983

Keen J, *Managing Systems Development*, Wiley, 1981

Lucas H, *The Analysis, Design and Implementation of Information Systems*, McGraw-Hill, 1981

Parkin A, *Systems Analysis*, 2nd edition, Edward Arnold, 1988

CHAPTER 8

Alavi M, An assessment of the prototyping approach to information systems development, *Communications of the ACM*, June 1984, vol 27, no 6

Alexander H, Potter B, Case Study: the use of formal specification and rapid prototyping to establish product feasibility, *Information and Software Technology*, September 1987, vol 29, no 7

Brancheau J, Wetherbe J, Key issues in information systems management, *MIS Quarterly*, March 1987

Checkland P, *Systems Thinking, Systems Practice*, Wiley, 1981

Janson M, Smith L, Prototyping for systems development; a critical appraisal, *MIS Quarterly*, December 1985

Jones N, Automating a systems development methodology: the LBMS experience. Benyon D, Skidmore S, *Automating Systems Development*, Plenum Press, 1988

Kimmerly W, Restricted vision, *Datamation*, 1984, pp 152–160

Kotarbinski T, *Praxiology: An Introduction to the Sciences of Efficient Action*, Pergamon, 1965

Macdonald I, Automating information engineering. Benyon D, Skidmore S, *Automating Systems Development*, Plenum Press, 1988

Prizzant A, Is prototyping counterproductive?, *Information and Software Technology*, September 1986, vol 28, no 7

Slusky L, Integrating software modelling and prototyping tools *Information and Software Technology*, September 1987, vol 29, no 7

Windsor J, Are automated tools changing systems analysis and design?, *Journal of Systems Management*, November 1986

Wroe B, *Successful Computing in a Small Business*, NCC Publications, 1987

Yourdon E, Whatever happened to structured analysis?, *Datamation*, 1 June 1986, pp 133–138

Zimmerman R, Phases, methods and tools – a triad of systems development. Davis, et al, eds, *Entity-Relationship Approach to Software Engineering*, Elsevier, 1983

Index